A Century
of American Historiography

A Century
of American Historiography

Edited by

James M. Banner, Jr.

BEDFORD/ST. MARTIN'S   BOSTON ◆ NEW YORK

For Bedford/St. Martin's

Publisher for History: Mary V. Dougherty
Executive Editor: William J. Lombardo
Director of Development: Jane Knetzger
Senior Developmental Editor: Sara Wise
Editorial Assistant: Jennifer Jovin
Production Associate: Samuel Jones
Executive Marketing Manager: Jenna Bookin Barry
Project Management: Books By Design, Inc.
Cover Design: Sara Gates
Composition: Books By Design, Inc.
Printing and Binding: RR Donnelley & Sons Company

President: Joan E. Feinberg
Editorial Director: Denise B. Wydra
Director of Marketing: Karen R. Soeltz
Director of Editing, Design, and Production: Marcia Cohen
Assistant Director of Editing, Design, and Production: Elise S. Kaiser
Manager, Publishing Services: Emily Berleth

Library of Congress Control Number: 2009928541

Manufactured in the United States of America
4 3
f e d

For information, write Bedford/St. Martin's, 75 Arlington Street, Boston, MA 02116 (617) 399-4000

ISBN-10: 0-312-53948-7
ISBN-13: 978-0-312-53948-1

PREFACE

A Century of American Historiography traces its origins to the April 2007 issue of the *OAH Magazine of History*, of which I was guest editor. That issue appeared during the centennial year of the Organization of American History, founded in 1907 as the Mississippi Valley Historical Association. Four essays in the issue reviewed the historiography of each of four subfields of American history—political, social, intellectual, and foreign relations history—over the century since 1907.[1] Subsequent to the issue's publication, Bedford/St. Martin's approached the OAH with the idea to expand the contents of the issue through the addition of essays on the historiography of other topics in American history, again over the course of approximately a century, and to publish those essays as a book. The volume you hold in your hands is the result.

The aim of these essays is to provide their intended readers—experienced scholars as well as undergraduate and graduate students seeking pathways into subjects they wish to explore—with current and authoritative guidance to the literature of particular topics of American history. In addition to the four original essays, this collection addresses the subfields of American cultural, military, legal, religious, regional, immigration, urban, and environmental history, as well as the historiography of African Americans, women, and American Indians. While major works from the past enjoy high stature and continuing influence

[1]The four essays appearing in that issue were Sean Wilentz, "American Political Histories"; Gary J. Kornblith and Carol Lasser, "More Than Great White Men: A Century of Scholarship on American Social History"; David A. Hollinger, "American Intellectual History, 1907–2007"; and Emily S. Rosenberg, "America and the World: From National to Global." Two other essays not relevant to this book but of great pertinence to the understanding of American secondary and collegiate history education over a hundred years—Diane Ravitch, "History's Struggle to Survive in the Schools," and Julie A. Reuben, "Going National: American History Instruction in Colleges and Universities"—also appeared in that issue.

that is unlikely to be taken from them, the comparative importance of the greatly increased number of works written nearer our own time cannot so easily be grasped, nor can their enduring effects be so confidently predicted. As a result, the shrewd assessment of the impact and significance of recent works of history by experts in discrete fields, such as the authors of these essays, is necessary. Those seeking counsel about where to dig into distinct bodies of historical litera- ture and how that literature has changed (and, equally important, how over time it has changed our view of the past) will find in the contents of this book indis- pensable up-to-date advice.[2]

Limiting the book's contents to the century from 1907, a restriction war- ranted by its origins during the OAH centenary, does not, in fact, limit its scope. The long twentieth century of modern American historiography commenced no later than in 1893 with Frederick Jackson Turner's epoch-making essay on the influence of the frontier in American history; and some of the authors in this vol- ume cite even earlier works as the origin points of their topics. The founding of the OAH a few years later drew upon the same impulse that actuated Turner—to separate American history as taught in schools and pursued by the then few, but growing number of, practicing professional historians of the United States from its fixed focus on the East Coast and on political and institutional developments. That broadening effort has us yet in thrall. For example, in, say, 1960, it would easily have been possible to include in a collection of this sort an essay on the literature of social history, but the subjects of that essay would not have ranged far, nor would its citations have been extensive. Since then, the fields of social and cultural history have exploded and splintered into many subfields, and the ancient topics of political, intellectual, and diplomatic history have taken on dimensions unimagined fifty years ago. We need frequent summaries of, as well as guidance through, this vastly expanded literature—summaries and guidance provided here—if we are to make any sense of it.

In reading and using these summaries, readers are likely to be struck, as I am, by a kind of convergence, or at least an overlap, that has begun to occur between most, perhaps all, of the subfields represented in this volume. It is no longer possible to distinguish most topics of American history by their distinct approaches. Yes, the history of American law remains tethered, as it must be, to case law and its peculiarities; yes, military historians must keep their eyes trained on past battlefield tactics and weaponry, historians of foreign relations upon the intricacies of negotiations and treaties. But it is difficult to discern a

---

[2]The authors of this book's essays were given no template to follow, no set of rules. Some of them, in keeping with the ways in which their subjects have developed, adopt an approach that emphasizes the larger phases of their topics' history. Others seek to reflect on individual works. One essay above all—that of Gary Kornblith and Carol Lasser on social history, one of the four original essays—stands out for the sheer challenge of its authors' assignment: taking a subject that spans so many other topics and providing the highlights of the literature of its many segments. Many of the other essays disaggregate their larger topic into some of its subtopics.

single subfield that does not now concern itself with issues of politics and power or any aspect of politics and political culture that is not suffused with consideration of race, gender, society, and class. Those who have sought to bring greater coherence to history through the return of narrative and synthetic sweep may have been looking to the wrong solution—or at least looking prematurely for what they so desire. It may instead be that, while the general history of the United States continues to splinter into subtopics and each of those subtopics to become ever more subdivided, our actual knowledge of each dimension of the American past is in fact becoming more implicated in knowledge of every other one. Increasingly, difficulty arises in keeping topics separated from each other more than it arises from keeping them linked. On the whole, this is promising.

It is important, however, to bear in mind that these essays do not provide guidance about the entire corpus of American historical literature. That would in any case be difficult to offer in an entire book, to say nothing of any set of short essays. Nor do they attempt to deal with any of the gradually emerging trans-topical subjects, like Atlantic or borderlands history, that have become increasingly important to a full understanding of the American past. They follow what remains the conventional way of organizing history curricula: They take as their unit of study the nation and then disaggregate its historical fields and literature into subtopics of the national whole. Increasingly, this way of dividing up the nation's history is becoming difficult to maintain—both in a book of this sort and in college and university undergraduate and graduate courses. Yet this manner of subdividing the literature remains justifiable because, while growing, the literature of young subfields (such as Atlantic or borderlands history) remains comparatively difficult to assess. Gradually, however, such assessment will become easier, and future collections like this one will carry essays on these newer topics.

It is also important to keep in mind that just as anyone seeking to know more about, say, American women's history cannot understand that subject without knowledge of its larger national historical context, so anyone pursuing knowledge of American history itself and all of its subfields is well served to place that history into its own larger frameworks. One of these is the history of historical knowledge. In its development and alterations since the emergence and institutionalization of history as a discipline in the nineteenth century, the historiography of the United States has paralleled that of Western historiography generally. One has only to read the three currently best accounts of Western historical thought and writing—Ernst Breisach, *Historiography: Ancient, Medieval, and Modern* (1984), the most comprehensive of the three; Donald R. Kelley's three volumes: *Faces of History: Historical Inquiry from Herodotus to Herder* (1998), *Fortunes of History: Historical Inquiry from Herder to Huizinga* (2003), and *Frontiers of History: Historical Inquiry in the Twentieth Century* (2006), the most searching and analytically perceptive; and John Burrow, *A History of Histories: Epics, Chronicles, Romances and Inquiries from Herodotus and Thucydides to the Twentieth Century* (2008), the most spirited and engaging[3] — to be struck by how all history written in Europe and the Americas has gone from being narrative, tribal, filiopietistic, philosophical, theoretically naïve, and nationalistic (as well as national) to being appreciably more disenthralled, universalistic, empirical, skeptical, critical, transnational, and theoretical (or at least revealing awareness of issues of objectivity, perspective, language, and the like). The essays here relate a similar story in all subjects — that of a growing capaciousness and sophistication of interpretation and view.

The essays also reveal, in all subjects, a continuing increase in the number of specialized works published and the continuing disintegration of larger fields of inquiry. History everywhere in the West emerged from a time in which interested readers could satisfy themselves with a few sweeping multivolume surveys of their nation's history. Today, that is no longer possible despite valiant and on the whole successful endeavors to provide narrative syntheses of discrete eras of the American past.[4] Even the most determined scholars struggle to keep up with their particular specialties. Everything has broken up; all is scatteration; and authors of surveys of particular topics in the history of the United States or of any other nation and people, like the authors of the essays here, have increasing difficulty gathering the outpouring of journal and book literature into manageable intellectual wholes. That the historians represented in this volume have managed to do so effectively is a tribute to their skills as well as to their knowledge.

The struggle to master an increasingly particularistic, specialized literature is matched by the struggle to maintain the largest perspective on the American past. If we must keep in mind how the historiography of the United States has always been embedded in that of the larger West and how what was written even

---

[3]Ernst Breisach, *Historiography: Ancient, Medieval, and Modern,* 2nd ed. (Chicago: University of Chicago Press, 1984); Donald R. Kelley, *Faces of History: Historical Inquiry from Herodotus to Herder* (New Haven, Conn.: Yale University Press, 1998), *Fortunes of History: Historical Inquiry from Herder to Huizinga* (New Haven, Conn.: Yale University Press, 2003), and *Frontiers of History: Historical Inquiry in the Twentieth Century* (New Haven, Conn.: Yale University Press, 2006); and John Burrow, *A History of Histories: Epics, Chronicles, Romances and Inquiries from Herodotus and Thucydides to the Twentieth Century* (New York: Knopf, 2008).

[4]One thinks especially of the ongoing appearance of volumes of the *Oxford History of the United States.* At the time of this writing, the following have appeared: Robert L. Middlekauff, *The Glorious Cause: The American Revolution, 1763–1789* (1982; 2nd ed., New York: Oxford University Press, 2005); Daniel Walker Howe, *What Hath God Wrought: The Transformation of America, 1815–1848* (New York: Oxford University Press, 2007); James M. McPherson, *Battle Cry of Freedom: The Civil War Era* (New York: Oxford University Press, 1988); David M. Kennedy, *Freedom from Fear: The American People in Depression and War, 1929–1945* (New York: Oxford University Press, 1999); James T. Patterson, *Grand Expectations: The United States, 1945–1974* (New York: Oxford University Press, 1996); and James T. Patterson, *Restless Giant: The United States from Watergate to Bush vs. Gore* (New York: Oxford University Press, 2005). Other volumes are in process. Some slated earlier for publication in the series were withdrawn and published outside of it. In many respects, one-volume textbooks now offer the best narrative and comprehensive interpretations of the nation's history.

2,500 years ago affects history still, we must also be sensitive to new efforts to return American history to its world context. The most far-reaching of these efforts is, in current language, to "globalize" American history—to interpret the history of the United States and its inhabitants through their origins in distant places and different times. This internationalizing of the nation's history occurs at a time when the entire world has become interconnected. It also represents a growing sense of dissatisfaction among American historians with what many see as an injurious provincialism in their subject. One is also justified in pointing out that internationalizing the nation's history makes knowledge of its past more relevant to today's conditions.

Historians of the United States have long been undertaking the internationalizing task in bits and pieces, as a growing literature demonstrates. Some of that literature has taken the form of comparative history—such as comparisons between American racism and slavery, racism, and bond servitude elsewhere and at other times (in, for example, George M. Fredrickson's *White Supremacy: A Comparative Study in American and South African History* [1981] and Peter Kolchin's *Unfree Labor: American Slavery and Russian Serfdom* [1987]).[5] Other portions of this literature have sought to set segments of the nation's past into their larger contemporary international framework—such as placing American colonial history in its Atlantic context (as in Alan Taylor's *American Colonies* [2001] and Bernard Bailyn's *Atlantic History: Concept and Contours* [2005]).[6] Yet others have situated the United States into the universe of the Western Hemisphere (as does Felipe Fernández-Armesto's *The Americas: A Hemispheric History* [2003]). All these approaches contribute to putting American history into its largest terrestrial context—that of the entire world. Exemplary in this regard are Thomas Bender's *A Nation among Nations: America's Place in World History* (2006) and Carl J. Guarneri's *America in the World: United States History in Global Context* (2006).[7]

Of one thing we can be certain—scholarship in American history will continue to change and to enlarge itself in consonance with developments both in the discipline of history and in the larger world. For now, the essays in this volume constitute the best guide we have to the state of American historical scholarship and understanding today.

---

[5]George M. Fredrickson, *White Supremacy: A Comparative Study in American and South African History* (New York: Oxford University Press, 1981); Peter Kolchin, *Unfree Labor: American Slavery and Russian Serfdom* (Cambridge, Mass.: Harvard University Press, 1987).

[6]Alan Taylor, *American Colonies* (New York: Viking, 2001); Bernard Bailyn, *Atlantic History: Concept and Contours* (Cambridge, Mass.: Harvard University Press, 2005).

[7]Felipe Fernández-Armesto, *The Americas: A Hemispheric History* (New York: Modern Library, 2003); Thomas Bender, *A Nation among Nations: America's Place in World History* (New York: Hill and Wang, 2006); Carl J. Guarneri, *America in the World: United States History in Global Context* (Boston: McGraw-Hill, 2006). A related work is Gary Reichard and Ted Dickson, *America on the World Stage: A Global Approach to U.S. History* (Champaign: University of Illinois Press, 2008).

ACKNOWLEDGMENTS

Members of the staff of Bedford/St. Martin's, colleagues without whom a work like this could not have come to fruition, have been indispensable in shepherding the work from conception to publishing. They are, especially, William Lombardo, who saw promise in the original idea; Sara Wise, whose shaping editorial skills are surely strengthened by her knowledge of the past; and Emily Berleth and Nancy Benjamin of Books By Design, who oversaw the book's production. That the work found a home at Bedford/St. Martin's is due to a timely suggestion from Gary J. Kornblith and Carol Lasser, participating authors in this volume and editors of *Teaching American History: Essays Adapted from the* Journal of American History, 2001–2007 (2009), also from Bedford/St. Martin's. Sincere thanks go to the Organization of American Historians for its generosity in letting us reprint four original essays, and to Phillip Guerty, Editor of the *OAH Magazine of History*. Lee Formwalt, former executive director of the Organization of American Historians, and Michael Regoli, also of the OAH, stood behind the project from the start.

James M. Banner, Jr.

Notes on Contributors

JEAN-CHRISTOPHE AGNEW teaches American studies and history at Yale University. He has published widely on the subjects of markets and culture, especially consumer culture, including *Worlds Apart: The Market and the Theater in Anglo-American Thought, 1550–1750* (1986). His most recent essay, "Capitalism, Culture, and Catastrophe," appears in James W. Cook, Lawrence B. Glickman, and Michael O'Malley, eds., *The Cultural Turn in U.S. History: Past, Present, Future* (2009).

DAVID J. FITZPATRICK is associate professor of history at Washtenaw Community College in Ann Arbor, Michigan, and adjunct professor at the University of Michigan. His research focuses on post–Civil War American military policy with an eye toward civil–military relations. The author of an award-winning journal article on Emory Upton, he is currently writing Upton's biography.

DONALD L. FIXICO is Distinguished Foundation Professor of History at Arizona State University. He has written and edited numerous books on American Indian history, the most recent of which is *American Indians in a Modern World* (2008).

TIMOTHY J. GILFOYLE is the author of *City of Eros: New York City, Prostitution, and the Commercialization of Sex, 1790–1920* (1992), *A Pickpocket's Tale: The Underworld of Nineteenth-Century New York City* (2006), and *Millennium Park: Creating a Chicago Landmark* (2006). He teaches American history at Loyola University Chicago.

ROBERT L. HARRIS, JR., is professor of African American History in the Africana Studies and Research Center and Vice Provost Emeritus at Cornell University. He is author of the *American Historical Association's Teaching African American History* (2000) and coeditor of *The Columbia Guide to African American History since 1939* (2006). He is currently writing a book on the Washington, D.C., Martin Luther King, Jr., National Memorial.

DAVID A. HOLLINGER is Preston Hotchkis Professor of History and Department Chair at the University of California at Berkeley. His recent books include *Postethnic America: Beyond Multiculturalism* (1995) and *Cosmopolitanism and Solidarity* (2006).

GARY J. KORNBLITH is professor of history at Oberlin College. He has published numerous articles and edited *The Industrial Revolution in America* (1998). He is currently working on *Slavery and Sectional Strife in the Early Republic* and, with Carol Lasser, *Elusive Utopia: A History of Race in Oberlin, Ohio*. He was coeditor of the Textbooks and Teaching section of the *Journal of American History* from 2001 to 2007.

CAROL LASSER is professor of history at Oberlin College. She was the coeditor, with Marlene Merrill, of *Friends and Sisters: Letters between Lucy Stone and Antoinette Brown Blackwell, 1846–93* (1987) and editor of *Educating Men and Women Together: Coeducation in a Changing World* (1987). She is currently working on *Antebellum American Women: Private, Public, Political* (with Stacey Robertson) and *Elusive Utopia: A History of Race in Oberlin, Ohio* (with Gary J. Kornblith). She was coeditor of the Textbooks and Teaching section of the *Journal of American History* from 2001 to 2007.

ALAN M. KRAUT is professor of history at American University and a nonresident fellow at the Migration Policy Institute. He has written or edited eight books, including *Silent Travelers: Germs, Genes, and the "Immigrant Menace"* (1995), which won the Theodore Saloutos award in immigration history, *Goldberger's War: The Life and Work of a Public Health Crusader* (2003), and, with Deborah A. Kraut, *Covenant of Care: Newark Beth Israel and the Jewish Hospital of America* (2007). Former president of the Immigration and Ethnic History Society, he is currently the chair of the History Advisory Committee of the Statue of Liberty–Ellis Island Foundation.

MARK A. NOLL is the Francis A. McAnaney Professor of History at the University of Notre Dame. His research focuses on issues of religion and society, primarily in the United States and Canada. His books include *American Evangelical Christianity: An Introduction* (2001), *The Civil War as a Theological Crisis* (2006), and *God and Race in American Politics: A Short History* (2008).

EMILY S. ROSENBERG is professor of history at the University of California, Irvine, and past president of the Society for Historians of American Foreign Relations. Most recently, she is the author of *A Date Which Will Live: Pearl Harbor in American Memory* (2003).

JOHN SHY is Professor Emeritus of History at the University of Michigan. Trained as a specialist in Early American history, his published work reflects his continuing interest in the subject of war and its history. He is currently working on an English edition of the last book written by Carl von Clausewitz, a study of Napoleon's first military campaign, in Italy in 1796.

CHRISTOPHER L. TOMLINS is research professor at the American Bar Foundation, Chicago. His interests are wide, ranging from sixteenth-century England to twentieth-century America, from the legal culture of work and labor to the interrelations of law and literature, from the early modern law of nations to the revolutionary Marxism of Walter Benjamin. He has written and edited six books, most recently the multivolume *Cambridge History of Law in America* (2008) coedited with Michael Grossberg, and more than a hundred other publications. He is completing a book on the legal culture of colonization and work in early Anglo-America and beginning another on the history of sovereignty and governance in Anglo-American law.

SUSAN D. WARE specializes in twentieth-century U.S. history and the history of American women. In addition to serving as the editor of *Notable American Women: A Biographical Dictionary Completing the Twentieth Century* (2004), she has published biographies of New Deal politician Molly Dewson, Amelia Earhart, and radio pioneer Mary Margaret McBride. She is currently writing a book about Billie Jean King, Title IX, and the revolution in women's sports. She is also the author of *Title IX: A Brief History with Documents* (2007) for the Bedford Series in History and Culture.

SEAN WILENTZ is Sidney and Ruth Lapidus Professor of the American Revolutionary Era at Princeton University and the author of several books, including most recently *The Rise of American Democracy: Jefferson to Lincoln* (2005), which received the Bancroft Prize in 2006.

DONALD WORSTER is the Hall Distinguished Professor of American History at the University of Kansas and has served as president of the American Society for Environmental History. His latest work is *A Passion for Nature: The Life of John Muir* (2008).

DAVID M. WROBEL is professor and chair of the History Department at the University of Nevada Las Vegas and a past president of the Pacific Coast Branch of the American Historical Association and of Phi Alpha Theta, the National History Honor Society. A historian of American thought and culture and the American West, his books include *The End of American Exceptionalism: Frontier Anxiety from the Old West to the New Deal* (1993), *Promised Lands: Promotion, Memory, and the Creation of the American West* (2002), and *Global West, American Frontier: Travelers' Accounts from the Nineteenth and Twentieth Centuries* (forthcoming).

ABOUT THE EDITOR

JAMES M. BANNER, JR., is an independent historian in Washington, D.C., whose scholarly interests have focused on the history of the United States between 1765 and 1865. A leader in the creation of the National History Center and cofounder and codirector of the History News Service, he is writing a book about what it means to be a historian today. He is most recently the coeditor, with John R. Gillis, of *Becoming Historians* (2009).

Contents

A Century
of American Historiography

Sean Wilentz

American Political Histories

It now seems as if an eon has passed, and not merely a century or so, since the eminent historian Herbert Baxter Adams's seminar room at Johns Hopkins was emblazoned with the motto "History is past Politics, and Politics present History." Whereas political history once dominated scholarship on all of American history, professional scholars in recent decades have turned skeptical, and at times hostile, to studies that stress mainstream politics (including parties and government institutions), let alone the lives and achievements of great political leaders and public officials. There has been, to be sure, a great deal written on these topics, as there continues to be today. But after the 1960s, an explosion of interest in other historical modes—social history, cultural history, anthropological history—relegated political history to the academic margins. As a field, political history lost its old sense of excitement, as well as the rewards of every variety that went with that excitement.[1]

Interestingly, the decline in professional political history has coincided with a burst of public interest in political biography in books broadly connected to politics and political history, including the history of warfare and military affairs. Given the regular appearances on the bestseller lists of works by David McCullough, Doris Kearns Goodwin, and other popular historians of politics, as well as the success of the History Channel, the reading and viewing public's appetite for traditional historical fare seems insatiable. Some critics have suggested that this renewed interest marks a mass yearning for an earlier, nobler, more glorious time in American history, and especially in American politics. If so, it is nostalgia most academic historians do not seem to share.

There are, however, grounds for believing that the gap between political history and other forms of historical writing may be less severe than is generally perceived and that it may be temporary. Any hard and fast division between traditional political history and social history creates, I believe, a false dichotomy.

---

[1] Over the years, several detailed appraisals of the historiography of American political history have appeared. One that I have found particularly useful is Richard J. Jensen, "Historiography of American Political History," in Jack P. Greene, ed., *Encyclopedia of American History* (New York: Scribner's, 1984), 1–25.

Just as certain individuals have more influence on history than others and give American politics its tone and shape, so in America leaders must draw their own tone and shape from those they would wish to lead. Neither the "top-down" nor "bottom-up" approach is fully intelligible without the other, a point I tried to make in a recent book on the rise of American democracy.[2] Additionally, a quick review of the historiography of American political history shows that, far from being complacent or conservative, the field has evolved dramatically over the past one hundred years, sometimes in response to developments among other scholars in other areas of American history, sometimes out of disagreements among political historians. It therefore makes more sense to speak of American political histories, rather than of American political history per se. Some of these histories have very close affinities with other subfields that may, at times, have seemed more avant-garde and glamorous. And, for a very long time, political historians have sought out the origins of political conflict and accommodation in social, economic, cultural, and intellectual history.

In 1907, political historians and approaches to American political history were very much in flux. An older, narrative mode, heavy on storytelling and historical moralizing, and usually spread over many volumes, still had a great deal of prestige. The studies ranged from the very first comprehensive national history, George Bancroft's *History of the United States of America from the Discovery of the Continent* (1834–1875) to James Ford Rhodes's *History of the United States from the Compromise of 1850* (1893–1906). The enduring masterpiece of this nineteenth-century genre, Henry Adams's *History of the United States during the Administrations of Thomas Jefferson and James Madison* (1889–1891), combined detailed political narrative with a remarkably sophisticated appreciation of the social, cultural, and intellectual changes that accompanied political developments.[3] But by 1907, the Germanic seminar style of "scientific" history, with its emphases on exacting analysis of primary documents aimed toward the discovery of larger forces in history, combined with a more critical approach to politics buoyed by the spirit of Progressive reform and pragmatic philosophy, was dramatically changing the sum and substance of political historians' writings. Above all, historians began describing deeper social, cultural, and economic causes of political change and conflict.

The turn to newer forms of historical inquiry is generally dated to the young Frederick Jackson Turner's reading of his famous paper, "The Significance of the Frontier in American History," at the annual meeting of the American Historical Association in 1893. A recent Ph.D. graduate of Johns Hopkins, Turner argued

[2]Sean Wilentz, *The Rise of American Democracy: Jefferson to Lincoln* (New York: W. W. Norton, 2005).

[3]George Bancroft, *History of the United States from the Discovery of the Continent* (Boston: Little, Brown, 1834–1875); James Ford Rhodes, *History of the United States from the Compromise of 1850* (New York: Macmillan, 1893–1906); Henry Adams, *History of the United States during the Administrations of Thomas Jefferson and James Madison* (New York: C. Scribner, 1889–1891).

that frontier settlement, and not institutional and spiritual inheritances from the Old World, accounted for the origins and peculiar development of American democracy. Here was a breathtaking interpretation of the social and cultural impulses behind American politics, more pointed than anything the old narrative historians had delivered. Turner thereafter devoted himself to teaching more than to writing, and he never developed the frontier thesis into a major historical work. But Turner's many students (notably Orin G. Libby) produced numerous important studies of the sectional influences on American politics from the ratification of the Constitution onward. And something of those sectional interpretations has survived over the decades, among political scientists and strategists as well as historians, in books ranging from V. O. Key's *Southern Politics in State and Nation* (1949) to Kevin Phillips's *The Emerging Republican Majority* (1969).[4]

Charles A. Beard was not immune to sectional explanations of politics; but like others of his generation he was drawn more to analyzing economic interests, which, he believed, sectional differences masked. And, unlike Turner, Beard focused more on changes wrought in the eastern cities than those in the developing West. His major early work, *An Economic Interpretation of the Constitution* (1913), postulated that ownership of different forms of property (essentially mercantile versus agrarian) accounted for different loyalties during the political struggles of 1787–1888. Beard would go on, with his wife, Mary Ritter Beard, to reinterpret all American history through this lens in *The Rise of American Civilization* (1927) — without question the best-known and most influential work of American historical scholarship from the 1920s through the Second World War. The Beards were hardly alone; the same broad interpretive framework emphasizing economic interest dominated the work of such important political historians as Carl Becker, Arthur M. Schlesinger, Sr., and John D. Hicks.[5]

The long retreat from radical Reconstruction to the age of Jim Crow also accompanied a basic revaluation of the Civil War and its aftermath. Whereas the grand narrator Rhodes approached the era from the standpoint of an antislavery, pro-big-business Republican, a new generation of professionally trained scholars reinterpreted slavery's demise in starkly materialistic terms as a Yankee effort to subjugate the South — an effort that ended only with the "redemption" of white

[4]Frederick Jackson Turner, *The Frontier in American History* (New York: Henry Holt, 1920); Orin G. Libby, *The Geographical Distribution of the Vote of the Thirteen States on the Federal Constitution, 1787–88* (1894; New York: Burt Franklin, 1969); V. O. Key, Jr., with the assistance of Alexander Heard, *Southern Politics in State and Nation* (New York: Knopf, 1949); Kevin Phillips, *The Emerging Republican Majority* (New Rochelle, N.Y.: Arlington House, 1969).

[5]Charles A. Beard, *An Economic Interpretation of the Constitution* (New York: Macmillan, 1913); Charles A. Beard and Mary R. Beard, *The Rise of American Civilization* (New York: Macmillan, 1927); Carl Becker, *The History of Political Parties in the Province of New York, 1760–1776* (1909; Madison: University of Wisconsin Press, 1960); Arthur M. Schlesinger, *The Colonial Merchants and the American Revolution* (n.p., 1917); John D. Hicks, *The Populist Revolt: A History of the Farmers' Alliance and the People's Party* (Minneapolis: University of Minnesota Press, 1931).

supremacy in the 1870s. At Columbia University, the Berlin-trained William A. Dunning became the leading proponent of this new view, through both his writings (especially *Reconstruction: Political and Economic, 1865–1877* [1907]) and the monographs of his many students. Something of the spirit and allegiances of the Dunning School would reappear in the 1930s and 1940s in the work of a younger group of historians, including James G. Randall and Avery O. Craven, who insisted that the Civil War itself could have been avoided were it not for the fanaticism of the abolitionists, the greed of domineering Yankees, and, above all, the incompetence of a "blundering generation" of politicians who came to the fore in 1850.[6]

Another strand of Progressive Era history writing melded political with intellectual and cultural history in ways roughly compatible with the writings of both Turner and Beard. The most prominent of these writers, Vernon L. Parrington, taught English rather than history, but he won enormous respect among historians. His massive three-volume *Main Currents in American Thought: An Interpretation of American Literature from the Beginnings to 1920* (1927–1930) presented a political history of American arts, letters, and philosophy that drew a sharp distinction between Hamiltonian pro-business elitists and Jeffersonian agrarian democrats. Comprehensive in its coverage, Parrington's masterwork also left no doubt about its author's Jeffersonian sympathies.[7]

After the Progressive historians, serious writers of American political history would never be tempted to render politics as a realm cut off from the wider worlds of economics, culture, social structure, and ideas (although some would stress certain of these connections more than others). But in the 1940s, a sustained assault commenced on the ways in which the Progressive historians had shoehorned all politics into simple dualisms (industrial–agrarian, Hamiltonian–Jeffersonian) and reduced political history into an unending conflict over either sectional or economic interests. As a generation, these historians shared in the desire to bring to the study of American politics what the literary critic Lionel Trilling famously called a sense of "variousness, possibility, complexity, and difficulty" that had eluded older historians. Yet while they rejected Progressive simplification, they also (as one of their leaders, Richard Hofstadter, later observed) built upon the Progressives' analytical breakthroughs.[8] And in their own variousness, they took the study of political history in many different directions, some of them contradictory.

[6]William A. Dunning, *Reconstruction: Political and Economic, 1865–1877* (New York: Harper & Brothers, 1907); J. G. Randall, *The Civil War and Reconstruction* (Boston: D. C. Heath, 1937); Avery O. Craven, *The Coming of the Civil War* (1942; Chicago: University of Chicago Press, 1957).

[7]Vernon L. Parrington, *Main Currents in American Thought: An Interpretation of American Literature from the Beginnings to 1920* (New York: Harcourt, Brace, 1927–1930).

[8]Lionel Trilling, *The Liberal Imagination: Essays on Literature and Society* (New York: Viking, 1950), xv; Richard Hofstadter, *The Progressive Historians: Turner, Beard, Parrington* (New York: Knopf, 1968).

The counter-Progressive scholarship with the least visible impact today was that of the so-called consensus school. Pioneered by Hofstadter in his iconoclastic book, *The American Political Tradition and the Men Who Made It* (1948), and given a more patriotic spin in Daniel J. Boorstin's *The Genius of American Politics* (1953), consensus history looked at the great clashes featured by the Progressives and found more basic agreement than disagreement, more cupidity than democratic idealism. The approach, at its strongest, was a by-product of the 1930s Marxist Left. Seeing nothing (or little enough) of European-style socialism in American political history, the consensus writers concluded that what looked like fierce conflict in the New World amounted to little more than battles between ins and outs, campaign jousts between candidates brandishing wooden spears. All of the political leaders Hofstadter discussed, from the Founders through FDR (except for the marginalized mid-nineteenth-century dissenter, Wendell Phillips) believed in capitalism. Boorstin's Americans held to no particular ideas worth mentioning but were engaged chiefly in the pragmatic exercise of finding out what worked best, sticking with it until something better came along.[9]

Appropriate enough for the late 1940s and 1950s, consensus history ran into trouble amid the political turbulence of the 1960s, which reconfigured the legacy of the Civil War—the cataclysmic, all-American conflict that confuted any idea that consensual harmony was the keystone of American politics, past or present. By 1956, when Kenneth M. Stampp's *Slavery: The Peculiar Institution* appeared, historians of the counter-Progressive cohort had begun adding their voices to the refutation of the Progressives on slavery and Reconstruction undertaken earlier by black historians such as W. E. B. Du Bois (and generally ignored by the historical profession in the 1930s and 1940s).[10]

Of more enduring influence was the counter-Progressives' search for non-economic factors to explain the vagaries of American political life. Borrowing liberally from the social sciences (especially the sociology of Max Weber), scholars as different as Hofstadter and David Herbert Donald deployed the concept of "status anxiety," as opposed to class interests, to understand political movements ranging from abolitionism to Progressivism.[11] Related interdisciplinary

[9]Richard Hofstadter, *The American Political Tradition and the Men Who Made It* (New York: Knopf, 1948); Daniel J. Boorstin, *The Genius of American Politics* (Chicago: University of Chicago Press, 1953).

[10]Kenneth M. Stampp, *Slavery: The Peculiar Institution* (New York: Knopf, 1956): W. E. B. Du Bois, *Black Reconstruction: An Essay toward a History of the Part Which Black Folk Played in the Attempt to Reconstruct Democracy in America, 1860–1880* (New York: Russell & Russell, 1935). Some of Stampp's themes and interpretations were anticipated by Richard Hofstadter, "U. B. Phillips and the Plantation Legend," *Journal of Negro History* 29 (1944): 109–24—a seeming irony given Hofstadter's later reputation as a consensus historian and a warning against taking the simplifications of general historiography (such as this essay) as the final word on the subject.

[11]Richard Hofstadter, *The Age of Reform: Bryan to FDR* (New York: Knopf, 1955); David Donald, *Lincoln Reconsidered* (1956; New York: Vintage, 1961).

efforts brought a number of new, more "scientific" methodologies to bear on historical research, including reference-group theory, multivariate analysis, and the structural-functionalist theories associated with sociologists Talcott Parsons at Harvard and Robert K. Merton at Columbia. Coupled with early innovations in computing technology in the 1960s, these adaptations led to a spate of new studies analyzing legislative roll-call voting patterns, the contents of political newspaper editorials, and, above all, the demographics of mass voting. By the late 1960s, these forays into the social sciences had fostered what is still known as the "new political history."

Although it covered a great deal of ground, the new political history became identified, first and foremost, with those studies that argued that ethnicity and religion, and not class, were the primary determinants of voting behavior. The breakthrough work, Lee Benson's *The Concept of Jacksonian Democracy: New York as a Test Case* (1961), looked intensively at voting returns in New York State in 1844 and showed that divisions between Protestants and Catholics, as well as natives and newcomers, overwhelmed those between rich and poor. Adapting the theme of political consensus, Benson also insisted that the class rhetoric of the parties amounted to so much "claptrap" and that, if anything, the supposedly conservative, pro-business Whigs, and not the Jacksonian Democrats, were the forerunner of FDR's New Dealers. Related studies of nineteenth-century politics by, among others, Michael F. Holt, Ronald P. Formisano, William G. Shade, Paul Kleppner, and Richard J. Jensen came to roughly similar conclusions about ethnic and religious voting at different times and in different places, enough so to identify these scholars, whether they liked it or not, as an ethnocultural school of American political history.[12]

Just as one group of counter-Progressives was maximizing the importance of cultural ascription in politics and minimizing the importance of political ideas, other scholars were rediscovering the connections between intellectual and political history. Inspired by, and in some cases actually taught by, Harvard's Perry Miller, perhaps the greatest twentieth-century American historian, these historians reversed the Parringtonian formulas about American ideas as the expression of politics by other means and tried to see American politics as, in large part, a product of ideas. Thus, in 1945, Arthur Schlesinger, Jr.'s, momentous *The Age of Jackson* not only challenged Turnerian interpretations of the Jacksonians as essentially

---

[12]Lee Benson, *The Concept of Jacksonian Democracy: New York as a Test Case* (Princeton, N.J.: Princeton University Press, 1961); Michael F. Holt, *Forging a Majority: The Formation of the Republican Party in Pittsburgh, 1848–1860* (New Haven, Conn.: Yale University Press, 1969); Ronald P. Formisano, *The Birth of Mass Political Parties: Michigan, 1827–1861* (Princeton, N.J.: Princeton University Press, 1971); William G. Shade, *Banks or No Banks?: The Money Issue in Western Politics* (Detroit: Wayne State University Press, 1972); Paul Kleppner, *The Cross of Culture: A Social Analysis of Midwestern Politics, 1850–1900* (New York: Free Press, 1970); Richard J. Jensen, *The Winning of the Midwest: Social and Political Conflict, 1888–1896* (Chicago: University of Chicago Press, 1971).

a Western sectional movement, but also reclaimed the importance of intellectuals and their ideas in forging the politics of Jacksonian democracy. Thus, a few years later, Edmund S. Morgan, with Helen M. Morgan, emphasized the importance of ideas in shaping the Stamp Act crisis of 1765 before he went on to expand the argument in a 1963 essay, "The American Revolution Considered as an Intellectual Movement."[13]

Later in the 1960s, a younger cohort combined intellectual history with a broadened sense of worldview as described, in particular, by sociologists and anthropologists, notably Karl Mannheim (who had influenced earlier historians, including Hofstadter) and Clifford Geertz. Whereas the Progressive generation was apt to dismiss political proclamations as mere camouflage for material interests, and "the new" political historians saw such appeals as populist claptrap, these historians probed the pamphlets and newspaper articles of the eighteenth and nineteenth centuries for clues about wider prejudices and aspirations that goaded Americans to act. Bernard Bailyn's *Ideological Origins of the American Revolution* (1967) and Gordon S. Wood's *The Creation of the American Republic, 1776–1787* (1969) fundamentally altered historians' views of the nation's formative years, substituting a British oppositionist, libertarian Whig outlook—known by the term "republicanism"—for the liberalism of John Locke as the guiding intellectual force behind American independence. Eric Foner's *Free Soil, Free Labor, Free Men: The Ideology of the Republican Party before the Civil War* (1970) brought a similar concept of ideology to the antislavery politics of the 1840s and 1850s by bridging material interests and morality and describing a free-labor ideology that united most of the North against the slave South.[14]

Foner's book appeared in 1970; thereafter, the social history boom seemed to sweep away most other forms of American historical study. There were abundant ironies to this, as well as some obvious connections to contemporaneous events. Much of the social history that emerged—called the "new social history" to distinguish it from the more anecdotal, impressionist studies by previous social historians—drew on social science methods and quantitative techniques every bit as enthusiastically as the new political history did. (Indeed, practitioners of both "new" histories would meet, if at times uneasily, at annual meetings of the newly formed Social Science History Association.) But coming in the wake of the civil

[13]Arthur M. Schlesinger, Jr., *The Age of Jackson* (Boston: Little, Brown, 1945); Edmund S. Morgan and Helen M. Morgan, *The Stamp Act Crisis: Prologue to Revolution* (Chapel Hill: University of North Carolina Press, 1953); Edmund S. Morgan, "The American Revolution Considered as an Intellectual Movement," in Arthur M. Schlesinger, Jr., and Morton White, eds., *Paths of American Thought* (Boston: Houghton Mifflin, 1963).

[14]Bernard Bailyn, *Ideological Origins of the American Revolution* (Cambridge, Mass.: Harvard University Press, 1967); Gordon S. Wood, *The Creation of the American Republic, 1776–1787* (Chapel Hill: University of North Carolina Press, 1969); Eric Foner, *Free Soil, Free Labor, Free Men: The Ideology of the Republican Party before the Civil War* (New York: Oxford University Press, 1970).

rights movement and the protests over the Vietnam War, the social historians
found little of interest in the work of the counter-Progressive political historians.
Every shred of the young social historians' own experience, of the history they
began to produce, told them that American consensus was a useless concept.
Accounts of voting and parties lay outside the history they wanted to discover,
much of it about blacks and women who were excluded from the polity for most
of American history. A neo-Marxist current, most visible among labor historians
and historians of slavery, aimed to recover the class dynamics that the social historians believed underlay the nation's social and political life, that the counter-
Progressives had allegedly obscured, and that American politics had supposedly
suffocated. ("The ballot box," according to one important study that combined
social and political history, "was the coffin of class consciousness."[15]) Some of the
social historians' work revived the spirit of the Progressive generation, but the
new generation, unlike the Progressive historians, focused either on the political
margins or outside politics completely.

And yet . . .

Even among the social historians, interest in politics never completely disap-
peared. Distinguished biographies of political radicals such as Eugene V. Debs
kept alive an interest in elections and voting; more recently, scholars who cut their
teeth on the social history of the 1970s and 1980s have turned their attention to the
likes of William Jennings Bryan. A select few among the feminist historians always
noticed that the great struggle of the woman's movement until 1920 was to secure
suffrage, which meant studying political history. Although historians of modern
America were slower, in general, to pick up on a possible merger of social and
political history, scholars such as Alan Brinkley and Lizabeth Cohen, starting
from different vantage points, found ways to integrate the two fields.[16]

All along, moreover, rumors of political history's death were greatly exaggerated. During the 1980s, the University of Kansas Press began releasing its distinguished American Presidency Series, followed soon after by the Henry Holt/
Times Books series on the presidents. Leading exponents of the new political history, now influenced by studies of ideology as well as by social history, wrote fresh
appraisals of subjects ranging from the Dorr War to the Whig Party. Among academic students of the early republic, there has recently arisen a "new new political history," which is trying to merge the cultural history of rituals and symbols
with the more traditional history of elections and lawmaking and is rekindling

---

[15]Alan Dawley, *Class and Community: The Industrial Revolution in Lynn* (Cambridge,
Mass.: Harvard University Press, 1976), 70.

[16]Nick Salvatore, *Eugene V. Debs: Citizen and Socialist* (Urbana: University of Illinois
Press, 1982); Michael Kazin, *Godly Hero: The Life of William Jennings Bryan* (New York:
Knopf, 2006); Ellen Carol Dubois, *Feminism and Suffrage: The Rise of an Independent Women's
Movement in America, 1848–1869* (Ithaca, N.Y.: Cornell University Press, 1979); Alan Brinkley,
The End of Reform: New Deal Liberalism in Recession and War (New York: Knopf, 1995); Liza-
beth Cohen, *Making a New Deal: Industrial Workers in Chicago, 1919–1939* (New York: Cam-
bridge University Press, 1990).

some of the earlier excitement about the field of political history. Other up-and-coming historians are reexamining topics ranging from the political economy of state-building (both locally and nationally) to the origins of the New Right conservatism of the age of Reagan. Even when political history supposedly fell into the doldrums, numerous historians, including Hugh Davis Graham, Alice Kessler-Harris, and the editors of and contributors to the impressive *Journal of Policy History*, produced major studies on various aspects of the history of public policy. A few distinguished historians, including Edmund Morgan, Gordon Wood, and Joseph J. Ellis, have attended to the popular interest in political narrative with books that combine scholarly precision with accessible, even vivid prose.[17]

What have we learned from these studies and the research of the past century? Every historian would answer the question differently, but I think most would agree about a few propositions. Above all, they would agree that American political competition has always involved rival coalitions, which cannot be reduced to a simple sociological or ideological formula. Second, no matter how irrational and intellectually barren American politics might seem, ideas, at least as cobbled together as ideologies, do play an important role in shaping both elections and the formulation of government policy. Third, American politics (like historical writing about American politics) is a perpetual argument over the meanings of certain first principles—freedom, equality, democracy—about which different groups of Americans disagree, sometimes furiously.

Where political history is headed, out of the current stew of styles and approaches, is much less clear. My guess is that it will advance fastest and farthest where the scholarly grudges, methodological obsessions, and political intrusions that have always haunted professional history can most quickly be put aside—and where the labels that have now become professional identifiers can be most safely ignored. If Americans generally, at least until very recently, have come to

---

[17]Ronald P. Formisano, "The Role of Women in the Dorr Rebellion," *Rhode Island History* 61 (1993): 88–104; Michael F. Holt, *The Rise and Fall of the American Whig Party: Jacksonian Politics and the Onset of the Civil War* (New York: Oxford University Press, 1999); Jeffrey L. Pasley et al., eds., *Beyond the Founders: New Approaches to the Political History of the Early Republic* (Chapel Hill: University of North Carolina Press, 2004); Sven Beckert, *The Monied Metropolis: New York City and the Consolidation of the American Bourgeoisie, 1850–1896* (New York: Cambridge University Press, 2001); Julian E. Zelizer, *Taxing America: Wilbur D. Mills, Congress, and the State, 1945–1975* (New York: Cambridge University Press, 1998); Lisa McGirr, *Suburban Warriors: The Origins of the New Republican Right* (Princeton, N.J.: Princeton University Press, 2001); Kevin M. Kruse, *White Flight: Atlanta and the Making of Modern Conservatism* (Princeton, N.J.: Princeton University Press, 2005); Hugh Davis Graham, *Collision Course: The Strange Convergence of Affirmative Action and Immigration Policy in America* (New York: Oxford University Press, 2002); Alice Kessler-Harris, *In Pursuit of Equity: Women, Men, and the Quest for Economic Citizenship in Twentieth-Century America* (New York: Oxford University Press, 2001); Edmund S. Morgan, *Benjamin Franklin* (New Haven, Conn.: Yale University Press, 2002); Gordon S. Wood, *Revolutionary Characters: What Made the Founders Different* (New York: Penguin Press, 2006); Joseph J. Ellis, *Founding Brothers: The Revolutionary Generation* (New York: Knopf, 2000).

hate politics because of ideological poisoning, American historians will reinvent political history where comity and large-mindedness prevail.

What is certain is that political history will remain essential to any general account of American history, no matter how much political historians may now feel slighted. The distinguished political historian John Morton Blum—who writes of society and culture, too—once observed that "even those who hate politics and the history of politics cannot escape the enduring involvement of politics in their lives."[18] As politics is inevitable, so, for historians, is political history.

---

[18]John Morton Blum, "History as It Should Be Taught," *Washington Monthly* 27 (May 1, 1995): 46.

Gary J. Kornblith and Carol Lasser

More Than Great White Men: A Century of Scholarship on American Social History

In 2005, the United States Congress voted to spend millions of dollars in federal funds to help K–12 students learn about their nation's past. Lawmakers were careful to specify that the money would go toward teaching "traditional American history," defined as "(A) the significant constitutional, political, intellectual, economic, and foreign policy trends and issues that have shaped the course of American history; and (B) the key episodes, turning points, and leading figures involved in the constitutional, political, intellectual, diplomatic, and economic history of the United States."[1] Notably absent from this list of topics suitable for the education of American schoolchildren was any mention of social history. The omission was not accidental. Social history has long been perceived by its champions and detractors alike as an alternative to "traditional" history—an alternative that some criticize as subversive and others applaud as more inclusive and engaging than standard narratives. Its practitioners claim that their methods, subjects, and sources hold the potential to challenge interpretations of the nation's past that emphasize the achievements of "great white men." Social historians focus either on the factors and forces that shape society as a whole or on the lives of ordinary people who are excluded from established centers of power. This essay traces how the writing of American social history has evolved over the last century.

In 1910, Frederick Jackson Turner, author of the famous essay "The Significance of the Frontier in American History," chose as the topic of his presidential address to the American Historical Association "Social Forces in American History."[2] Turning his gaze to his own moment, the Progressive Era—the period since the frontier was said to have closed in 1890—he declared, "The revolution

---

[1] Senate Committee on Health, Education, Labor, and Pensions, *Higher Education Amendments of 2005*, 109th Cong., 2d sess., 2005, S. Rep. 26-249 to accompany S. 1614, Sec. 851. <http://thomas.loc.gov/cgi-bin/cpquery/T?&report=sr218&dbname=109&> (accessed October 25, 2006).

[2] Frederick Jackson Turner, "The Significance of the Frontier in American History," in *Annual Report of the American Historical Association for the Year 1893* (Washington, D.C.: U.S. Government Printing Office, 1894), 199–227.

in the social and economic structure of this country during the past two decades is comparable to what occurred when independence was declared and the Constitution was formed, or to the changes wrought . . . by the era of Civil War and Reconstruction."[3] For Turner, his revolutionary times demanded new approaches to historical analysis. Historians needed to reach out to the social sciences as well as the humanities to write the kind of history that would make sense of the great transformation going on around them, changes not captured in more purely political narratives. In calling on American historians to focus on social forces rather than discrete political events, formal institutions, or heroic actions, Turner laid out an ambitious agenda for future scholarly research. Yet it was not Turner's address but the publication three years later of *An Economic Interpretation of the Constitution of the United States* (1913) by Charles A. Beard that triggered a public firestorm over how American history should be investigated, analyzed, and presented. Beard challenged previous interpretations of constitution making, arguing that the process was not a grand intellectual exercise undertaken by demigods; it was, instead, a process driven by social forces in their economic manifestation and evidenced in the behavior of individuals. Identifying the property holdings of the Constitution's framers, Beard argued that they stood to benefit financially from the governmental framework they had devised. More generally he found a "line of cleavage" between farmers and debtors on the one hand and nascent business interests on the other. By his provocative account, social and economic dynamics—Beard considered them essentially identical—shaped political developments, not vice versa.[4]

While Beard and Turner focused on fundamental social forces that they believed drove history, other scholars in the Progressive Era pursued the alternate approach to social history: the study of everyday life, or what the English historian G. M. Trevelyan later called "the history of a people with the politics left out."[5] While antiquarians and connoisseurs catalogued the silver and china of elites, these scholars sought to understand the elements of ordinary people's experience. Noteworthy examples of this genre included Alice Morse Earle's *Colonial Dames and Good Wives* (1895), Lucy Salmon's *Domestic Service* (1897), and Arthur W. Calhoun's *A Social History of the American Family from Colonial Times to the Present* (1917).[6] As these titles indicate, this sort of apolitical social history encompassed the circumstances of women and children, not just men. By addressing groups of Americans largely ignored by political historians, social

[3]Frederick Jackson Turner, "Social Forces in American History," *The American Historical Review* 16 (January 1911): 217.

[4]Charles A. Beard, *An Economic Interpretation of the Constitution of the United States* (New York: Macmillan, 1913).

[5]G. M. Trevelyan, *English Social History: A Survey of Six Centuries* (New York: Longmans, Green and Co., 1942), vii.

[6]Alice Morse Earle, *Colonial Dames and Good Wives* (New York: Houghton, Mifflin & Company, 1895); Lucy Maynard Salmon, *Domestic Service* (New York: Macmillan, 1897); Arthur W. Calhoun, *A Social History of the American Family from Colonial Times to the Present* (Cleveland: Arthur H. Clark, 1917).

historians propelled people without public power or fame to center stage. Some scholars self-consciously sought to promote social reform by drawing academic attention to the oppressed. Thus John R. Commons and his colleagues produced the multivolume *Documentary History of American Industrial Society* (1910) to illuminate the history and enhance the conditions of American workers. Carter Woodson wrote *The Education of the Negro prior to 1861* (1915) and founded the *Journal of Negro History* to promote the African American struggle for equality.[7]

Over the next generation, Arthur Meier Schlesinger brought the work of social historians to the general reading public. In 1922, he published *New Viewpoints in American History*, which included synthetic essays on "The Influence of Immigration on American History," "Economic Influences in American History," and "The Role of Women in American History," among other topics.[8] For the next quarter century, Schlesinger collaborated with Dixon Ryan Fox in editing the multivolume series *A History of American Life*, which ranged chronologically from 1492 to 1941. In his own contribution to the series, *The Rise of the City, 1878–1898* (1933), Schlesinger employed urbanization as the central organizing principle and relegated his discussion of political events to a single chapter. For Schlesinger, as for Turner and Beard, the engine of historical change lay in large-scale social processes that political figures and governmental policies could influence but not really control.[9]

Against the backdrop of the Great Depression, social historians turned their attention to earlier phases of American industrial development. Three scholars undertook carefully wrought case studies of nineteenth-century New England that remain classic accounts: Caroline Ware's *The Early New England Cotton Manufacture* (1931), Vera Shlakman's *Economic History of a Factory Town: A Study of Chicopee, Massachusetts* (1935), and Constance McLaughlin Green's *Holyoke, Massachusetts: A Case History of the Industrial Revolution in America* (1939).[10] Social historians in the 1930s increasingly framed their analyses of social change in terms of class and class conflict. W. E. B. Du Bois began *Black Reconstruction* (1935) with a chapter titled "The Black Worker" and termed the black response to the Civil War "The General Strike."[11] Roger Shugg focused on southern

[7]John R. Commons et al., *A Documentary History of American Industrial Society* (Cleveland: The A. H. Clark Company, 1910); Carter Godwin Woodson, *The Education of the Negro prior to 1861: A History of the Education of the Colored People of the United States from the Beginning of Slavery to the Civil War* (London: G. P. Putnam's Sons, 1915).

[8]Arthur M. Schlesinger, *New Viewpoints in American History* (New York: Macmillan, 1922).

[9]Arthur M. Schlesinger, *The Rise of the City, 1878–1898* (New York: Macmillan, 1933).

[10]Caroline F. Ware, *The Early New England Cotton Manufacture: A Study in Industrial Beginnings* (New York: Houghton Mifflin, 1931); Vera Shlakman, *Economic History of a Factory Town: A Study of Chicopee, Massachusetts* (Northampton, Mass.: Department of History of Smith College, 1935); Constance McLaughlin Green, *Holyoke, Massachusetts: A Case History of the Industrial Revolution in America* (New Haven, Conn.: Yale University Press, 1939).

[11]W. E. B. Du Bois, *Black Reconstruction: An Essay toward a History of the Part Which Black Folk Played in the Attempt to Deconstruct Democracy in America, 1860–1880* (New York: Russell & Russell, 1935).

white experience in *Origins of Class Struggle in Louisiana: A Social History of White Farmers and Laborers during Slavery and after, 1840–1875* (1939).[12]

Because so many American workers were themselves first-generation Americans or their children, scholars sought to recover their stories by studying the historical dynamics of ethnicity and immigration. Carl Wittke published *We Who Built America: The Saga of the Immigrant* in 1939, and the following year Marcus Hansen's *The Atlantic Migration, 1607–1860: A History of the Continuing Settlement of the United States* appeared posthumously.[13] In 1941, Oscar Handlin published *Boston's Immigrants, 1790–1865: A Study in Acculturation*, a pathbreaking historical analysis of one immigrant group's experience in a major American city. Handlin sought to bring social scientific methodologies to bear on his subject, but he also insisted on the need for historical imagination to convey the experiences of anonymous individuals. "Lacking the sociologist's or anthropologist's direct access to the subject by questionnaires or observation," he explained, the historian "must piece together his story from widely diversified sources, and, tethered within the limits of that which is known, impale upon a rigid page the intimate lives and deepest feelings of humble men and women who leave behind few formal records."[14]

American entry into World War II brought an end to the Great Depression and prompted a broad-based groundswell of patriotism. For the rising generation of Americans, a mutual commitment to win the fight for freedom against fascism—and, later, communism—took precedence over any internal disagreements. With this political and cultural shift, historians in the late 1940s and 1950s turned their attention to historical factors that brought Americans together by putting aside, at least for the moment, their study of forces that drove them apart. Conflicts between classes and other social groups no longer seemed as important as the values that Americans of different backgrounds shared in common. To explain the apparent agreement among Americans, historians developed new models of what made American society exceptional when compared to European societies. The result was a kind of historical analysis commonly referred to as the "consensus" interpretation.

Among the major works of consensus historiography was David Potter's *People of Plenty* (1954), which drew on the research of contemporary social scientists and identified "economic abundance" as the key to the distinctive American character. "America," Potter declared, "has had a greater measure of social equality and social mobility than any other highly developed society in human history."[15] Louis Hartz offered a more complex explanation for American

[12]Roger W. Shugg, *Origins of Class Struggle in Louisiana: A Social History of White Farmers and Laborers during Slavery and after, 1840–1875* (University: Louisiana State University Press, 1939).

[13]Carl F. Wittke, *We Who Built America: The Saga of the Immigrant* (New York: Prentice-Hall, 1939); Marcus Lee Hansen, *The Atlantic Migration, 1607–1860: A History of the Continuing Settlement of the United States* (Cambridge, Mass.: Harvard University Press, 1940).

[14]Oscar Handlin, *Boston's Immigrants, 1790–1865: A Study in Acculturation* (Cambridge, Mass.: Harvard University Press, 1941), x.

[15]David M. Potter, *People of Plenty: Economic Abundance and the American Character* (Chicago: University of Chicago Press, 1954), 95.

exceptionalism in his enormously influential *The Liberal Tradition in America* (1955). Although primarily a study of political thought rather than social history, Hartz's book contended that the absence of feudalism in colonial America set American history on a peculiar trajectory. Unlike the European case, Hartz argued, in the United States liberal ideology—the belief in private property, limited government, and individual freedom—reigned unchecked by either aristocratic notions on the Right or socialistic ideas on the Left.[16] In a somewhat similar vein, Daniel Boorstin in *The Americans: The Colonial Experience* (1958) suggested that the openness of the New World environment eroded the European habits of mind that the colonists brought with them, thereby allowing Americans to develop into a peculiarly free, pragmatic, and inventive people.[17]

One work of consensus historiography deserves special notice. While it confirmed conventional wisdom about the fluidity of American society, Merle Curti's *The Making of an American Community: A Case Study of Democracy in a Frontier County* (1959) broke new ground methodologically. Subjecting Turner's frontier thesis to a close empirical test, Curti and his associates used "modern calculating machines" (not yet computers) to analyze quantitative data from nineteenth-century Trempealeau County, Wisconsin. Curti demonstrated that quantitative social science methods could illuminate the lives of ordinary Americans who had all too often left behind nothing more than ghostly statistical traces. He thereby established a template for the quantitative community studies that would become a central feature of the "new social history" of the 1960s and 1970s.[18]

What set the new social history apart from the old? To some extent it was the quest to apply the methods and theories of the social sciences more systematically and more rigorously than had earlier social historians. But in retrospect the main distinction appears to have been that the old social history came before the interregnum of consensus historiography while the new social history came after it.[19] The civil rights movement played a major, albeit indirect, role in the rise of the new social history. Press reports of sit-ins, freedom rides, and violent white resistance to black demands for equal rights appeared to contradict the consensus historians' notion that American society was marked by broad agreement on fundamental values. Like Progressive scholars before them, the new social historians of the 1960s and 1970s sought to recover a "usable past" that

[16]Louis Hartz, *The Liberal Tradition in America: An Interpretation of American Political Thought since the Revolution* (New York: Harcourt, Brace, 1955).

[17]Daniel J. Boorstin, *The Americans: The Colonial Experience* (New York: Random House, 1958).

[18]Merle E. Curti, *The Making of an American Community: A Case Study of Democracy in a Frontier County* (Stanford, Calif.: Stanford University Press, 1959). The reference to "modern calculating machines" appears on p. 7.

[19]For a discussion that emphasizes how the new social history differed from the old social history, see Peter N. Stearns, "The Old Social History and the New," in Mary Kupiec Cayton, Elliott J. Gorn, and Peter W. Williams, eds., *Encyclopedia of American Social History*, 3 vols. (New York: Scribner's, 1993), 1: 237–50. On the continuities between the old and new social history, see Ellen F. Fitzpatrick, *History's Memory: Writing America's Past, 1880–1980* (Cambridge, Mass.: Harvard University Press, 2002).

would provide models of success and inspiration for contemporary social activists. In his 2005 presidential address to the Organization of American Historians, James Oliver Horton recalled, "When I entered graduate school in the late
1960s, the buzz among my fellow history students was all about something
we called New Left history—what came to be called the new social history."
"We focused on everyday working people and the families and communities
in which they lived," he explained. "They were women and men—including
Native Americans, African Americans, and a host of immigrants—whose historical experiences differed fundamentally from those of the elite minority about
which most historical accounts had been written."[20] Horton's rising generation of
social historians set out to analyze history "from the bottom up" in order to promote a more just and democratic social order.

Not all new social historians embraced the politics of the New Left, but most
believed that ordinary people, including the poor, exploited, and oppressed, possessed the agency—the self-directed capacity—as well as the right to make decisions for themselves. A number of scholars reacted strongly against Stanley
Elkins's *Slavery: A Problem in American Institutional and Intellectual Life* (1959),
which portrayed American slaves as docile and then explained their failure to
rebel with the help of a provocative analogy between southern plantations and
Nazi concentration camps.[21] Turning, like Elkins himself, to the social sciences
for models and methodologies, his critics recovered dimensions of slave culture
and slave behavior that had been invisible to the nineteenth-century white
observers on whom Elkins had relied for evidence. Key works that refuted
Elkins's thesis and offered new interpretations of the black experience under
slavery included John Blassingame's *The Slave Community* (1972), George P.
Rawick's *From Sundown to Sunup* (1972), Eugene Genovese's *Roll, Jordan, Roll*
(1974), Herbert Gutman's *The Black Family in Slavery and Freedom, 1750–1925*
(1977), and Lawrence Levine's *Black Culture and Black Consciousness* (1977).[22]
This scholarship was joined by pioneering works on slave women, including
Angela Davis's "Reflections on the Black Woman's Role in the Community of
Slaves" (1971) and Gerda Lerner's pathbreaking collection, *Black Women in White
America* (1972).[23]

[20]James Oliver Horton, "Patriot Acts: Public History in Public Service," *Journal of American History* 92 (December 2003): 806.

[21]Stanley M. Elkins, *Slavery: A Problem in American Institutional and Intellectual Life*
(Chicago: University of Chicago Press, 1959).

[22]John W. Blassingame, *The Slave Community: Plantation Life in the Antebellum South*
(New York: Oxford University Press, 1972); George P. Rawick, *From Sundown to Sunup: The
Making of the Black Community* (Westport, Conn.: Greenwood, 1972); Eugene D. Genovese,
Roll, Jordan, Roll: The World the Slaves Made (New York: Pantheon, 1974); Herbert G. Gut-
man, *The Black Family in Slavery and Freedom, 1750–1925* (New York: Vintage, 1977);
Lawrence W. Levine, *Black Culture and Black Consciousness: Afro-American Folk Thought
from Slavery to Freedom* (New York: Oxford University Press, 1977).

[23]Angela Y. Davis, "Reflections on the Black Woman's Role in the Community of Slaves,"
Black Scholar 3 (December 1971): 2–15; Gerda Lerner, *Black Women in White America: A Documentary History* (New York: Pantheon, 1972).

Colonial historians developed their own variant of the new social history. Influenced by French scholars associated with the journal *Annales*, they turned to vital records and other quantifiable evidence to produce community studies challenging easy generalizations about American society's having been "born liberal"—that is, valuing individualism and personal choice over tradition and social stability. In *A New England Town* (1970), Kenneth Lockridge argued that Dedham, Massachusetts, began as a "Christian Utopian Closed Corporate Community," while in *Four Generations* (1970) Philip Greven concluded that the early settlers of Andover, Massachusetts, created "extended patriarchal families" that were "as deeply rooted to the land and the community as it is possible for families to be."[24] Other colonial historians focused on more famous communities. In *A Little Commonwealth* (1971), John Demos examined family life in seventeenth-century Plymouth; in *Salem Possessed* (1974), Paul Boyer and Stephen Nissenbaum found the origins of America's most notorious witchcraft scare in localized community conflict; and, in *The Minutemen and Their World* (1976), Robert Gross explored why the farmers of Concord, Massachusetts, rallied to the patriot cause in the 1770s after having largely ignored the imperial crisis during the previous decade.[25]

New urban historians explored whether the nineteenth-century myth of the self-made man who rose from rags to riches had much basis in social reality. In 1964, Stephan Thernstrom's *Poverty and Progress* applied the statistical techniques pioneered by Curti to study the careers of unskilled workers in Newburyport, Massachusetts, and a flood of social mobility studies soon followed.[26] Sam Bass Warner in *Streetcar Suburbs* (1962) and David Ward in *Cities and Immigrants* (1971) borrowed from the toolboxes of sociologists and geographers to show how economic and technological changes reshaped urban spatial arrangements.[27] New labor historians turned for analytical models to British historians Eric Hobsbawm and E. P. Thompson, who emphasized the cultural dimensions

---

[24]Kenneth A. Lockridge, *A New England Town: The First Hundred Years, Dedham, Massachusetts, 1636–1736* (New York: W. W. Norton, 1970), 16; Philip J. Greven, *Four Generations: Population, Land, and Family in Colonial Andover, Massachusetts* (Ithaca, N.Y.: Cornell University Press, 1970), 168–69.

[25]John Demos, *A Little Commonwealth: Family Life in Plymouth Colony* (New York: Oxford University Press, 1971); Paul S. Boyer and Stephen Nissenbaum, *Salem Possessed: The Social Origins of Witchcraft* (Cambridge, Mass.: Harvard University Press, 1974); Robert A. Gross, *The Minutemen and Their World* (New York: Hill and Wang, 1976).

[26]Stephan Thernstrom, *Poverty and Progress: Social Mobility in a Nineteenth-Century City* (Cambridge, Mass.: Harvard University Press, 1964). Other social mobility studies included Peter R. Knights, *The Plain People of Boston, 1830–1860: A Study in City Growth* (New York: Oxford University Press, 1971); Howard P. Chudacoff, *Mobile Americans: Residential and Social Mobility in Omaha, 1880–1920* (New York: Oxford University Press, 1972); Michael B. Katz, *The People of Hamilton, Canada West: Family and Class in a Mid-Nineteenth-Century City* (Cambridge, Mass.: Harvard University Press, 1975); Clyde Griffen and Sally Griffen, *Natives and Newcomers: The Ordering of Opportunity in Mid-Nineteenth-Century Poughkeepsie* (Cambridge, Mass.: Harvard University Press, 1978).

[27]Sam Bass Warner, Jr., *Streetcar Suburbs: The Process of Growth in Boston, 1870–1900* (Cambridge, Mass.: Harvard University Press, 1962); David Ward, *Cities and Immigrants: A Geography of Change in Nineteenth-Century America* (New York: Oxford University Press, 1971).

of working-class formation. Herbert Gutman traced the persistence of preindustrial work habits in his essay "Work, Culture and Society in Industrializing America" (1973), while Alan Dawley offered a new answer to the perennial question, "Why is there no socialism in the United States?" in *Class and Community: The Industrial Revolution in Lynn* (1976).[28] Studies of working-class formation in turn stimulated innovative scholarship on middle-class formation. Most notably, Paul Johnson's *A Shopkeeper's Millennium* (1978) and Mary Ryan's *Cradle of the Middle Class* (1981) both focused on developments in antebellum upstate New York, where religious revivals led to middle-class campaigns for temperance, abolition, and other social reforms.[29]

At the same time, the second wave of American feminism interacted with the burgeoning interest in social history to stimulate a rich array of scholarship proclaiming the importance of ordinary women's lives. In 1969, Gerda Lerner's "The Lady and the Mill Girl: Changes in the Status of Women in the Age of Jackson" shifted scholarly attention from "women worthies" and traditional suffrage history to the ways in which gender and class jointly shaped women's experiences.[30] Carroll Smith-Rosenberg's pathbreaking article "The Female World of Love and Ritual" (1975) revealed an autonomous female culture that had escaped the attention of previous historians.[31] Nancy Cott's *The Bonds of Womanhood* (1977) examined how middle-class women in New England developed a fledgling consciousness of sisterhood during the early nineteenth century, while Thomas Dublin's *Women at Work* (1979) showed how gender shaped the contents of working women's lives in the same region by providing a foundation for solidarity.[32]

By the early 1980s, the use of social-historical concepts and approaches was commonplace among professional historians. *A People and a Nation*, the first college-level survey text to focus on the social history of ordinary Americans, appeared in 1982 and quickly proved a huge commercial success.[33] Within a few years, every major textbook publisher offered at least one social history survey. *Who Built America?*—a collaborative work undertaken by the American Social

[28]Herbert G. Gutman, "Work, Culture, and Society in Industrializing America, 1815–1919," *American Historical Review* 78 (June 1973): 531–88; Alan Dawley, *Class and Community: The Industrial Revolution in Lynn* (Cambridge, Mass.: Harvard University Press, 1976).

[29]Paul E. Johnson, *A Shopkeeper's Millennium: Society and Revivals in Rochester, New York, 1815–1837* (New York: Hill and Wang, 1978); Mary P. Ryan, *Cradle of the Middle Class: The Family in Oneida County, New York, 1790–1865* (New York: Cambridge University Press, 1981).

[30]Gerda Lerner, "The Lady and the Mill Girl: Changes in the Status of Women in the Age of Jackson," *American Studies Journal* 10 (Spring 1969): 5–15.

[31]Carroll Smith-Rosenberg, "The Female World of Love and Ritual: Relations between Women in Nineteenth-Century America," *Signs* 1 (Autumn 1975): 1–29.

[32]Nancy F. Cott, *The Bonds of Womanhood: "Woman's Sphere" in New England, 1780–1835* (New Haven, Conn.: Yale University Press, 1977); Thomas Dublin, *Women at Work: The Transformation of Work and Community in Lowell, Massachusetts, 1826–1860* (New York: Columbia University Press, 1979).

[33]Mary Beth Norton et al., *A People and a Nation: A History of the United States* (Boston: Houghton Mifflin, 1982).

History Project of the City University of New York—explicitly put "working people" at the center of a narrative that emphasized the popular struggles to make
history "from the bottom up."[34] Meanwhile practitioners of the new social history
won the discipline's most prestigious awards with increasing frequency. Indeed,
since 1980 the Bancroft Prize has been conferred on works of social history more
often than it has on works of either political or intellectual history.[35] The United
States Congress still may not consider social history to be traditional, but within
academe it has achieved orthodox status over the past quarter century.

Yet as social history matured, it faced new challenges. During the 1980s,
scholars paid increasing attention to the interactions of race, gender, and class as
factors shaping American society.[36] They explored the heterogeneity of women's
experiences and added the study of sexuality to social history's agenda.[37] In 1988,
John D'Emilio and Estelle Freedman published *Intimate Matters*, a pioneering
synthesis that challenged older narratives of the ongoing liberation of individuals
from a "puritanical" past and traced the creation of sexual identities and sexual
communities within which physical practices took on different social meanings.[38]
Younger historians questioned older approaches to race and ethnicity and focused instead on the history of "racial formations," analyzing how racial categories were framed differently under different historical circumstances.[39] Much
of the recent scholarship on race and gender has moved away from the study of
social behavior and toward a kind of literary analysis that deconstructs ideologies
that uphold systems of established power.

In the last decade, many new cultural historians have raised doubts about
the adequacy of social-historical approaches that emphasize the potential of ordinary people to resist oppression and take charge of their own destinies. These

[34]Bruce Levine et al., *Who Built America?* (New York: Pantheon, 1989).

[35]"The Bancroft Prizes: Previous Awards," Columbia University Libraries Subject Guides.
<http://www.columbia.edu/cu/lweb/eguides/amerihist/bancroftlist.html> (accessed October 25,
2006).

[36]Deborah Gray White, *Ar'n't I a Woman? Female Slaves in the Plantation South* (New
York: W. W. Norton, 1985); Suzanne Lebsock, *The Free Women of Petersburg: Status and Culture in a Southern Town, 1784–1860* (New York: W. W. Norton, 1984); Paula Giddings, *When
and Where I Enter: The Impact of Black Women on Race and Sex in America* (New York:
William Morrow, 1984); Jacqueline Jones, *Labor of Love, Labor of Sorrow: Black Women, Work,
and the Family from Slavery to the Present* (New York: Basic Books, 1985).

[37]Nancy F. Cott and Elizabeth H. Pleck, eds., *A Heritage of Her Own: Toward a New
Social History of American Women* (New York: Simon & Schuster, 1979) brought together articles from the early phases of this project. Ellen DuBois and Vicki Ruiz, eds., *Unequal Sisters: A
Multicultural Reader in U.S. Women's History* (New York: Routledge, 1990) carried the project
forward. It has been revised several times to include new scholarship in these vibrant fields.
Martin Bauml Duberman, Martha Vicinus, and George Chauncey, Jr., eds., *Hidden from History: Reclaiming the Gay and Lesbian Past* (New York: New American Library, 1984) also continues to be updated to reflect new directions.

[38]John D'Emilio and Estelle Freedman, *Intimate Matters: A History of Sexuality in America* (New York: Harper & Row, 1988).

[39]Michael Omi and Howard Winant, *Racial Formation in the United States: From the
1960s to the 1980s* (New York: Routledge, 1986).

scholars contend that the manipulative effects of mass culture and the coercive power of the modern state tightly constrain human action at most levels of the American social order. Yet at the same time, other historians have moved in a very different direction—toward the reintegration of social and political history. For example, in *Parlor Politics* (2000), Catherine Allgor shows how, though denied the vote, women in Washington, D.C., helped to shape the course of national politics in the early nineteenth century.[40] In *A Nation under Our Feet* (2003), Steven Hahn locates the sources of black political strength and determination during the travails of Reconstruction and Redemption in the families, communities, and lived experiences of rural African Americans.[41]

Today's social historians, like those before them, review and rework, alter and amplify received historical accounts to better encompass the full complexity of the past. Are these scholars, then, guilty of promoting "revisionist history"—a kind of anti-American history—as some politicians and cultural commentators have alleged? During the 1990s, efforts to craft National History Standards, an outline of the content that teachers and educators might consider essential for America's schoolchildren, foundered on disputes over whether the standards' authors had substituted "interpretation" for "facts" and had paid too much attention to minority groups and too little to the nation's leading statesmen. Lynne Cheney, former chair of the National Endowment for the Humanities, charged that the standards' authors "pursu[ed] their revisionist agenda [and] no longer bothered to conceal their great hatred of traditional history."[42] Other critics complained that the National History Standards did not sufficiently celebrate the foundations of America's distinctive identity and would undermine young people's patriotic pride.

More recently, in June 2006, Florida Governor Jeb Bush signed into law legislation requiring that "American history shall be viewed as factual, not as constructed, shall be viewed as knowable, teachable and testable, and shall be defined as the creation of a new nation based largely on the universal principles stated in the Declaration of Independence."[43] The law's supporters saw it as a weapon to beat back the onslaught of revisionist history. Yet in mandating a focus on political history rooted in a particular ideology, the Florida state government obscures the true diversity of American history and prevents young citizens from understanding the multicultural dimensions of their nation's past. A century after Frederick Jackson Turner called for the development of new historical approaches suitable to a new era, the study of American social history remains a deeply contested yet also wonderfully stimulating field of scholarly enterprise.

[40]Catherine Allgor, *Parlor Politics: In Which the Ladies of Washington Help Build a City and a Government* (Charlottesville: University Press of Virginia, 2000).

[41]Steven Hahn, *A Nation under Our Feet: Black Political Struggles in the Rural South from Slavery to the Great Migration* (Cambridge, Mass.: Harvard University Press, 2003).

[42]Cheney is quoted on p. 4 of Gary B. Nash, Charlotte Crabtree, and Ross E. Dunn, *History on Trial: Culture Wars and the Teaching of the American Past* (New York: Knopf, 1997).

[43]David Davisson, "Florida Education," History News Network. <http://hnn.us/blogs/entries/26616.html> (accessed October 28, 2006).

David A. Hollinger

American Intellectual History, 1907–2007

Intellectual history became a major recognized subfield of United States history only in the 1950s, midway through the century. Conveniently, in 1957—the exact midpoint between 1907 and 2007—the *Mississippi Valley Historical Review* (as the *Journal of American History* was titled until 1964) published John C. Greene's methodological essay, "Objectives and Methods in Intellectual History." This article marked the incorporation of intellectual history into the mainstream of the larger field of United States history.[1] Greene invited his colleagues to follow the example already being set by students of European history and by scholars in other disciplines. They were already engaged in the study of conscious, articulate, public reflection on the part of historical actors about human society, the economy, the natural world, race, God, political obligation, and a host of other topics. Previous generations of historians had studied ideas in America, but usually in strict relation to politics. George Bancroft, Francis Parkman, and Henry Adams, to cite three great nineteenth-century historians, attended to some of the ideas held by the presidents and generals who dominated their great narratives. Yet for these historians and their successors down through the generation of Charles A. Beard in the first half of the twentieth century, the central subjects were most often the state, political movements, the economy, diplomacy, and warfare.[2] What happened in the 1950s was a greater acceptance of the reality of *thinking* as a human activity like voting, fighting, farming, manufacturing, exploring, fishing,

[1]John C. Greene, "Objectives and Methods in Intellectual History," *Mississippi Valley Historical Review* (MVHR) 44 (June 1957): 58–74. Another article of the same epoch by John Higham is also a marker of this incorporation, but since it appeared in the *American Historical Review*, the journal for the whole discipline rather than for specialists in United States history, Higham's essay was a less striking sign of the times. Europeanists were generally more oriented to the study of ideas in history than were Americanists. See John Higham, "The Rise of Intellectual History," *American Historical Review* 56 (April 1951): 453–71.

[2]There were exceptions to this pattern, but the most influential historical studies of ideas in America, such as V. L. Parrington's *Main Currents in American Thought* (New York: Harcourt, Brace, 1927), were written by professors of English. Prior to the 1940s, one of the few widely noted books by a leading professional historian written in the mode of what would later be called intellectual history was Albert Bushnell Hart, *National Ideals Historically Traced,*

and litigating. No longer "a thing apart" left to philosophers and literary scholars, theoretical discourse as such became part of the history that historians study.

Philosophers and literary scholars helped historians of Greene's generation to see the importance of ideas in history. The very concept of the history of ideas was popularized by philosopher Arthur O. Lovejoy in the 1930s, especially through *The Great Chain of Being* (1936).[3] This study traced the development over many centuries in many cultures of the metaphysical idea of a hierarchy of life forms. Lovejoy's rigorous approach to the historical study of thought flowered in *The Journal of the History of Ideas*, an important interdisciplinary journal founded in 1940 by Lovejoy and a group of philosophers and literary scholars he recruited. During the 1940s and early 1950s, Lovejoy's journal published a series of dazzling analyses of Renaissance Europe and Mediterranean antiquity, many written by European émigrés whose work commanded instant and rapt attention from the learned world. These included Hans Baron, Ernst Cassirer, Alexander Koyre, Paul Oskar Kristeller, and Leo Spitzer. American thought was marginal to the specific engagements of *The Journal of the History of Ideas*, but in 1949 one of its early contributors, philosopher Morton White, published *Social Thought in America: The Revolt against Formalism*, a book that won immediate and lasting attention from historians interested in the philosophical underpinnings of liberal politics in the Progressive Era and after.[4]

The methodological impact of White's book in particular and of *The Journal of the History of Ideas* in general increased in the mid-1950s in the context of a series of historically focused books of breathtaking ambition and erudition written by literary scholars and political theorists. Chief among these landmark books—which, along with White's, long defined the meaning of intellectual history for professional historians even though written outside the discipline of history—were *The Liberal Tradition in America*, by political theorist Louis Hartz, and a series of books about Puritanism by the literary scholar Perry Miller. Hartz's sweeping study of how a highly specific set of liberal ideas had controlled much of American political history appeared in 1954, the year after the publication of Miller's most influential book, *The New England Mind: From Colony to Province*.[5] In that book, Miller analyzed the changes in theology and political

1607–1907 (New York: Harper and Brothers, 1907). The study of United States history during Hart's generation was heavily influenced by the deeply anti-intellectual frontier thesis of Frederick Jackson Turner, according to which material conditions, especially free land and population density, were the determining forces in the development of the United States.

[3]Arthur O. Lovejoy, *The Great Chain of Being* (Cambridge, Mass.: Harvard University Press, 1936).

[4]Morton G. White, *Social Thought in America: The Revolt against Formalism* (Boston: Viking Press, 1949). This book appeared in an expanded second edition in 1957 and a third edition in 1976. It was a study of five leading Progressive Era thinkers: John Dewey, Thorstein Veblen, James Harvey Robinson, Charles Beard, and Oliver Wendell Holmes, Jr.

[5]Louis Hartz, *The Liberal Tradition in America: An Interpretation of American Political Thought since the Revolution* (New York: Harcourt, Brace, 1954); Perry Miller, *The New England Mind: From Colony to Province* (Cambridge, Mass.: Harvard University Press, 1953).

doctrine of New England intellectuals in the late seventeenth and early eighteenth centuries. But once historians started attending to Miller, who was a writer of exceptional intensity and muscle, they found themselves caught up also in his earlier works, *The New England Mind: The Seventeenth Century* (1939), *Jonathan Edwards* (1949), and, soon thereafter, his most accessible work, a collection of essays published in 1956, *Errand into the Wilderness*.[6]

If it was the philosopher Lovejoy who more than any other single scholar popularized the history of ideas, it was the literary scholar Miller who did more than anyone else to make historians of the United States aware of how those ideas could be studied in their social context. Miller focused not on ideas in their disembodied state, as Lovejoy and his followers often did. Rather, Miller studied how leading intellectuals had worked out their basic ideas in a series of specific historical settings, especially the changing economic and political circumstances of British North America. Historians were quick to see the promise of this more contextual approach to ideas once the approach had been practiced commandingly by Miller. Although some work on American thought followed the classical Lovejoyan model of studying ideas as passed from one thinker to another regardless of the historical setting, most of the scholars who came to be known as American intellectual historians in the 1950s and after were concerned with the dialectical relation between thought and its immediate social environment. This was true, for example, of Merle Curti, who, as early as 1943 in the first edition of his textbook, *The Growth of American Thought*, linked intellectual history closely with social history.[7] The same link preoccupied John Higham, Curti's most prominent student. Higham's *Strangers in the Land* (1955) explained the ebb and flow of ethnic and racial prejudice in terms of the social and political setting of successive generations of Anglo-Protestants.[8] But Miller, Hartz, and White differed from Curti and Higham in the rigor with which they analyzed ideas and in the attention they devoted to the most highly developed philosophical, theological, and political theoretical discourses. Curti and Higham studied general ideas that had broad popular appeal, but Miller, Hartz, and White were willing to address the most sophisticated writings of leading American thinkers who were full participants in the intellectual history of the Europe-centered North Atlantic West. Miller, Hartz, and White showed that theoretical discussion in the United States invited, and indeed vindicated, the same kind of rigorous analysis being devoted to European thinkers at that historiographical moment by such contemporary historians as H. Stuart Hughes, Leonard Krieger, and Carl Schorske.[9]

[6]Perry Miller, *The New England Mind: The Seventeenth Century* (Cambridge, Mass.: Harvard University Press, 1939); *Jonathan Edwards* (New York: W. Sloane Associates, 1949); *Errand into the Wilderness* (Cambridge, Mass.: Belknap Press of Harvard University Press, 1956).

[7]Merle Curti, *The Growth of American Thought* (New York: Harper and Brothers, 1943), was expanded in editions of 1951 and 1964.

[8]John Higham, *Strangers in the Land* (New Brunswick, N.J.: Rutgers University Press, 1955).

[9]The work of European intellectual history that most influenced historians of the United States during this era was H. Stuart Hughes, *Consciousness and Society: The Reconstruction of European Social Thought, 1890–1930* (New York: Knopf, 1958).

The importance of ideas to an understanding even of American political history—a field that had been dominated by scholars who even while acknowledging ideas focused more on economic interests and political parties—was established by yet another scholar of Greene's generation, Richard Hofstadter. In a book of 1948 destined to be one of the most influential books ever written about the history of the United States, *The American Political Tradition*, Hofstadter delivered a series of vividly etched chapters on the ideas of leading presidents and their attendant political movements. Although Hofstadter had already written an important work on political ideologies (his 1944 volume, *Social Darwinism in American Thought*), his study of political ideologies throughout American history gave new and striking credibility to the basic methodological postulate that political ideas were not merely epiphenomenal—the consequences of some prior economic or social conditions—but were forces that could define a political movement and explain the popular appeal of a given political leader.[10]

Hofstadter integrated the study of political ideas into the study of basic American political history as no previous scholar had done. He did not pursue in any detail the work of political philosophers like John Dewey or Walter Lippmann, who later became canonical for the study of American intellectual history as carried out in the wake of Miller, Hartz, and White. But Hofstadter was a crucial influence in the growth of American intellectual history because, after *The American Political Tradition*, it proved very difficult to study the history of American politics without taking seriously the ideas expressed by leading political actors. In sharp contrast to the behaviorally focused political scientists of the era—who often instructed others, "Don't tell me what a politician said, tell me what he did"—Hofstadter insisted that the ideological self-representation of political actors was vital to understanding their role in history.

Even more important for the growth and standing of intellectual history as a subfield recognized by professional historians of the United States, however, was *The End of American Innocence*, by Henry F. May. This book of 1959, subtitled *A Study of the First Years of Our Time*, surveyed the entire panorama of public discourse about politics, religion, and literature in the United States during the five-year period, 1912 to 1917. It was much broader than Hofstadter's work, encompassing the thought of educated Americans about virtually all the topics they discussed in their magazines and books. While Hartz, Miller, and White focused on a relatively small number of obviously important texts, May analyzed the ideas of a host of what came to be called "middlebrow" thinkers and demonstrated that these journalists and popular writers participated in the same large conversation that engaged major thinkers like William James, Mark Twain, and Charles Beard. May's work, while capacious, was thus more specialized than most previous work

---

[10]Richard Hofstadter, *The American Political Tradition* (New York: Knopf, 1948); *Social Darwinism in American Thought* (1944; revised edition, Boston: Beacon Press, 1955).

in the field; by concentrating on a short time span, May offered a virtual ethnography of the educated classes of the United States in a sharply defined era.[11]

Having achieved this maturity, intellectual history has flourished within the ranks of United States history specialists from the 1950s to the present, but the subfield's relation to other subfields has changed considerably during this half-century, and so, too, has its relation to the study of other societies, especially those of Europe. The remainder of this essay concerns these developments in the period since Greene's essay of 1957 and May's striking book of 1959.

The growth of social history during the 1970s and 1980s is perhaps the single most widely noted development within the discipline in the last fifty years. This is not the place to do justice to the emergence of social history, but in order to understand the destiny of intellectual historians it is vital to keep in mind that a sharper division of labor between intellectual historians and other specialists in United States history was a major consequence of the rise of social history. The latter attended more to everyday life than to public affairs and less to elites than to the vast non-elite population of the country. Social historians were especially concerned with groups defined by gender, race, ethnicity, and economic function. Just as the intellectual historians of the 1950s sometimes advanced their position in the discipline by calling attention to important topics that had been ignored by the political and diplomatic historians who dominated the discipline's major departments, journals, and professional organizations, so, too, did the social historians of the 1970s and 1980s call attention to topics left out of accounts by the intellectual, as well as the political and diplomatic, historians.

To this the intellectual historians generally responded by articulating more sharply than they had before the sense that intellectual history did not claim to embrace all thinking, but focused more on the discourse of intellectuals, and on the historical acts of people who made history by arguing. This clarification of the character of the field of American intellectual history was marked by a 1979 volume coedited by Higham and Paul Conkin, *New Directions in American Intellectual History*.[12] Hence by the 1980s it was rare to see titles invoking the "American mind," because intellectual historians were more conscious than before that the intellectual leaders they studied were not necessarily representatives of the national population as a whole.[13] Intellectual historians, who in the middle decades of the twentieth century had written sweeping books and articles attributing this or that cluster of ideas to American society as a whole, produced instead a flurry of specialized studies clarifying particular episodes, careers, and traditions.

---

[11] Henry F. May, *The End of American Innocence: A Study of the First Years of Our Time, 1912–1917* (New York: Knopf, 1959). In a 1993 edition May revisited the issues he had addressed more than three decades before.

[12] John Higham and Paul Conkin, eds., *New Directions in American Intellectual History* (Baltimore: Johns Hopkins University Press, 1979).

[13] A prime example of what was later seen as the overreach of the American intellectual historians of the 1950s was Henry Steele Commager, *The American Mind: An Interpretation of American Thought and Character since the 1890s* (New Haven, Conn.: Yale University Press, 1950).

Bruce Kuklick's study of philosophy in and around Harvard University between 1860 and 1930 is one prominent example of this trend. Another is Thomas Bender's study of intellectual life in New York City. A third is Dorothy Ross's history of late-nineteenth- and early-twentieth-century sociology, economics, and political science.[14] This sharpening of the division of labor was also a mark of the maturity of American intellectual history as a field. It had less to prove, it was established as a subfield, and its practitioners were known for their skill. These specialized works made explicit that their subject matter was not so much thinking as the traces left by thinking: the documents—such as books, letters, and diaries—that registered in some material and thus accessible form the thoughts that produced them. This more methodologically austere practice produced an enduring body of carefully documented and closely argued monographic work. Simultaneously, intellectual historians began to design and execute their projects with much greater attention to the learned discourses of the North Atlantic West. A prominent feature of the work of intellectual historians of the middle decades of the twentieth century had been its intensely American focus, congruent with and in many ways constituent of the American Studies movement that began in American higher education at that time. The founding of *The American Quarterly* in 1949 and of the American Studies Association shortly thereafter institutionalized the preoccupation of many literary scholars and historians with the distinctness of the culture of the United States. Hartz's *The Liberal Tradition in America* was among the most famous of many ambitious treatises claiming to explain how and why the United States differed from both Western Europe and Soviet Russia and its satellite nations. The Cold War was not the only impetus for this preoccupation, but it was a crucial matrix for the American exceptionalism that dominated the American Studies movement. This persuasion emphasized the uniqueness of American culture and sometimes extended to the claim that the United States was an exception to the apparent laws of historical development that affected other nations. Literary scholars Henry Nash Smith (in *Virgin Land* [1950]) and R. W. B. Lewis (in *The American Adam* [1955]) led this American Studies movement, along with historians Daniel J. Boorstin (in *The Genius of American Politics* [1953]) and David Potter (in *People of Plenty*, 1954).[15]

[14]Bruce Kuklick, *The Rise of American Philosophy: Cambridge, Massachusetts, 1860–1930* (New Haven, Conn.: Yale University Press, 1977); Thomas Bender, *New York Intellect: A History of Intellectual Life in New York City, from 1750 to the Beginnings of Our Time* (New York: Knopf, 1987); Dorothy Ross, *The Origins of American Social Science* (New York: Cambridge University Press, 1991).

[15]Henry Nash Smith, *Virgin Land: The American West as Symbol and Myth* (Cambridge, Mass.: Harvard University Press, 1950); R. W. B. Lewis, *The American Adam: Innocence, Tragedy, and Tradition in the Nineteenth Century* (Chicago: University of Chicago Press, 1955); Daniel J. Boorstin, *The Genius of American Politics* (Chicago: University of Chicago Press, 1953); David Potter, *People of Plenty: Economic Abundance and the American Character* (Chicago: University of Chicago Press, 1954).

But well before the end of the Cold War, the most widely discussed works in the field of American intellectual history had taken on a much different cast. In the 1980s and after, scholars treated the intellectual life of the United States in much closer relation to Europe and emphasized the continuities rather than the contrasts between what intellectuals were doing in the United States and Europe. In this new perspective, the intellectual life of the United States held to Europe a relationship not so different from that held to it by the intellectual life of Great Britain or Russia or France. There were indeed national traditions, but the thinkers who sustained and critically revised those national traditions also participated in the larger discourse of the North Atlantic West. James T. Kloppenberg's *Uncertain Victory: Progressivism and Social Democracy in the United States and Europe, 1870–1920* (1986) exemplified the new internationalism of intellectual historians. Kloppenberg offered a close comparative analysis of the epistemologies and political theories developed during the era of rapid industrialization in Germany, France, and Great Britain as well as the United States. Kloppenberg did acknowledge national differences, but his work was profoundly contrary to the Americocentric approach of White, who covered many of the same American intellectuals. Indeed, in 2000 when a popular book by literary scholar Louis Menand advanced an unreconstructed American exceptionalist interpretation of the pragmatist philosophers who were central figures in Kloppenberg's book as well as in White's, he made no mention at all of Kloppenberg. Menand's *The Metaphysical Club* (2000) was much appreciated by specialists for its accessible, deeply engaging account of the American intellectuals who created pragmatist philosophy, but these specialists complained with good reason that Menand had harvested a generation of detailed monographic work but missed its meaning: The United States was but one of many national settings in which the idea that ideas were tools for coping rather than mirrors of reality developed in the late nineteenth and early twentieth centuries.[16]

The international frame of reference taken increasingly for granted by American intellectual historians was part of the design of *Modern Intellectual History*, a new journal founded in 2004 devoted to the period since the Enlightenment. This journal is coedited by three leading intellectual historians, one a specialist in the United States (Charles Capper), one in the history of Great Britain and other English-speaking countries (Nicholas Phillipson), and one in the history of continental Europe (Anthony LaVopa). In its first four years, *Modern Intellectual History* published more than one hundred research articles and review essays, by younger scholars as well as by the most senior of intellectual historians, thus revealing the maturity and depth of the subfield of intellectual history. In the pages of this new journal, scholars engaged the intellectual history of Asia as well as that of Europe and the United States. In 2007 it published an

[16]James T. Kloppenberg, *Uncertain Victory: Progressivism and Social Democracy in Europe and America, 1870–1920* (New York: Oxford University Press, 1986); Louis Menand, *The Metaphysical Club* (New York: Farrar, Straus and Giroux, 2000).

entire issue devoted to the intellectual history of India in dialectical relation to that of the Europe-centered West. Hence, exactly at a time when other subfields of United States history are struggling to meet the challenge of a more global history, intellectual historians, along with diplomatic historians, have already charted part of the way.

This same internationalism also characterizes *Modern Intellectual History*'s older sibling, *The Journal of the History of Ideas*, which continues its distinguished tradition of nearly eighty years, now more responsive to American history than in decades past. A new editorial collective published its first issue of *The Journal of the History of Ideas* in 2006 and immediately signaled a new openness to scholarship beyond the ancient, medieval, and early modern European subfields in which that journal had made its reputation. In its April 2008 issue, this reanimated, expanded journal published contributions by no fewer than five specialists in American history.

The sustained attention to international communities of discourse found in the pages of these two journals helps to mark off intellectual history from cultural history. Cultural historians are largely concerned with patterns of meaning found in local, regional, or national communities and less often with the learned elites who participate in international argumentation. Cultural history emerged out of social history during the last quarter of the twentieth century, in response to the widespread feeling that quantitatively oriented social historians had left out of account the ways in which the non-elite populations studied by social historians assigned meaning to their lives. The emergence of cultural history repeats in some ways the same professional dynamic displayed earlier in the development of intellectual history and social history. Each such movement advances by pointing to aspects of history insufficiently taken into account, ostensibly, at least, by other historians. In the process, divisions of labor are sharpened. Cultural history's complaint against intellectual history was that the latter, while studying the arguments of intellectuals, left largely unexplored the cognitive life of ordinary people.[17]

The division of labor between intellectual historians and other subgroups within the discipline is illustrated by the materials used in teaching. The basic text assigned in most college classes in American intellectual history is *The American Intellectual Tradition: A Source Book*, which reprints classical, "canonical" works by Jonathan Edwards, Thomas Jefferson, Randolph Bourne, Margaret Mead, Hannah Arendt, Thomas Kuhn, James Baldwin, Richard Rorty, and dozens of comparable figures. This textbook, now in its fifth edition, does not deal with popular culture at all, but rather focuses on leading intellectuals, the people who made history by arguing.[18] Hence American intellectual history has become, more avowedly than ever, the history of American intellectuals.

[17]The relations between cultural, intellectual, social, and political history as currently understood by historians of the United States are displayed in a roundtable discussion of nine historians in the *Journal of American History* 90 (September 2003): 576–611.

[18]David A. Hollinger and Charles Capper, eds., *The American Intellectual Tradition: A Sourcebook*, 5th ed. (New York: Oxford University Press, 2006).

Yet this sharpening of focus has not meant a retreat to the margins of the discipline. Students of diplomatic, business, and labor history have all begun to take more account of theoretical discourse and have formed new alliances with intellectual historians. Within the pages of a recent book edited by Nelson Lichtenstein, one of the nation's leading historians of unionized workers, labor historians and intellectual historians are seen interacting with one another to the mutual benefit of their subfields. Lichtenstein and his contributors to *American Capitalism: Social Thought and Political Economy in the Twentieth Century* (2006) illustrate the ability of the subfields of United States history to pool their strengths while practicing the specialized skills promoted by a refined division of professional labor.[19]

At a time when many educators worry about the "dumbing down" of the American population, intellectual historians explore and reinforce the most critically engaged, theoretically intensive aspects of the United States. In their capacity as students of the history of the use of evidence and reasoning, intellectual historians remind us that evidence and reasoning are not foreign objects, exotic arts suitable only for Vienna and Paris, but are as American as apple pie.

[19]Nelson Lichtenstein, ed., *American Capitalism: Social Thought and Political Economy in the Twentieth Century* (Philadelphia: University of Pennsylvania Press, 2006).

Emily S. Rosenberg

America and the World: From National to Global

Today, many professional historians and educators urge introducing students to a subject they call "America and the world."[1] Their refrain extends many historians' earlier entreaties to broaden a field of scholarly inquiry and instruction once designated as "U.S. diplomatic history." To trace the changing nature and content of this field over a century, this short sketch highlights several prominent schools within U.S. diplomatic history. Then it traces efforts to expand the field's bounds to encompass American foreign relations, American international relations, and, most recently, America and the world. The increasingly diverse scholarship that has accompanied these shifts has shaped—and continues to reshape—teaching at every level of the curriculum.

During the late nineteenth and early twentieth centuries, when educators sought to divide history curricula into coherent sequences of individual courses, they organized their subject matter around nation-states. Professional history itself had developed in conjunction with other projects of national consolidation, and historians considered diplomacy conducted by leaders of nation-states to be the primary way in which peoples interacted with other peoples in the world.

While national distinctiveness constituted the guiding framework for historical inquiry in the late nineteenth and early twentieth centuries, human progress provided a common theme. Histories of this period generally presented the United States as the latest chapter in an unfolding story of liberty that could be traced from its beginnings in the ancient world, through Europe, then through England, to the continent of America. In this developmental view of history as unfolding progress, historians often used states and cultures to exemplify supposed stages of human advancement along a continuum that ran from the

---

[1] Also called "United States and the world." The choice of whether to use *America* or *United States* presents a conundrum. Some scholars object to using *America* to designate only the United States when the entire hemisphere is actually America. Yet *United States* often carries a connotation designating the government, rather than the people. There is no English word such as "United Stateseans," and "U.S. Americans" seems cumbersome. While acknowledging the problems, I prefer "America and the world" to other options.

"primitive" to the "civilized." U.S. expansion across the continent, from this perspective, seemed consistent with a story of U.S. national destiny and the spread of "civilization."

Although many U.S. historians writing before World War I closely examined their country's consolidation of territory in the U.S. West—the area of that generation's most substantial military and political involvement—the history of the U.S. West developed largely as a subfield of U.S. domestic (not diplomatic) history. This division, which conceived relations with Indian nations to the west to be domestic history and relations with European nations to the east to be diplomatic history, in effect has inscribed the idea of manifest destiny (that is, the notion that the United States was providentially destined to create a sea-to-sea landed empire) into the very fabric of how historical fields have been conceptualized and taught.[2]

The field of U.S. diplomatic history that emerged around 1900 focused primarily on state-to-state relations between the United States and the well-consolidated states of Western Europe. Much of it revolved around the U.S. commitment to the Monroe Doctrine, a policy that declared the Western Hemisphere to be a sphere of U.S. special influence and warned European nations against any interference in its affairs. Policy elites and military leaders, the presumed custodians of the nation-state, constituted the major subjects of history, and official state archives provided the most important sources for research.[3]

This emphasis on U.S. diplomacy with Europe was reinforced after World War I, when a large number of American diplomatic histories examined the causes and consequences of the war and tried to suggest lessons for future policy makers. Although some historical work defended President Woodrow Wilson, many historians concluded that he had been unsuccessful in fulfilling his promises to abolish the "old diplomacy" of secret intrigue, to produce new international peacekeeping institutions, and to usher in a more democratic world. They split, however, over the causes of the president's failure. Some blamed Wilson for betraying his own ideals and for political ineptitude in being unable to gain Senate approval of U.S. membership in the League of Nations. Others stressed the clever manipulations of Old World leaders or of Republican senators like Henry Cabot Lodge, who led the opposition to the League. A school of historians called "revisionists," led by Harry Elmer Barnes, concluded that the United States had lacked any compelling national interest to enter the war and faulted Wilson for

---

[2] Robert Orrill and Linn Shapiro, "From Bold Beginnings to an Uncertain Future: The Discipline of History and History Education," *American Historical Review* 110 (June 2005): 727–50. On this general point, see Ian Tyrrell, "American Exceptionalism in an Age of International History," *American Historical Review* 96 (October 1991): 1031–55; Daniel A. Segal, "'Western Civ' and the Staging of History in American Higher Education," *American Historical Review* 105 (June 2000): 770–804.

[3] See works by Henry Cabot Lodge, such as *The War with Spain* (New York: Macmillan, 1899) and *One Hundred Years of Peace* (New York: Macmillan, 1913), on relations between the United States and Great Britain.

ever abandoning neutrality.[4] The greatest issues of statecraft—those dealing with war and peace—seemed to be, as they remain, the appropriate central subjects for diplomatic history. This traditional diplomatic history often had an elitist cast because of its emphasis on well-consolidated nation-states and high policy.

The strong reformist currents after World War I, however, profoundly affected the field. In the era between World Wars I and II, Charles A. Beard and Herbert E. Bolton altered, each in a very different way, the prevailing interpretive paradigms of scholarship and teaching. Beard's concerns emerged from the broad intellectual movement Progressivism. Post–World War I Progressive historians, often influenced by John Dewey's pragmatism, drew upon the emerging social sciences in an attempt to render history relevant to current social problems such as industrialization, immigration, urbanization, and international conflict. Beard had emphasized "the economic basis of politics" in his influential study of the making of the U.S. Constitution and in a series of lectures published as a book in 1922.[5] His *Idea of National Interest* (1934) elaborated the connection he saw between economic interests and international conflict. Beard had resigned from Columbia University in 1917 in protest over wartime restrictions on academic freedom, and the book built on his conviction that economic interests, war, and a growing state bureaucracy would ultimately imperil the nation's democracy.

The Idea of National Interest rejected the common notion that a liberalized "open-door" world—that is, one relatively free of economic restrictions—contributed to peace and global prosperity. By trying to force open-door policies on other countries and then pushing the sale of goods and the lending of money abroad, Beard argued, Republican administrations of the 1920s had turned government into an agency of private interests operating overseas. Defining national interest as global economic expansion, in his view, would lead to war, as nations were bound to clash over markets, resources, and territory. Moreover, an ever-growing military establishment would eventually threaten the republic. His companion volume, *The Open Door at Home* (1934), suggested that investments in new technologies at home would promote both economic growth and the pursuit of greater social justice.[6] The views of Charles Beard and his wife Mary R. Beard, a pioneer in social and women's history, were especially influential

[4]Compare, for example, Ray Stannard Baker, *Woodrow Wilson and World Settlement* (Garden City, N.Y.: Doubleday, Page and Co., 1922), with Harry Elmer Barnes, *The Genesis of the World War: An Introduction to the Problem of War Guilt* (New York: Knopf, 1926). Baker, a close friend of Wilson who was the press officer for the American peace commission in Paris, became editor of Wilson's papers and addresses. Barnes was the leading World War I revisionist. See Warren I. Cohen, *The American Revisionists: The Lessons of Intervention in World War I* (Chicago: University of Chicago Press, 1967) for more on the historical scholarship of World War I.
[5]Charles A. Beard, *An Economic Interpretation of the Constitution of the United States* (New York: Macmillan, 1913); *The Economic Basis of Politics* (New York: Knopf, 1922).
[6]Charles A. Beard, *The Idea of National Interest: An Analytical Study in American Foreign Policy* (New York: Macmillan, 1934); *The Open Door at Home* (New York: Macmillan, 1934).

because they coauthored school textbooks widely used during the period between the world wars.[7]

From the late 1930s on, Beard became vehemently opposed to President Franklin D. Roosevelt, who he thought plotted to involve the United States in war. In fact, Beard became so obsessed with blaming Roosevelt personally for U.S. involvement in World War II that his histories began to seem inconsistent with his own systemic analysis of the economic basis of politics. During World War II and the early Cold War, as the nation fought fascism and confronted communism, Beard's critique attracted fewer followers. His economic interpretation, however, would emerge influential again in the antiwar critiques of the 1960s and 1970s.

Although not a diplomatic historian, Herbert E. Bolton of the University of California stands out as another important figure in interwar historiography. Bolton focused on the "essential unity" of nations in the Western Hemisphere by pointing to the similarities in their histories, first as colonized territories with indigenous populations, then as newly independent states. Bolton offered his first course on Greater America in 1920, teaching American history as the history of the hemisphere, rather than of the United States (a practice that continues today in International Baccalaureate high school curricula). The so-called Bolton thesis provided an alternative to the traditional histories that had focused U.S. history on its Anglo-Saxon and British heritage. Though not without its own problems and contradictions, Bolton's insistence on casting American history within a broader framework than that of a single nation-state and conceptualizing it within larger global forces presaged some of the concerns of later America and the world scholars.[8]

The Second World War dealt a setback to both Beard's and Bolton's interpretations. Many diplomatic historians enlisted in national service in some capacity during World War II and subsequently wrote histories that returned the focus of scholarship to high policy and diplomacy. Some tended to see public service, rather than adversarial critique, as their proper role and feared a relapse into isolationism in the face of the postwar Communist threat. Diplomatic history textbooks of the 1950s, therefore, generally encouraged students to join a

---

[7]On American historiography generally, including that of the interwar era, see John Higham, *History: Professional Scholarship in America* (Baltimore: Johns Hopkins University Press, 1986); Peter Novick, *That Noble Dream: The "Objectivity Question" and the American Historical Profession* (Cambridge: Cambridge University Press, 1988); Ellen Fitzpatrick, *History's Memory: Writing America's Past, 1880–1980* (Cambridge, Mass.: Harvard University Press, 2002). Charles A. Beard and Mary R. Beard, *History of the United States: A Study in American Civilization* (New York: Macmillan, 1921) and *The Rise of American Civilization* (New York: Macmillan, 1927) went through many editions in the 1920s, 1930s, and 1940s.

[8]See Herbert E. Bolton, *History of the Americas* (Boston: Ginn and Co, 1928). Bolton's best-known book was *The Spanish Borderlands* (New Haven, Conn.: Yale University Press, 1921). David J. Weber, *The Spanish Frontier in North America* (New Haven, Conn.: Yale University Press, 1992), 353–60, discusses some of the contradictions of the Bolton school.

new consensus that supported their country's exercise of its "responsibilities" in the world and rejected any kind of disengagement, "appeasement," or antiwar "revisionism."[9] This so-called consensus history looked away from social and economic divisions in America and emphasized the nation's exceptional leadership on the world stage.

During the early Cold War, a new "realist" critique of U.S. policy also appeared. Especially prominent in political science, this critique entered U.S. diplomatic history primarily through George F. Kennan's widely read and assigned *American Diplomacy, 1900–1950* (1951). Kennan had been in the State Department and watched the breakdown of Europe on the eve of World War II. After the war he headed the State Department's Policy Planning staff but resigned in 1950, went into academic life, and wrote his short history of American diplomacy. The book presented an extended critique of the moralistic and idealistic approach that he felt Woodrow Wilson had bequeathed to U.S. policy. To Kennan and other realists, World War II taught the clear lesson that the United States needed to be involved in the world in a tough-minded way. In Kennan's view, open-ended and idealistic crusades, accompanied by overblown rhetoric, constituted the central problem of U.S. diplomacy. A cultural conservative, Kennan had little confidence in democratic public opinion and saw diplomacy as the proper realm of educated elites who could deal with subtlety, set priorities, and astutely weigh means and ends. He came to decry the global and highly militarized anti-Communist crusading of the early Cold War and Vietnam War eras. Ill-defined commitments to contain communism everywhere, he believed, failed to establish wise strategic priorities or to carefully allocate always-limited resources. Kennan's anti-Wilsonian realist critique permeated much of the historical work on foreign policy during the Cold War, although it seemed to have had a limited impact on policy making.[10]

Although diplomacy-centered histories shaped by the anti-Communist consensus and by the realist tradition held sway in most classrooms during the early Cold War, a Beardian legacy continued to flourish among a group of historians at the University of Wisconsin. William Appleman Williams elaborated a Beardian-type analysis in *The Tragedy of American Diplomacy* (1959) and thereby sparked a controversy that would shape two decades of diplomatic history scholarship.

[9]Novick, *That Noble Dream*, 305–9. Widely used texts of the 1950s, which went through many editions, included Julius W. Pratt, *A History of United States Foreign Policy* (New York: Prentice-Hall, 1954); Thomas A. Bailey, *A Diplomatic History of the American People* (New York: Appleton-Century-Crofts, 1942); Samuel Flagg Bemis, *A Diplomatic History of the United States* (New York: Henry Holt, 1936).

[10]George F. Kennan, *American Diplomacy, 1900–1950* (Chicago: University of Chicago Press, 1951; expanded edition, 1985); Richard L. Russell, *George F. Kennan's Strategic Thought: The Making of an American Political Realist* (New York: Praeger, 1999); Wilson D. Miscamble, *George F. Kennan and the Making of American Foreign Policy, 1947–1950* (Princeton, N.J.: Princeton University Press, 1992). Norman A. Graebner's work elaborates the realist position in several different diplomatic contexts; see, for example, his *America as a World Power: A Realist Appraisal from Wilson to Reagan* (Wilmington, Del.: Scholarly Resources, 1984).

Williams, who began to teach at the University of Wisconsin in 1957 and whose views subsequently influenced a generation of scholars called the "Wisconsin school," argued that economic expansion in search of new markets lay at the core of the American experience. Integrating foreign economies into the U.S. market system, he explained, constituted a new form of "open door" or "informal" empire that brought American policy into "tragic" conflict with professed ideals of democracy and self-determination. Although his economic interpretation drew heavily on Beard's warnings that the power of globalized capital interests would eclipse democratic traditions, many opposing historians conflated Williams's economic interpretation with Marxism and portrayed him as a dangerous purveyor of "New Left" ideology. In the years that followed, Wisconsin school students produced much significant work. Walter LaFeber's *The New Empire* (1963), for example, examined the economic forces behind expansionist foreign policy in the late nineteenth century.[11]

The Wisconsin school stood at odds with most of the prevailing historical interpretations. Postwar consensus and realist historians portrayed the United States as an often isolationist power that now needed to accept its global responsibilities to build a liberalized economic order and a strong military force. Williams, like Beard, suggested that the United States had long been an outward-looking empire driven by economic interests, which used the state to push an open-door order that brought militarism, repression, and war. Like Beard, the Wisconsin school paid close attention to large economic and social forces and presented policy as flowing from these pressures more than from external threats.

The debates over the role of economics in foreign policy animated the field of diplomatic history during the 1960s and 1970s. Discussions became especially heated in the context of the Vietnam War because each side articulated a very different conception of America's role in the world. Was U.S. involvement in Vietnam driven by a commitment to freedom or by open-door imperialism? Did conflicts such as that in Vietnam arise from Communist aggression, or did the United States contribute to tensions through its vigorous postwar push for an open-door world that it could dominate?

Attacking and defending the Wisconsin school (often also labeled "revisionist" or "New Left" by critics) set the agenda for much of the diplomatic history written between the 1960s and the 1980s, and most historians became caught up in the cross fire. Teachers and students should be aware that many of the books from this era will generally address, overtly or more subtly, this debate—by whether they present economic concerns as the primary drivers of foreign policy and by the degree of their critical posture toward U.S. policies.

While these Vietnam era controversies raged, scholarship pushed in other directions as well. In 1967, some leading U.S. diplomatic historians who did not embrace an economic interpretation, such as Alexander DeConde, Richard W.

---

[11]William Appleman Williams, *The Tragedy of American Diplomacy* (Cleveland: World Publishing Co., 1959); Walter LaFeber, *The New Empire: An Interpretation of American Expansion, 1860–1898* (Ithaca, N.Y.: Cornell University Press, 1963).

Leopold, Robert H. Ferrell, and Ernest R. May, formed the Society for Historians of American Foreign Relations (SHAFR). SHAFR's creation signaled two themes that would significantly reorient the field.

First, many historians of diplomacy sought to break from what DeConde, in his presidential address to SHAFR in 1969, called the "elitism and self-satisfying patriotism" of earlier generations. They called for more multinational archival research and greater language competency, both of which would militate against national, and overtly nationalistic, histories. SHAFR soon dropped the image of the seal of the U.S. Department of State, which had initially adorned the cover of its newsletter.[12]

Second, as the new organization's name implied, the "history of foreign relations" slowly began to replace "diplomatic history" as the descriptor of the field. This new designation suggested how historians were moving away from studying "what one clerk said to another," which had become an uncharitable description of the terrain of diplomatic history. Many people in SHAFR (both those who associated their work with the Wisconsin school and those who did not) stretched their concerns beyond government policy making and elite diplomacy to encompass the agents of American influence that worked outside government—individuals and groups that political scientists called "non-state actors." These included religious missionaries, investors, traders, educators, media institutions, technocrats and advisers, labor unions, tourists, service and cultural organizations, and major philanthropic foundations.[13]

The turn toward foreign relations, especially visible from the 1980s on, received a boost from the new social and cultural emphasis that was simultaneously altering the entire discipline of history. Once the role of non-state actors in the global arena came into focus, new topics and methodologies followed. Taking cues from labor history, gender theory, critical race studies, cultural studies, and work exploring the construction of nationalisms, historians of American foreign relations began to examine policy documents in new ways. More important, they increasingly looked beyond the arena of foreign policy making toward transnational networks—economic, religious, cultural—that enlisted people's allegiances. Simultaneously, diplomatic history's reputation as a preserve of white males (a reputation not always deserved) began to change. Although the diversity of a new generation of practitioners remained less visible than in other

[12]Peter L. Hahn, "The Last Word," *Passport* 9 (December 2005): 55. *Passport* is the newsletter of SHAFR. When SHAFR's official journal was established in 1977, it was titled *Diplomatic History*, a name that has provoked ongoing discussions about boundaries and designations in the field. See, for example, Michael J. Hogan, "The 'Next Big Thing': The Future of Diplomatic History in a Global Age," *Diplomatic History* 28 (January 2004): 1–22.

[13]Two works that pointed in this direction were Frank Costigliola, *Awkward Dominion: American Political, Economic, and Cultural Relations with Europe, 1919–1933* (Ithaca, N.Y.: Cornell University Press, 1984), and Emily S. Rosenberg, *Spreading the American Dream: American Economic and Cultural Expansion, 1890–1945* (New York: Hill and Wang, 1982).

subfields of history, the broadened field attracted more women and people of diverse racial and ethnic backgrounds than in the past.[14]

The late-twentieth-century revolutions in markets, technology, media, and migration, all of which accelerated contacts among citizens and cultures, prompted other descriptive terms. "Foreign relations" seemed to imply that non-Americans were, well, too *foreign*. Did not the connectivity and circulation of the modern (or postmodern) era point toward tangled networks of both international and transnational relationships that fit poorly within the spoke-and-wheel pattern implied in the term "American foreign relations"? The phenomenon called "globalization," a word suddenly seen everywhere as a descriptor of the post–Cold War 1990s, offered new terms and paradigms for conceptualizing complex state and non-state relationships.

The more U.S. historians pondered the processes of transnationalism and globalization, the more they recognized that those phenomena had always been a feature of U.S. life. Every era, after all, had formal and informal networks forged through migration, travel, media, religion, trade, investment, advertising, and cultural interactions. Akira Iriye's many books, especially *Global Community* (2002), exemplify diplomatic historians' move toward an interest in culture and globalization.[15] Iriye and many others have urged U.S. historians to become more involved in globalization studies and world history. Even international history that tends to focus on governmental policies has significantly enlarged its geographical scope as growing numbers of scholars have concentrated on areas outside Europe.

This global focus has prompted new projects to broaden the study of U.S. history. In the 1990s David P. Thelen, as editor of the *Journal of American History*, reached out to historians throughout the world by sponsoring a number of international initiatives and bringing scholars from outside the United States into an advisory role. In 2000 a group headed by Thomas Bender—a collaboration between New York University and the Organization of American Historians—produced a report that called on historians to transcend "the nation as the container of American history" and to link the U.S. experience to transnational and global developments.[16] Bender's group advocated a study of U.S. history *within*

---

[14]For an extensive discussion of influential works illustrating the inclusion of social and cultural history in the field of foreign relations, see Brenda Gayle Plummer, "The Changing Face of Diplomatic History: A Literature Review," *The History Teacher* 38 (May 2005): 1–16; Michael J. Hogan, "The 'Next Big Thing.'" in Michael J. Hogan and Thomas G. Paterson, eds., *Explaining the History of American Foreign Relations* (New York: Cambridge University Press, 2004) contains useful essays that explore the many new approaches to the field.

[15]Akira Iriye, *Global Community: The Role of International Organizations in the Making of the Contemporary World* (Berkeley: University of California Press, 2002).

[16]Thomas Bender, *La Pietra Project on Internationalizing the Study of American History* (Bloomington, Ind.: Organization of American Historians, 2000), 3; see <http://www.oah.org/activities/lapietra/index.html>; Thomas Bender, ed., *Rethinking American History in a Global Age* (Berkeley: University of California Press, 2002). Bender's latest book, *A Nation among Nations: America's Place in the World* (New York: Farrar, Straus and Giroux, 2006), places American history within a broad world context.

world history and suggested organizing themes related to, for example, poverty, disease, environmental issues, resources, demography, consumerism, communications networks, and human rights.

The history of America and the world—and the vastly expanded agenda that such a term entails—will not replace diplomatic history or foreign relations history. Both remain important components of the broader category. Scholars such as John Lewis Gaddis and Melvyn P. Leffler, for example, continue to research—and contest—important diplomatic and policy issues related to the origins and end of the Cold War.[17] Still, "America and the world" does seem likely to become, in the words of Michael Hogan's SHAFR presidential address of 2003, the "next big thing."

The shift in historical focus to a broadly conceived America and the world approach brings both hazard and possibility. It may be worth considering whether this new big thing might represent an unsettling accompaniment to U.S. global power. Critics of globalization have asked probing questions about the onset of globalization studies at precisely the moment of America's victory in the Cold War and its apex of power in the world. It may be easy for Americans to appear to set aside a national focus and state-centered historical frameworks when they dominate so many global systems. On the other hand, teachers in schools and universities may, if self-aware, be able to embrace the broader scope of America's relations with the world as a way to counter provincialism in their classrooms and as a means to engage ethnically diverse students. The "next big thing" may help move history curricula toward an approach that is neither ethnocentric nor primarily celebratory.

[17]Contrast John Lewis Gaddis, *We Now Know: Rethinking Cold War History* (New York: Oxford University Press, 1998) and *The Cold War: A New History* (New York: Penguin, 2005) with Melvyn P. Leffler, *The Specter of Communism: The United States and the Origins of the Cold War, 1917–1953* (New York: Hill and Wang, 1994) and *For the Soul of Mankind: The United States, the Soviet Union, and the Cold War* (New York: Hill and Wang, 2008). For a more globalized look at the Cold War emphasizing the Third World, see Odd Arne Westad, *The Global Cold War* (New York: Cambridge University Press, 2005).

Jean-Christophe Agnew

Main Currents in American Cultural History

As an approach to the past, cultural history is as old as Herodotus. Yet a little more than a decade ago, historians were announcing the triumphant arrival of the "new cultural history" as if it were new because it was cultural. Why? Might the sense of novelty have sprung from residual confusions and disagreements about what the word *culture* meant? *Culture*, as the British critic Raymond Williams once remarked, "is one of the two or three most complicated words in the English language," and those complications have both driven and dogged the practice of American cultural history—new and old—over the past century.[1]

In the early decades of the twentieth century, historians and literary critics were less likely to invoke American culture when they could as well write of American *civilization*, with all of that word's suggestions of intellectual and technological progress. This preference was, if anything, strengthened by historians' experience of the First World War and of the creation of "war aims" courses in Western or Contemporary Civilization at Columbia College and elsewhere. The epic, evolutionary, and encompassing implications of civilization were also visible in the most prominent historical syntheses of the 1920s, Vernon L. Parrington's *Main Currents in American Thought* (1927–1930) and Charles and Mary Beard's best-selling *The Rise of American Civilization* (1927).[2]

Social and intellectual history furnished the two headings under which most historians were content to distribute the contents of American Civilization in the years before the Second World War, with social institutions and practices clustering at one pole of their analysis and arts and letters at the other. The title of Lewis Mumford's pathbreaking *The Golden Day: A Study in Experience and Culture* (1926) hinted at a melding of the social and intellectual into a third element, a cultural organicism.[3] Years later, that promise would inspire the American Studies

---

[1]Raymond Williams, *Keywords: A Vocabulary of Culture and Society* (New York: Oxford University Press, 1976), 76.

[2]Vernon L. Parrington, *Main Currents in American Thought: An Interpretation of American Literature from the Beginnings to 1920* (3 vols.; New York: Harcourt, Brace, 1927–1930); Charles A. Beard and Mary R. Beard, *The Rise of American Civilization* (2 vols.; New York: Macmillan, 1927).

[3]Lewis Mumford, *The Golden Day: A Study in Experience and Culture* (New York: Boni and Liveright, 1926).

movement, but Mumford's 1926 study remained a largely literary enterprise. In the years before the stock market crash of 1929, American folklore and the vernacular arts drew little more than the occasional nod from historians and critics preoccupied with explaining the nation's geopolitical ascendancy and vindicating its literary tradition.

Hard times, the New Deal, and the antifascist struggles of the 1930s soon reshaped the priorities of a generation of intellectuals by weaning American historians from the evaluative concept of civilization as a nation's ancestral gift, divine mission, or evolutionary destiny. Eugenic theories of American civilization that had once legitimized immigration restriction suddenly became an academic embarrassment as reports of racist persecutions made their way from Germany to the United States. An unabashedly racialized concept of culture as a collective biosocial inheritance quickly gave way to an ethnographic concept of cultures as plural, unranked, and site-specific patterns of beliefs, values, and symbolic practices.

The notion of culture as a whole way of life—an autonomous and complex whole—had first been ventured in 1871 by the British ethnologist Edward B. Tyler. But it was the German emigré and ethnographer Franz Boas, together with his Columbia graduate students (such as Ruth Benedict, Margaret Mead, and Melville Herskovitz), who introduced a conspicuously symbolic, holistic, and plastic view of society into American anthropology and, indirectly, into the practice of history. Benedict's widely read *Patterns of Culture* (1934) marked the arrival of this new model of culture into the mainstream. With its tripartite scheme of "primitive peoples" (Zuñi, Dobu, and Kwakiutl), each located along the "great arc of potential human purposes and motivations," *Patterns* brought the culture concept home by inviting American readers to reflect on their own national character. "A culture, like a person, is a more or less consistent pattern of thought and action," Benedict wrote.[4]

As Warren I. Susman later pointed out in a pioneering series of essays on the 1930s, the culture concept entered popular usage during the Great Depression as Americans encountered the arts and documentary initiatives of the New Deal and the Popular Front, as they followed the intensifying debates over propaganda and public opinion, and as they tried to gauge the impact in their own lives of the new mass culture industries—what Susman called "the culture of sight and sound." The culture concept, he argued, allowed a once "lost" generation of intellectuals and artists to repatriate themselves, to rediscover their native grounds. These returning "exiles," Susman concluded, helped domesticate the concept of culture, and the concept in turn helped domesticate them.[5]

[4]Ruth Benedict, *Patterns of Culture* (Boston: Houghton Mifflin, 1934), 237, 46.
[5]See especially "The Culture of the Thirties" (1983) in Warren I. Susman, *Culture as History: The Transformation of American Society in the Twentieth Century* (New York: Pantheon, 1984), 150–83. This collection of Susman's essays, published posthumously, was itself an announcement of cultural history's arrival.

In 1939, New Deal activist and historian Caroline F. Ware pressed to have the American Historical Association's annual meeting highlight "the study of history from the standpoint of total culture"—a culture, that is, in lower case—a concept as attuned to the industrial realities and popular pastimes of the "inarticulate and semi-articulate masses" as to the loftier traditions of art and literature. Such an approach was itself a "cultural phenomenon," she acknowledged, an "obvious product of a society with an increasingly collectivist base." Ware gathered some of the meeting's papers into a volume titled *The Cultural Approach to History* (1940), only to see her gritty, plebeian model of cultural history almost immediately lost to the ideological exigencies of wartime mobilization.[6] While the holism of the culture concept survived, it did so chiefly as a testament to home-front unity as expressed in the softer, more nostalgic, and consumerist iconography of the "American way of life."

With the war drawing to a close, anthropologists Ralph Linton and Cora Du Bois and psychiatrist Abram Kardiner began to refine Benedict's broad concept of culture as "personality writ large" into a psychodynamic theory that promised to identify and classify cultures by their characteristic or "modal personalities."[7] With the notable exception of David M. Potter, however, few historians were prepared to speak, much less write, in this idiom. "Thou shalt not sit with statisticians," W. H. Auden had warned Harvard undergraduates in 1946, "or commit a social science." But eight years later, Potter's *People of Plenty: Economic Abundance and American Character* (1954) was riding the high tide of social science's postwar prestige, and Potter took his fellow historians to task for their evidentiary eclecticism, their conceptual imprecision, and their lack of theoretical reflection when writing about national character.[8]

For all that, *People of Plenty* offered its readers little more than a sequel to Frederick Jackson Turner's frontier thesis, with the western wilderness literally yielding pride of place to the "secondary environment" of man-made wealth. Modern Americans had become what they were, Potter argued, in response to an economy *and a culture* of abundance. Although the word *capitalism* appeared only once in his index—and then only as a "product of abundance"—Potter had carefully crafted his argument to negotiate the Cold War imperatives to celebrate the capitalist system that were bearing down on him as a Charles Walgreen lecturer at the University of Chicago and as director of the new American Studies

[6]Caroline F. Ware, ed., *The Cultural Approach to History* (New York: Columbia University Press, 1940), 7–13.

[7]Abram Kardiner, *The Individual and His Society* (New York: Columbia University Press, 1939); Cora Alice Du Bois, *The People of Alor: A Social-Psychological Study of an East Indian Island* (2 vols.; Cambridge, Mass.: Harvard University Press, 1944); Ralph Linton, *The Cultural Background of Personality* (New York: D. Appleton-Century, 1945); Abram Kardiner, with Ralph Linton, Cora Du Bois, and James West, *The Psychological Frontiers of Society* (New York: Columbia University Press, 1945).

[8]David M. Potter, *People of Plenty: Economic Abundance and the American Character* (Chicago: University of Chicago Press, 1954).

program at Yale, institutions that had been created and endowed to promote the virtues of the free-enterprise system.[9]

As an avowedly interdisciplinary venture, the early American Studies movement (of which Potter was a leader) emerged as a domestic counterpart to the area studies programs springing up in the Cold War university system. Historians like Potter were thus intellectually and, in some instances, institutionally partnered with the "mandarins of the future" — Nils Gilman's artful label for the behavioral scientists who promoted modernization theory as a "high-concept version of Americanism," meaning "materialism without class conflict, secularism without irreverence, democracy without disobedience."[10] For the so-called consensus historians of the 1950s, the specter of class conflict that had haunted the work of Vernon Parrington and the Beards quietly dissolved when class was transmuted into status, ideology into culture, and culture into "personality writ large." If Americans were divided, then, it was within themselves. Or so it seemed in studies like Daniel Boorstin's *The Genius of American Politics* (1953), Marvin Meyers's *The Jacksonian Persuasion* (1957), Richard Hofstadter's *The Paranoid Style in American Politics* (1965), and Michael Kammen's *People of Paradox* (1972), perhaps the last noteworthy effort to inquire into the origins of American civilization.[11]

What was to become the most influential encapsulation of this quiet drift from the prewar currents-of-thought model of culture to the postwar collective-syndrome model appeared in a widely circulated 1964 essay, "Ideology as a Cultural System," written by Clifford Geertz, a cultural anthropologist trained in Harvard's Department of Social Relations, the institutional heartland of modernization theory. Ideologies, Geertz argued, were improvised cognitive and affective maps of the world, "symbolic frames" that, at junctures of great social and economic strain, rendered "otherwise incomprehensible social situations meaningful" so as to make possible the formation of "collective conscience" and political action. Ideologies were culture's transformers and switchboards, converting the paralysis of cognitive dissonance into the energy of collective mobilization.[12]

[9]On these imperatives, see especially Sigmund Diamond, "The American Studies Program at Yale: *Lux, Veritas, et Pecunia*," *Prospects* 16 (1991): 41–55; Michael Holzman, "The Ideological Origins of American Studies at Yale," *American Studies* 40 (Summer 1999): 71–99.

[10]Nils Gilman, *Mandarins of the Future: Modernization Theory in Cold War America* (Baltimore: Johns Hopkins University Press, 2003), 13.

[11]Daniel J. Boorstin, *The Genius of American Politics* (Chicago: University of Chicago Press, 1953); Marvin Meyers, *The Jacksonian Persuasion: Politics and Belief* (Stanford, Calif.: Stanford University Press, 1957); Richard Hofstadter, *The Paranoid Style in American Politics, and Other Essays* (New York: Knopf, 1965); Michael G. Kammen, *People of Paradox: An Inquiry concerning the Origins of American Civilization* (New York: Knopf, 1972). Michael A. Lebowitz was one of the first to challenge this divided-character model in "The Jacksonians: Paradox Lost?" in a bellwether collection of New Left articles titled *Towards a New Past: Dissenting Essays in American History*, ed. Barton J. Bernstein (New York: Pantheon, 1968).

[12]Clifford Geertz, "Ideology as a Cultural System," (1964) reprinted in *The Interpretation of Cultures* (New York: Basic Books, 1973).

Unexceptional as Geertz's formulation may seem today, it furnished the novel theoretical lens through which Bernard Bailyn reenvisioned *The Ideological Origins of the American Revolution* (1967).[13] Bailyn's bold and bleak reinterpretation of transatlantic republicanism swept aside the conventional, agent-driven, social, and intellectual interpretations in favor of an account that treated the revolutionaries as the misguided victims of their own mental maps and the Revolution as the misbegotten child of an immature modernization. It was as if the whole area-studies apparatus of American exceptionalism, development theory, and cultural-systems analysis had been turned back against its source in one grand, albeit unintentional, patricidal gesture.

The moment was thick with irony. The cultural approach that Caroline Ware had enthusiastically championed to the AHA for its democratic methodology had evolved over three decades into a dispassionate retrospective diagnosis of what Bailyn's colleague, Samuel P. Huntington, labeled the "democratic distemper."[14] Pathbreaking as *Ideological Origins* was, it also signaled the imminent exhaustion of the Cold War cultural methodology that had informed historical practice to that moment. By 1967, the year of the anti-Vietnam War march on the Pentagon, historians were already looking elsewhere for new models of political culture and cultural politics.

More than a decade of social and political activism—the black freedom struggle, the peace movement, the free-speech movement, and the women's movement—lay behind the growing dissatisfaction with the Cold War consensus and its aging arsenal of models and methodologies; but equally important had been the explosive growth of the postwar university, whose students were more blue-collar, more "ethnic," and more comfortable with the mass-cultural media and genres that had been a source of wonder and anxiety to their teachers. For these students, a sufficient number of unanswered questions about culture had accumulated, to paraphrase Thomas S. Kuhn's influential *Structure of Scientific Revolutions* (1962), to set the stage for a "paradigm shift."[15] Predictably, the consensus (history's "normal science") unraveled at the two poles of cultural historical practice to that point: social and intellectual history.

Social history became new during the 1970s in several ways, first among them being the full-bore deployment of social scientific models and quantification techniques to recover the material conditions, life cycles, and survival strategies of the "inarticulate and semi-articulate masses." But social history became new, too, in its lively transatlantic engagement with the Annales school of historians in France and the Marxist historians' group in England: Christopher Hill,

[13]Bernard Bailyn, *The Ideological Origins of the American Revolution* (Cambridge, Mass.: Harvard University Press, 1967).

[14]Samuel P. Huntington, "The Democratic Distemper," *The Public Interest* 41 (Fall 1975): 9–38.

[15]Thomas S. Kuhn, *The Structure of Scientific Revolutions* (Chicago: University of Chicago Press, 1962).

George Rudé, Eric Hobsbawm, and E. P. Thompson. Thompson's *The Making of the English Working Class* (1963) was easily the most influential exemplar in launching the new labor history in the United States.[16] In that spirit, historians like David Montgomery and Herbert Gutman shifted the focus away from the behavior of workingmen and women and toward their experience, away from the study of working-class tribunes and toward the interpretation of working-class cultures, native and immigrant, slave and waged, cultures that were in one way or another resistant, "distempered."

If aspects of the Geertzian model persisted, for example, in Herbert Gutman's *Work, Culture, and Industrializing America* (1976), Eugene Genovese looked elsewhere—to a Gramscian model of hegemony—in his controversial but elegant account of slaveholder law and paternalism in *Roll, Jordan, Roll* (1974). Meanwhile, Lawrence Levine drew freely on folk cultural theories in his equally groundbreaking *Black Culture and Black Consciousness* (1977). And nowhere was the exemplary impact of the civil rights experience more visible than in Lawrence Goodwyn's dynamic model of Populism's grassroots insurgency as a "movement culture," a framework introduced in *The Democratic Promise* (1976), in order to rescue the agrarian radicals from the condescension implicit in Richard Hofstadter's earlier accounts of their "status anxiety," their "agrarian myths," and their "paranoid style."[17]

That said, Goodwyn's subtitle, "The Populist Moment in America," betrayed the sense of contingency—of roads not taken, of promises foreclosed, of worlds lost and houses fallen—that ran through so much of the first generation of new sociocultural history at the moment of the bicentennial. Most of the studies stopped around the First World War, at the birth of radio and Hollywood. Mass culture was jurisdictionally ceded to the Popular Culture Association, which, under the leadership of Ray Browne and Russell Nye, had spun off from the American Studies movement in the late 1960s. At the threshold of mass consumer culture—Potter's culture of "plenty"—the new social and labor historians, like the American Studies movement, momentarily balked.

Meanwhile, intellectual history had reached an impasse of its own as a new generation wrestled to bring Arthur O. Lovejoy's history of ideas down to earth, or at least into conversation with social history "from the bottom up." Little

---

[16]E. P. Thompson, *The Making of the English Working Class* (New York: Pantheon, 1963).

[17]Eugene D. Genovese, *Roll, Jordan, Roll: The World the Slaves Made* (New York: Pantheon, 1974); Herbert G. Gutman, *Work, Culture, and Industrializing Society: Essays in Working-Class and Labor History* (New York: Knopf, 1976); Lawrence Goodwyn, *The Democratic Promise: The Populist Moment in America* (New York: Oxford University Press, 1976); Lawrence W. Levine, *Black Culture and Black Consciousness: Afro-American Folk Thought from Slavery to Freedom* (New York: Oxford University Press, 1977); David Montgomery, *Workers' Control in America: Studies in the History of Work, Technology, and Labor Struggles* (New York: Cambridge University Press, 1979); for Richard Hofstadter's views on populism, see *The Age of Reform: From Bryan to FDR* (New York: Knopf, 1955), especially chapters 1 and 2.

progress on that front was visible in a major state-of-the-field anthology published in 1979, but John Higham's and Paul Conkin's collection was organized in a sequence of articles that moved promisingly from the "history of ideas" to the "history of culture" and that introduced sociologically friendly concepts like David Hollinger's "communities of discourse."[18] Still, it was left to students then in graduate school to extend these contextualist gestures further, inspired not so much by Thomas Kuhn's model of paradigm shifts as by the new hybrid genre of intellectual history and cultural sociology associated with Warren Susman and Christopher Lasch.

Lasch's *The New Radicalism in America, 1889–1963* (1965) electrified this cohort of historians in part because of the deftness with which he used the familiar form of the biographical sketch to track the emergence of the "intellectual as a social type" in turn-of-the-century America. "New radicals" like Jane Addams, Mabel Dodge, and Lincoln Steffens, Lasch argued, were mostly internal exiles drawn from a small-town and suburban middle-class, men and women who had seized upon a self-consciously cultural politics as their principal means of personal renewal, class recognition, and social control. But if this heady mixture of culture and politics had provided the existential glue binding this new subculture together, Lasch insisted that it had also bonded (and blinded) the new intelligentsia to the seductive powers of the modern liberal state—the welfare and warfare state—as the vehicle of their own personal and political ambitions.[19]

Because *The New Radicalism* arrived a mere two years before the press exposé of the CIA's covert sponsorship of the anti-Communist Congress of Cultural Freedom, the National Student Association, and *Encounter* magazine, Lasch's history seemed almost prescient. He had managed to isolate and identify the subcultural genealogy—the experiential dynamic—of modern liberalism's on-again-off-again romance with state power. To be sure, Lasch's thesis was not entirely new; a neo-Marxist version of it had been pioneered by the so-called corporate liberal school of historians writing in the journal *Studies on the Left* (1959–1967). And in 1977 the argument expanded yet again with Barbara and John Ehrenreich's influential article in *Radical America* on the formation in the United States of a new professional-managerial class ("salaried mental workers who do not own the means of production") standing between labor and capital. Engrossing as Lasch's biographical vignettes were, historians turned to works like Burton J. Bledstein's *The Culture of Professionalism* (1976) and David Noble's *America by Design* (1977) to sort through the different institutional and cultural transformations underwriting the rise of the professional-managerial class, the P-MC for short. Thomas L. Haskell's *The Emergence of Professional Social Science* (1977)

---

[18]John Higham and Paul K. Conkin, eds., *New Directions in American Intellectual History* (Baltimore: Johns Hopkins University Press, 1979). The articles had been delivered as papers at a Wingspread Conference in Racine, Wisconsin, two years earlier.

[19]Christopher Lasch, *The New Radicalism in America, 1889–1963: The Intellectual as a Social Type* (New York: Knopf, 1965).

likewise inspired a rich array of articles and monographs on the culture of expertise and the formation of academic disciplines.[20]

Discipline itself took on a power-steeped double meaning as the philosopher Michel Foucault's meditations on the asylum, the clinic, and the "archeology of knowledge" were translated and circulated during the 1970s. Yet, until the end of the 1980s, recognizably Foucauldean concepts such as his causality-free notion of "genealogy" and his agent- or subject-free idea of "power/knowledge" made little headway among American cultural historians, and even then chiefly among literary scholars associated with the so-called new historicism.[21]

Instead, the last years of the 1970s—years of stagflation and academic unemployment—brought historians back to the question and the critique of consumer culture, first in Stuart Ewen's *Captains of Consciousness* (1976), then in Ann Douglas's withering *The Feminization of American Culture* (1977), and finally in Lasch's neo-Freudian jeremiad *The Culture of Narcissism* (1979), the surprise best-seller that won him an invitation to Camp David to advise Jimmy Carter on the eve of his 1979 "national malaise" speech. Ironically, Lasch's book owed a good part of its success to his having reverted to the familiar formula of the culture-and-personality model.[22] By contrast, T. J. Jackson Lears mixed his Freud with Max Weber and Antonio Gramsci in the cultural biographies that enriched *No Place of Grace* (1981), his influential study of Victorian antimodernism as the unwilling and unwitting parent of modern consumerism, while the collection he edited with Richard Wightman Fox two years later, *The Culture of Consumption* (1983), treated early consumer culture as a psychosocial episode in the rise of a Protestant professional-managerial class.[23]

[20]Barbara and John Ehrenreich, "The Professional-Managerial Class: Part 1," *Radical America* 11 (March–April 1977): 7–31; "The Professional-Managerial Class: Part 2," *Radical America* 11 (May–June 1977): 7–22. See also Pat Walker, ed., *Between Labor and Capital* (Boston: South End Press, 1979); Burton J. Bledstein, *The Culture of Professionalism: The Middle Class and the Development of Higher Education in America* (New York: W. W. Norton, 1976); David F. Noble, *America by Design: Science, Technology, and the Rise of Corporate Capitalism* (New York: Knopf, 1977); Thomas L. Haskell, *The Emergence of Professional Social Science: The American Social Science Association and the Nineteenth-Century Crisis of Authority* (Urbana: University of Illinois Press, 1977); also, Alexandra Oleson and John Voss, eds., *The Organization of Knowledge in America, 1860–1920* (Baltimore: Johns Hopkins University Press, 1979); Thomas L. Haskell, ed., *The Authority of Experts: Studies in History and Theory* (Bloomington: Indiana University Press, 1984).

[21]One influential example was Walter Benn Michaels, *The Gold Standard and the Logic of Capitalism: American Literature at the Turn of the Century* (Berkeley: University of California Press, 1987), especially 177–79.

[22]Stuart Ewen, *Captains of Consciousness: Advertising and the Social Roots of Consumer Culture* (New York: McGraw-Hill, 1976); Ann Douglas, *The Feminization of American Culture* (New York: Knopf, 1977); Christopher Lasch, *The Culture of Narcissism: American Life in an Age of Diminishing Expectations* (New York: W. W. Norton, 1979).

[23]T. J. Jackson Lears, *No Place of Grace: Antimodernism and the Transformation of American Culture, 1880–1920* (New York: Pantheon, 1981); Richard Wightman Fox and T. J. Jackson Lears, eds., *The Culture of Consumption: Critical Essays in American History* (New York: Pantheon, 1983).

A quite different, more multicultural, and decidedly affirmative model of a class's collective (and political) unconscious appeared in George Lipsitz's synoptic study of working-class militancy and popular culture in the 1940s, *Class and Culture in Cold War America* (1981).[24] Lipsitz's book almost single-handedly thrust the new social and labor historians across the threshold of mass culture; yet its subtitle—"A Rainbow at Midnight"—suggested the Left's growing unease, its sense of déjà vu, as the Reagan era's culture wars and antiunion backlash got under way. Figuratively speaking, American cultural history went underground and overseas in search of secret sharers in different disciplines and on other soil.

Across the Atlantic, the work of European cultural historians like Peter Burke, Roger Chartier, Robert Darnton, Natalie Zemon Davis, and Carlo Ginzburg added its measure of centrifugal force to the cultural turn that historians were taking during this period. And when Rhys Isaac published his Pulitzer Prize–winning study of the American Revolution, *The Transformation of Virginia, 1740–1790* (1982), its stunning sequence of close readings in eighteenth-century visual and performative culture—above all, the architectural display and ritual enactment of the social order—registered something more than the second coming of Clifford Geertz to the historiography of the American Revolution (this time in the culture-as-text mode of Geertz's landmark 1973 essay on "thick description"). Isaac's book marked as well the transpacific impact of the so-called Melbourne school of ethnographic history associated with Isaac, Greg Dening, Inga Clendinning, and Donna Merwick.[25]

An even more inspirational impulse behind the cultural turn—or return—in American history and American studies was to be found in the British cultural studies movement that Richard Hoggart and Raymond Williams had inspired during the late 1960s and that Stuart Hall nurtured through the next decades as director of Birmingham's Center for Contemporary Cultural Studies. Michael Denning's study of dime novels and nineteenth-century working-class culture, *Mechanic Accents* (1987), was but one example of this influence. Denning drew on his Birmingham experience and Fredric Jameson's critical theory of cultural form to go underground, so to speak, to dig below the surface of a reviled popular genre and locate (as Lipsitz had before him) a "political unconscious"—a narrative resolution to class anger and yearning that took the form of a covert fantasy of labor's virtuous triumph over capital. Janice Radway (1984)—a Russell Nye student—and Jane Tompkins (1985) offered comparably bold arguments about the

[24]George Lipsitz, *Class and Culture in Cold War America: A Rainbow at Midnight* (New York: Praeger, 1981).

[25]Rhys Isaac, *The Transformation of Virginia, 1740–1790* (Chapel Hill: University of North Carolina Press, 1982); Clifford Geertz, "Thick Description: Toward an Interpretive Theory of Culture," in *Interpretation of Cultures*, 3–30. See also Jean-Christophe Agnew, "History and Anthropology: Scenes from a Marriage," *Yale Journal of Criticism* 3 (Spring 1990): 28–50; Rhys Isaac, "Power and Meaning: Event and Text: History and Anthropology," in Donna Merwick, ed., *Dangerous Liaisons: Essays in Honor of Greg Dening* (Parkville, Australia: University of Melbourne, 1994), 297–315.

subculture of middle-class women readers in their analysis of nineteenth-century sentimental and twentieth-century romance novels.[26] The supply-side version of cultural history, as it was called, now had its demand side.

And it had its feminist side as well. Diagnostic readings of cultural patterns, syndromes, or pathologies had become familiar protocols in cultural history, as we have seen. But by the mid-1980s, it was no longer the politics that were being read symptomatically as latent cultural systems so much as it was cultures that were being read symptomatically as latent politics. Cultural politics, the hybrid symbolic practice that Christopher Lasch had indicted in the new radicals, the New Left, and the new social movements that followed, entered the political mainstream during the 1980s along with the then-decade-old radical feminist axiom of consciousness-raising: "The personal is political." For cultural historians, feminist theory effectively recharged the subterranean social grid of ordinary experience, infusing every personal bond, every exchange of favors, and every circuit of gossip or shoptalk with intimations of power. Small wonder, then, that the culture concept fairly glowed with significance.

Carroll Smith-Rosenberg (1975), Blanche Wiesen Cook (1977), and Nancy Cott (1977) were among the first historians to venture a retrospective social anthropology of white women's "support networks" by giving special attention to the ritual ordering of Victorian "women's culture." Almost immediately, though, the model was challenged by feminist historians reeling from the failure of the Equal Rights Amendment and divided over questions of race, class, and sexuality. Debates over the historical reality and reach of men's and women's "separate spheres" soon turned into arguments over the meaning of gender itself.[27]

A pivotal point was reached in 1986, when a widely discussed journal article by Joan Wallach Scott called on historians to treat gender as something more than a mere topic, field, or ideology. Gender, the former "new social historian" insisted, was an "element" that implanted, ranked, and legitimized sexed differences in social relationships and in the history written of them. What kind of

---

[26]Janice A. Radway, *Reading the Romance: Women, Patriarchy, and Popular Literature* (Chapel Hill: University of North Carolina Press, 1984); Jane P. Tompkins, *Sensational Designs: The Cultural Work of American Fiction, 1790–1860* (New York: Oxford University Press, 1985); Michael Denning, *Mechanic Accents: Dime Novels and Working-Class Culture in America* (New York: Verso, 1987).

[27]Carroll Smith-Rosenberg, "The Female World of Love and Ritual: Relations between Women in Nineteenth-Century America," *Signs* 1 (Autumn 1975): 1–29, reprinted in Nancy F. Cott and Elizabeth Hafkin Pleck, eds., *A Heritage of Her Own: Toward a New Social History of American Women* (New York: Simon & Schuster, 1979), 311–42; Blanche Wiesen Cook, "Female Support Networks and Political Activism: Lillian Wald, Crystal Eastman, and Emma Goldman," *Chrysalis* 3 (Autumn 1977): 43–61, reprinted in Cott and Pleck, eds., *A Heritage of Her Own*, 412–44; Nancy F. Cott, *The Bonds of Womanhood: "Woman's Sphere" in New England, 1780–1835* (New Haven, Conn.: Yale University Press, 1977); Linda K. Kerber, "Separate Spheres, Female Worlds, Woman's Place: The Rhetoric of Women's History," *Journal of American History* 75 (June 1988): 9–39.

element was it? Drawing on the philosopher Michel Foucault and the sociologist Pierre Bourdieu, Scott defined gender as a field or discourse of "culturally available symbols, norms, and identities" by means of which power relations were imagined, scripted, enacted, and affirmed. Causality was moot in this model, for culture (writ large or small) was better understood as the categorical *condition* of possibility for politics, society, and the economy.[28]

As this accumulation of abstract terms suggests, Scott's article also served notice to mainstream historians that there was another disciplinary route to cultural history besides the paths of anthropology and cultural studies—namely, poststructuralist theory or theory *tout court*. That, too, added to the newness of the new cultural history in the 1980s. And though Scott's own cultural turn angled more toward a neo-Lovejoyan intellectual history—the genealogy of conceptual categories—the model of gender she championed quickly became an indispensable tool for cultural historians. The victory was a mixed one for feminist historians, though, as they watched gender (a term that had once served as a "synonym for women") provide the intellectual aegis for numerous cultural histories of manhood and masculinity. Black studies scholars witnessed a similar turn of events during the 1990s when the discursive model of race sanctioned a raft of cultural studies of whiteness.[29]

The rising tide of the new cultural history was perhaps best signaled by the anthology that another former social historian, Lynn Hunt, published under that title in 1989.[30] But the ripples could be felt across the broad span of history's constituent fields—in religious history, for example, where the work of Robert Anthony Orsi (1985), David Hall (1989), Jon Butler (1990), Leigh Schmidt (1995),

---

[28]Joan Wallach Scott, "Gender: A Useful Category of Historical Analysis," *American Historical Review* 91 (December 1986): 1053–75. The journeys out of the new social history are related in Geoff Eley, *A Crooked Line: From Cultural History to the History of Society* (Ann Arbor: University of Michigan Press, 2005).

[29]See, for example, Anthony E. Rotundo, *American Manhood: Transformations in Masculinity from the Revolution to the Modern Era* (New York: Basic Books, 1993); Robert L. Griswold, *Fatherhood in America: A History* (New York: Basic Books, 1993); Gail Bederman, *Manliness and Civilization: A Cultural History of Gender and Race in the United States, 1880–1917* (Chicago: University of Chicago Press, 1995); Michael Kimmel, *Manhood in America: A Cultural History* (New York: Free Press, 1996); Ralph LaRossa, *The Modernization of Fatherhood: A Social and Political History* (Chicago: University of Chicago Press, 1997); Stephen M. Frank, *Life with Father: Parenthood and Masculinity in the Nineteenth-Century American North* (Baltimore: Johns Hopkins University Press, 1998). On whiteness, see David R. Roediger, *The Wages of Whiteness: Race and the Making of the American Working Class* (New York: Verso, 1991); Eric Lott, *Love and Theft: Blackface Minstrelsy and the American Working Class* (New York: Oxford University Press, 1993); Matthew Frye Jacobson, *Whiteness of a Different Color: European Immigrants and the Alchemy of Race* (Cambridge, Mass.: Harvard University Press, 1999); and the special issue of *International Labor and Working Class History* 60 (October 2001).

[30]Lynn Hunt, ed., *The New Cultural History* (Berkeley: University of California Press, 1989).

and Colleen McDannell (1995) led the way.[31] Or in political history, where Daniel Walker Howe (1979), Jean H. Baker (1983), Susan G. Davis (1986), Simon P. Newman (1997), David Waldstreicher (1997), and Joanne B. Freeman (2001) were among the leading innovators.[32] Or in the history of foreign relations, where concepts of gender, cultural imperialism, and the cultural Cold War figured prominently in the work of Emily S. Rosenberg (1982, 1990), Kristin L. Hoganson (1998), Matthew Frye Jacobson (2000), Melani McAlister (2001), Mary A. Renda (2001), Robert D. Dean (2001), Christina Klein (2003), and Penny von Eschen (2004).[33] And just as literary history had reopened itself to more "culturalist" work in the form of the new historicism, so art history expanded to embrace the study of visual, material, and performance culture.

In that spirit, the essays of Robin D. G. Kelley and Shane and Graham White's *Stylin': African American Expressive Culture from Its Beginning to the Zoot Suit* (1998) exemplified the ways in which historians of the African American past

---

[31]Robert A. Orsi, *The Madonna of 115th Street: Faith and Community in Italian Harlem, 1880–1950* (New Haven, Conn.: Yale University Press, 1985); David D. Hall, *Worlds of Wonder, Days of Judgment: Popular Religious Belief in Early New England* (New York: Knopf, 1989); Jon Butler, *Awash in a Sea of Faith: Christianizing the American People* (Cambridge, Mass.: Harvard University Press, 1990); Leigh Schmidt, *Consumer Rites: The Buying and Selling of American Holidays* (Princeton, N.J.: Princeton University Press, 1995); Colleen McDannell, *Material Christianity: Religion and Popular Culture in America* (New Haven, Conn.: Yale University Press, 1995).

[32]Daniel Walker Howe, *The Political Culture of the American Whigs* (Chicago: University of Chicago Press, 1979); Jean H. Baker, *Affairs of Party: The Political Culture of Northern Democrats in the Mid-Nineteenth Century* (Ithaca, N.Y.: Cornell University Press, 1983); Susan G. Davis, *Parades and Power: Street Theatre in Nineteenth-Century Philadelphia* (Philadelphia: Temple University Press, 1986); Simon P. Newman, *Parades and the Politics of the Street: Festive Culture in the Early American Republic* (Philadelphia: University of Pennsylvania Press, 1997); David Waldstreicher, *In the Midst of Perpetual Fetes: The Making of American Nationalism, 1776–1820* (Chapel Hill: University of North Carolina Press, 1997); Joanne B. Freeman, *Affairs of Honor: National Politics in the New Republic* (New Haven, Conn.: Yale University Press, 2001).

[33]Emily S. Rosenberg, *Spreading the American Dream: American Economic and Cultural Expansion, 1890–1945* (New York: Hill and Wang, 1982), and "Gender, A Round Table: Explaining the History of American Foreign Relations," *Journal of American History* 77 (June 1990): 116–24; Kristin L. Hoganson, *Fighting for American Manhood: How Gender Politics Provoked the Spanish-American and Philippine American Wars* (New Haven, Conn.: Yale University Press, 1998); Matthew Frye Jacobson, *Barbarian Virtues: The United States Encounters Foreign Peoples at Home and Abroad, 1876–1917* (New York: Hill and Wang, 2000); Melani McAlister, *Epic Encounters: Culture, Media, and U.S. Interests in the Middle East, 1945–2000* (Berkeley: University of California Press, 2001); Mary A. Renda, *Taking Haiti: Military Occupation and the Culture of U.S. Imperialism, 1915–1940* (Chapel Hill: University of North Carolina Press, 2001); Robert D. Dean, *Imperial Brotherhood: Gender and the Making of Cold War Foreign Policy* (Amherst: University of Massachusetts Press, 2001); Christina Klein, *Cold War Orientalism: Asia in the Middlebrow Imagination, 1945–1961* (Berkeley: University of California Press, 2003); Penny S. von Eschen, *Satchmo Blows Up the World: Jazz Ambassadors Play the Cold War* (Cambridge, Mass.: Harvard University Press, 2004).

were increasingly drawing on cultural studies methods in order to cross and recross the historical threshold of mass culture from which an earlier generation of social historians had held back and, at the same time, to revisit the practice of symbolic or cultural politics that Christopher Lasch had once disparaged. Similarly, Michael Denning's *The Cultural Front* (1997), his landmark study of a multicultural intelligentsia in the age of the CIO, cast aside the conservative reading that Warren Susman had given to the culturalism of 1930s intellectuals and instead identified a large social democratic coalition of labor, intellectuals, and cultural industry personnel working together to swing the nation's cultural apparatus to the left.[34] It was a coalition—a bloc—that included Caroline Ware. For as she had acknowledged in 1940, the cultural approach to history was itself an artifact of the increasingly collectivist features of modern life.

Coalition, bloc, front: Denning's strategic terms highlighted the degree to which the action in cultural history had quietly shifted over two decades from the cultural work performed by a text to the cultural workers and culture industries themselves. As another century turned and historians plugged into a global market in cultural commodities, many found themselves gravitating toward an open-source, agent-driven model of cultural production and consumption and moving away from a model tied to the nation-state. Today, one can scarcely imagine the publication of a national cultural history with the epic ambitions of a Parrington, a Beard, a Potter, or a Kammen. Cultural history remains site-specific, but, like anthropology and world literature, it is increasingly likely to be specific to multiple sites.

All this may go some way toward explaining why, in contrast to social and intellectual historians, cultural historians have founded no journals of their own. The boundaries of its object have shifted, while its methods have been incorporated into virtually every other field of history. True, some observers might say that transnational and transdisciplinary history have swamped the new cultural history; yet these movements would never have emerged in the absence of the culturalist currents that continue to run so strongly beneath them. And if it is the case, as I have tried to suggest, that the new cultural history arose out of the convergent crises in social, intellectual, and women's history—a perfect storm, so to speak—who is to say that we may not reach that high-water mark again? Weather permitting.

[34]Shane White and Graham White, *Stylin': African American Expressive Culture from Its Beginnings to the Zoot Suit* (Ithaca, N.Y.: Cornell University Press, 1998); Robin D. G. Kelley, *Race Rebels: Culture, Politics, and the Black Working Class* (New York: Free Press, 1994); Michael Denning, *The Cultural Front: The Laboring of American Culture in the Twentieth Century* (New York: Verso, 1997).

ROBERT L. HARRIS, JR.

The Changing Contours of African American History during the Twentieth Century

The great black intellectual W. E. B. Du Bois, in his masterful book *The Souls of Black Folk* (1903), identified two themes that have influenced the writing of African American history since the early twentieth century. Du Bois observed that "one ever feels his twoness, — an American, a Negro; two souls, two thoughts, two unreconciled strivings; two warring ideals in one dark body." He asserted that "the history of the American Negro is the history of this strife, — this longing to attain self-conscious manhood, to merge his double self into a better and truer self. In this merging he wishes neither of the older selves to be lost." This first theme raised the question of black identity in the United States, exclusion and inclusion, acculturation and assimilation, self-definition and self-determination. Toward the end of the book, Du Bois mused: "Your country? How came it yours? Before the Pilgrims landed we were here." He wrote of the special gifts of story and song, sweat and brawn, and spirit that black people brought to America. He challenged the country and historians with the question "Would America have been America without her Negro people?"[1] This second theme called for examining the role that African Americans had played in the development of the United States, artistically, physically, intellectually, and spiritually. Du Bois's two themes evoked the need to study black America from the inside out and in relation to the trajectory of the nation's history.

Since 1900, historians have addressed Du Bois's themes in different ways and have given us a more intricate understanding of the African American past. In *The Negro in Our History* (1922), Carter G. Woodson, often referred to as the Father of Black History, explored Du Bois's second theme of active African American participation in the development of the United States for the average reader. Jacqueline Goggin's *Carter G. Woodson: A Life in Black History* (1993) and Pero G. Dagbovie's *The Early Black History Movement: Carter G. Woodson and Lorenzo Johnston Greene* (2007) both evaluated Woodson's role in writing and promoting African American history.[2] Woodson founded the Association for the

---

[1]W. E. B. Du Bois, *The Souls of Black Folk* (1903; New York: Penguin, 1996), 5, 215.
[2]Carter G. Woodson, *The Negro in Our History* (Washington, D.C.: The Associated Publishers, 1922); Jacqueline Goggin, *Carter G. Woodson: A Life in Black History* (Baton Rouge: Louisiana State University Press, 1993); Pero G. Dagbovie, *The Early Black History Movement: Carter G. Woodson and Lorenzo Johnston Greene* (Urbana: University of Illinois Press, 2007).

Study of Negro (now African American) Life and History in 1915 to collect and preserve materials related to the black past. A year later, he published the first issue of *The Journal of Negro History* to promote research and writing about black history.[3] In 1926, Woodson inaugurated Negro History Week to increase interest in black history by the black masses, to inform the nation about blacks' accomplishments, and to inspire black youth to greater achievement. He launched *The Negro History Bulletin* in 1937 to reach black schoolchildren, their teachers, and their parents. Woodson also wrote *The African Background Outlined or Handbook for the Study of the Negro* (1936), which dispelled the notion that the history of black people in the United States began with the slave trade, European conquest, and assumptions of racial inferiority.[4] The theme of black identity, of relationship to Africa, has been a more vexing problem in writing African American history since 1900 than the role of African Americans in the development of the United States.

There has been some tension among scholars of the African American experience between emphasis on Africa and on America. Many early black historians, such as Woodson, considered the African background important as a corrective to assumptions that people of African ancestry had made no contributions to world civilization. More recently, proponents of Afrocentricity have placed greater emphasis on Africa than on America. Molefi Kete Asante, in *The Afrocentric Idea* (1998), defines the concept as a critical perspective that places "African ideals at the center of any analysis that involves African culture and behavior." He suggests that African Americans are culturally more African than American. For him, the goal of Afrocentricity is not exclusion but inclusion based on "mutual respect for the cultural agency of all people." Maghan Keita, in *Race and the Writing of History: Riddling the Sphinx* (2000), explains that Afrocentricity challenges the construction of knowledge that supports Western interpretations as universal and that disallows multiple perspectives based on non-Western traditions. In *Afrotopia: The Roots of African American Popular History* (1998), Wilson Jeremiah Moses criticizes Afrocentricity as being overly romantic in its focus on ancient Egypt and its implication that "the worth of a people is demonstrated by its capacity for 'civilization.'"[5] Although many black historians wrote in opposition to the exclusion of African Americans from freedom, justice, and equality in the United States, they argued that African Americans were a central part of the nation's history and that they were integral to its cultural, economic, political, and social development.

Most historians of black America prior to the late 1960s wrote in a contributionist or vindicationist vein similar to Woodson. They wanted to demonstrate

[3]The journal has since been renamed *The Journal of African American History*.

[4]Carter G. Woodson, *The African Background Outlined or Handbook for the Study of the Negro* (Washington, D.C.: The Association for the Study of Negro Life and History, 1936).

[5]Molefi Kete Asante, *The Afrocentric Idea* (Philadelphia: Temple University Press, 1998), xi; Maghan Keita, *Race and the Writing of History: Riddling the Sphinx* (New York: Oxford University Press, 2000), 162–65; Wilson Jeremiah Moses, *Afrotopia: The Roots of African American Popular History* (New York: Cambridge University Press, 1998), 229.

that African Americans made significant contributions to the nation's progress. And they sought to justify and vindicate the African American claim to freedom, justice, and equality. Many of these early historians—such as John H. Russell, *The Free Negro in Virginia* (1913), James M. Wright, *The Free Negro in Maryland* (1921), Luther Porter Jackson, *Free Negro Labor and Property-Holding in Virginia* (1942), and John Hope Franklin, *The Free Negro in North Carolina* (1943)— wrote about African Americans who had acquired their freedom before the Civil War to illustrate that enslavement was not African Americans' natural condition.[6] Benjamin Quarles's *The Negro in the American Revolution* (1961) revealed the contributions that African Americans made in securing American independence, while his *The Negro in the Civil War* (1953) told us about their part in preserving the Union.[7]

Historians of the African American experience did not fully examine the enslavement of black people until the 1970s. Scholars of American history such as U. B. Phillips, *American Negro Slavery* (1918), had studied the institution of slavery without much attention to the lives of the enslaved, except to suggest that they were naturally suited for enslavement, which supposedly rescued them from Africa and introduced them to Western civilization.[8] Three books published in the 1940s began a shift in the interpretation of African American history. The anthropologist Melville J. Herskovits, in *The Myth of the Negro Past* (1941), examined evidence of African culture in the New World.[9] Although he reported that such evidence was stronger in the Caribbean and in Brazil than in North America, he identified traces of African culture in the United States. The slave trade and enslavement, he argued, did not erase former languages, religions, and cultures. Although much African culture did not survive in the United States, strongly recognizable remnants could be found in religion, cuisine, speech patterns, music, dance, burial practices, and social customs. Herskovits's work influenced historians to study more deeply the theme of black identity, the transition from Africa to America, and the development of African American culture.

Black identity and culture became manifest in many ways, a principal one of which was resistance to slaveholders. Herbert Aptheker, in *American Negro Slave Revolts* (1944), recorded the large number of slave conspiracies and revolts.[10]

---

[6]John H. Russell, *The Free Negro in Virginia, 1619–1865* (1913; New York: Dover Publications, 1969); James M. Wright, *The Free Negro in Maryland, 1634–1860* (1921; New York: Octagon Books, 1977); Luther Porter Jackson, *The Free Negro Labor and Property-Holding in Virginia, 1830–1860* (New York: Appleton, 1942); John Hope Franklin, *The Free Negro in North Carolina, 1790–1860* (Chapel Hill: University of North Carolina Press, 1943).

[7]Benjamin Quarles, *The Negro in the American Revolution* (Chapel Hill: University of North Carolina Press, 1961), and *The Negro in the Civil War* (Boston: Little, Brown, 1953).

[8]Ulrich B. Phillips, *American Negro Slavery: A Survey of the Supply, Employment and Control of Negro Labor as Determined by the Plantation Regime* (New York: Appleton, 1918).

[9]Melville J. Herskovits, *The Myth of the Negro Past* (New York: Harper and Brothers, 1941).

[10]Herbert Aptheker, *American Negro Slave Revolts* (New York: Columbia University Press, 1944).

After Aptheker, historians have generally agreed that African Americans did not passively accept their plight but actively resisted enslavement with recalcitrance and armed struggle. Aptheker opened a new dimension for the study of African Americans in looking at their interior lives, at what they did for themselves to resist racial oppression. John Hope Franklin's groundbreaking textbook *From Slavery to Freedom* (1947) furthered this approach. In his preface to the first edition, he explained the need to start with ancient African beginnings to understand the development of "Afro-American institutions in the Old World and the New." Franklin's work was in many respects revisionist as he sought "to re-tell the story of the evolution of the people of the United States in order to place the Negro in his proper relationship and perspective." In the spirit of Herskovits and Aptheker, he sought a balance between "the deeds of outstanding persons," and "the fortunes of the great mass of Negroes." He was moving away from the contributionist and vindicationist mode of many early historians to a greater concern with the interior world of African Americans while maintaining the goal of telling "the story of the process by which the Negro has sought to cast his lot with an evolving American civilization."[11]

One of the great problems in studying the history of the black masses was the paucity of known sources. The civil rights movement occasioned a major change in black life and culture beyond the dismantling of legal segregation. It led also to efforts for greater inclusion of African Americans in the story of the nation. Du Bois had written in *The Souls of Black Folk* that "actively we have woven ourselves with the very warp and woof of this nation."[12] But this was a story that was not well known by most Americans, black or white, despite the earlier efforts of Woodson and his successors to demonstrate the part that African Americans played in building and preserving the United States. The story was not told in most American history textbooks, exhibited in most museums, or referenced in most newspapers. With the rise of the civil rights movement in the 1950s and the advent of fresh scholarship and thinking under the general term Black Studies in the 1960s, however, there was a thirst for more knowledge about African Americans. Many Americans wanted to know about the increase in black activism and the context of the black struggle for equality. Many federal, state, and local archivists combed their libraries for materials on the African American experience and published useful guides to their collections. They sought and assembled the papers of black leaders and organizations. Through these efforts, there was soon abundant material (print, sound, and visual) to reconstruct and to interpret the African American past.[13]

One of the most important projects to help document and reconstruct the African American past was George P. Rawick's *The American Slave: A Composite*

[11]John Hope Franklin, *From Slavery to Freedom: A History of American Negroes* (New York: Knopf, 1947), vii–viii.

[12]Du Bois, *The Souls of Black Folk*, 215.

[13]Robert L. Harris, Jr., and Rosalyn Terborg-Penn, eds., *The Columbia Guide to African American History since 1939* (New York: Columbia University Press, 2006).

Autobiography (1972). This nineteen-volume collection was based on interviews
of former slaves conducted by the Federal Writers' Project of the New Deal's
Works Progress Administration from 1936 to 1938. In addition to the interviews,
Rawick reminded us, "There were at least eighty published slave narratives
which appeared before the Civil War and probably many more."[14] John W. Blassingame's *The Slave Community* (1972) drew on slave testimony to offer a compelling view of life among the enslaved in their own words.[15] For the first time,
historians engaged slavery as social rather than institutional history by giving cre-
dence to African Americans' own thoughts, feelings, and observations. In expanding our knowledge of the slave community, historians such as Herbert G.
Gutman, in *The Black Family in Slavery and Freedom* (1976), and Brenda E.
Stevenson, in *Life in Black and White: Family and Community in the Slave
South* (1996), suggested that there had been greater stability among slave families
than previously thought. Wilma A. Dunaway, in *The African American Family in
Slavery and Emancipation* (2003), more recently questioned the persistence of
slave families, especially on small plantations. In *From Rebellion to Revolution*
(1979), Eugene Genovese used a comparative study of slave resistance in the
Western Hemisphere to argue that slaves in the United States were basically
pre-political.[16] Unlike other studies that gave the enslaved a revolutionary consciousness in resisting slavery, Genovese attributed the absence of a large-scale
successful slave revolt in the United States similar to the Palmares Republic in
Brazil or the Haitian Revolution to the lack of well-articulated or defined political objectives.

Many other dimensions of slave society have gained historians' attention.
Deborah Gray White's *Ar'n't I a Woman?* (1985) probed the intersection of race
and gender in the lives of female slaves and the myths that emerged about black
women. Wilma King, in *Stolen Childhood* (1995), examined the absence of
childhood among enslaved children because they entered the workplace at a
young age. She found that, despite their early introduction to the world of work,
enslaved children did enjoy some leisure activities, informal education, and religious instruction within the slave community. Marie Jenkins Schwartz's *Born in
Bondage* (2000) investigated the tension between slave owners and slave parents
about how to raise enslaved children and how the children perceived their own
lives. John Hope Franklin and Loren Schweninger, in *Runaway Slaves* (1999),

---

[14]George P. Rawick, *The American Slave: A Composite Autobiography*, 19 vols. (Westport,
Conn.: Greenwood, 1972).

[15]John W. Blassingame, *The Slave Community: Plantation Life in the Antebellum South*
(New York: Oxford University Press, 1972).

[16]Herbert G. Gutman, *The Black Family in Slavery and Freedom, 1750–1925* (New York:
Pantheon, 1976); Brenda E. Stevenson, *Life in Black and White: Family and Community in the
Slave South* (New York: Oxford University Press, 1996); Wilma A. Dunaway, *The African Amer-
ican Family in Slavery and Emancipation* (New York: Cambridge University Press, 2003);
Eugene D. Genovese, *From Rebellion to Revolution: Afro-American Slave Revolts in the Mak-
ing of the Modern World* (Baton Rouge: Louisiana State University Press, 1979).

based in large measure on advertisements for fugitive slaves, offered descriptions of fleeing slaves, including physical features, skills, age, region of the country, and what slave owners thought about them. Albert J. Raboteau's *Slave Religion* (1978) and Margaret Washington Creel's *A Peculiar People* (1988) discussed the centrality of religion to the slave community.[17] Religion, Raboteau and Washington demonstrated, helped sustain the slaves, gave them a sense of self-worth, and reinforced the idea that they were equal to whites in the sight of God despite whites' efforts to denigrate them.

Generations of Captivity (2003), Ira Berlin's masterful synthesis of enslavement, emphasized slavery as a dynamic rather than a static institution. Berlin demonstrated changes over time and space in the making and remaking of slavery during three centuries of development in North America. Although slavery in large measure was abolished in the North during the formation of the new nation, Berlin, like Leon Litwack in *North of Slavery* (1961), considered the institution of slavery as important to the history of the antebellum North as it was to the history of the North during the colonial and revolutionary periods. Berlin acknowledged that "slaveholders severely circumscribed the lives of enslaved people, but they never fully defined them." A major problem in studying enslavement is how to balance the power, force, and violence of the slaveholders and the nation that protected them against the humanity, integrity, self-definition, and resourcefulness of those who were enslaved. Although U.S. slaves were not able to overthrow slavery as in Haiti, Berlin also demonstrated that slaves in the United States also did not become "socially dead, 'absolute aliens,' 'genealogical isolates,' 'deracinated outsiders,' 'pre-political,' or unreflective 'sambos.'"[18]

Lawrence W. Levine's *Black Culture and Black Consciousness* (1977) heralded a methodological and interpretive breakthrough for studying African Americans. Levine drew on the work of anthropologists, ethnomusicologists, and folklorists to unveil "the contours of slave folk thought on the eve of emancipation and . . . the effects of freedom upon that thought." Levine's work departed from past studies that "rendered black history an unending round of degradation and pathology." Like many other historians after the 1960s, he argued that African Americans were not objects but rather actors who forged and nurtured a

---

[17]Deborah Gray White, *Ar'n't I a Woman? Female Slaves in the Plantation South* (New York: W. W. Norton, 1985); Wilma King, *Stolen Childhood: Slave Youth in Nineteenth-Century America* (Bloomington: Indiana University Press, 1995); Marie Jenkins Schwartz, *Born in Bondage: Growing Up Enslaved in the Antebellum South* (Cambridge, Mass.: Harvard University Press, 2000); John Hope Franklin and Loren Schweninger, *Runaway Slaves: Rebels on the Plantation* (New York: Oxford University Press, 1999); Albert J. Raboteau, *Slave Religion: The "Invisible Institution" in the Antebellum South* (New York: Oxford University Press, 1978); Margaret Washington Creel, *A Peculiar People: Slave Religion and Community among the Gullahs* (New York: New York University Press, 1988).

[18]Ira Berlin, *Generations of Captivity: A History of African-American Slaves* (Cambridge, Mass.: Harvard University Press, 2003), 3–4, 18; Leon F. Litwack, *North of Slavery: The Negro in the Free States, 1790–1860* (Chicago: University of Chicago Press, 1961).

distinctive culture. Historians were beginning to broaden and deepen John Hope Franklin's effort to uncover the story of the black masses and to reveal the voice and agency of African Americans. In *Exodusters: Black Migration to Kansas after Reconstruction* (1977), Nell Irvin Painter contrasted the interests of "representative men of color" and "the authentic voices of rural Blacks." Leon Litwack, in *Been in the Storm So Long* (1979), explored how ordinary black men and women perceived their freedom and how they acted to shape their future. He also provided evidence to substantiate his argument that "the distant voices of Africa still echoed in their music, in their folk tales, in the ways they worshipped God, and in their kinship relationships. But in 1860 they were as American as the whites who lorded over them."[19]

Many historians have studied the transition of Africans to African Americans. Sterling Stuckey, in *Slave Culture* (1987), explained how disparate groups from Africa melded into a community with a set of essentially African values that bound them together and helped to sustain them under the brutal conditions of oppression. Michael Gomez, in *Exchanging Our Country Marks* (1998), explored the transition from different ethnicities that were transported from Africa to the emergence of a race in the United States. According to Gomez, not all Africans experienced slavery in the same way. Different mixes of Africans in each colony and state resulted in distinctive, though related, cultural forms. Gomez found evidence that, by the 1830s, the African American community was becoming bifurcated along class lines, with different visions of African elements in African American culture. The black elite in many respects sought to divorce itself from its African heritage to gain inclusion into American society, while the masses saw this exclusion as a rejection of Africa and their identity as a people.[20]

The persistent theme of African American agency, which contradicted the contributionist tilt of early scholarship, required historians to revise previous studies to allow greater inclusion of African Americans in the story of the United States. In *Black Reconstruction in America* (1935), Du Bois called into question the prevailing interpretation of the Reconstruction era, which depicted black people as ignorant, lazy, dishonest, extravagant, and responsible for bad government in the South after the Civil War. This depiction was used to justify disfranchisement, segregation, and later resistance to civil rights legislation and school desegregation. John Hope Franklin, in *Reconstruction: After the Civil War* (1961), Kenneth M. Stampp, in *The Era of Reconstruction* (1965), and Lerone Bennett,

---

[19]Lawrence W. Levine, *Black Culture and Black Consciousness: Afro-American Folk Thought from Slavery to Freedom* (New York: Oxford University Press, 1977); Nell Irvin Painter, *Exodusters: Black Migration to Kansas after Reconstruction* (New York: Knopf, 1977), 16; Leon F. Litwack, *Been in the Storm So Long: The Aftermath of Slavery* (New York: Knopf, 1979), xi.

[20]Sterling Stuckey, *Slave Culture: Nationalist Theory and the Foundations of Black America* (New York: Oxford University Press, 1987); Michael A. Gomez, *Exchanging Our Country Marks: The Transformation of African Identities in the Colonial and Antebellum South* (Chapel Hill: University of North Carolina Press, 1998).

Jr., in *Black Power U.S.A.* (1967), provided a different view of Reconstruction, followed more recently by James M. McPherson's *Ordeal by Fire* (1982) and Eric Foner's *Reconstruction: America's Unfinished Revolution* (1988). These and other historians have concluded that Reconstruction was a period of significant advances for African Americans, that federal protection was essential to their advances, and that the former slaves had helped bring about substantial reform of southern government and society. McPherson argued that "neither the black leaders nor their constituents were so ignorant or incompetent as the traditional image of Reconstruction has portrayed them." Foner emphasized that "no part of the American experience has, in the last twenty-five years, seen a broadly accepted point of view so completely overturned as Reconstruction."[21]

The role of black women has entered more fully into the story of African Americans as actors in history. Darlene Clark Hine's multivolume reference work, *Black Women in American History* (1990), much like Rawick's *The American Slave: A Composite Autobiography*, opened numerous possibilities for studying black women. Hine provided little-known information about black women and their organizations, which helped to make the history of black women more visible. Rosalyn Terborg-Penn's *African American Women in the Struggle for the Vote* (1998) reviewed the often stormy relationship between black women and white feminists in the effort to secure women's right to vote. Tera Hunter, in *To 'Joy My Freedom* (1997), covered the domestic labor of southern black women after the Civil War as cooks, maids, children's nurses, and laundresses. She probed their strategies and struggles to resist oppression and to achieve self-sufficiency in their neighborhoods, families, churches, organizations, dance halls, and theaters. Michelle Scott's *Blues Empress in Black Chattanooga* (2008) examined how urban migration and black life in Chattanooga, Tennessee, nurtured the emergence of Bessie Smith as the Empress of the Blues.[22]

The black church has been the most powerful institution for self-help among African American women. Evelyn Brooks Higginbotham, in *Righteous*

[21]W. E. B. Du Bois, *Black Reconstruction in America: An Essay toward a History of the Part Which Black Folk Played in an Attempt to Reconstruct Democracy in America, 1860–1880* (New York: Russell & Russell, 1935), especially Du Bois's last chapter, "The Propaganda of History"; John Hope Franklin, *Reconstruction: After the Civil War* (Chicago: University of Chicago Press, 1961); Kenneth M. Stampp, *The Era of Reconstruction, 1865–1877* (New York: Knopf, 1965); Lerone Bennett, Jr., *Black Power U.S.A.: The Human Side of Reconstruction, 1867–1877* (Chicago: Johnson Publishing Co., 1967); James M. McPherson, *Ordeal by Fire: The Civil War and Reconstruction* (New York: Knopf, 1982), 556; Eric Foner, *Reconstruction: America's Unfinished Revolution, 1863–1877* (New York: Harper & Row, 1988), xix–xxi.

[22]Darlene Clark Hine, ed., *Black Women in American History* (Brooklyn, N.Y.: Carlson, 1990); Rosalyn Terborg-Penn, *African American Women in the Struggle for the Vote, 1850–1920* (Bloomington: Indiana University Press, 1998); Tera W. Hunter, *To 'Joy My Freedom: Southern Black Women's Lives and Labors after the Civil War* (Cambridge, Mass.: Harvard University Press, 1997); Michelle R. Scott, *Blues Empress in Black Chattanooga: Bessie Smith and the Emerging Urban South* (Urbana: University of Illinois Press, 2008).

Discontent (1993), argued that black women were critical to making the black church such a strong and important institution. Martha S. Jones's *All Bound Up Together* (2007) vividly analyzed the story of black women's involvement in the major issues of the nineteenth century, such as slavery and abolition, women's rights, war, emancipation, institution building, the Fourteenth Amendment, and Jim Crow. Black women, Jones argued, were active participants in African American public culture, a "contested space in which activists self-consciously wrestled with the meanings of manhood and womanhood and the implications of those ideas for the structures and practices of institutions."[23]

Two recent books, *Emerging Voices and Paradigms* (2008) and *Telling Histories: Black Women Historians in the Ivory Tower* (2008), illuminate the development of black women's history as a field of study during the late twentieth century and the evolution of the black woman scholar. *Emerging Voices and Paradigms* presents the work of many young black women historians. Most of the essays represent works in progress and fresh directions in the field of black women's history. They provide new information and interpretations about social uplift, philanthropic strategies, and shared leadership responsibilities. *Telling Histories: Black Women Historians in the Ivory Tower* provides the reflections of black women historians who entered a white- and male-dominated profession during the late twentieth century.[24] Black women had to confront issues of legitimacy and assumptions about their level of objectivity in writing black women's history. They faced a pull between traditional history departments and emerging black and women's studies departments. The book signals the maturation of the field of black women's history and the growth of the black woman as historical scholar.

The writing of black history during the late twentieth century became more complex in taking up realities within the black community itself. In *Uplifting the Race* (1996), Kevin K. Gaines addressed black nationalism, tensions among black males and females, and the intersection of racial discourses between African Americans and mainstream society. He explored "the origins of racial liberalism, civil rights, the myth of color blindness, and the reactive black messianism that circumscribes black struggle and distorts its history." There has always been heterogeneity in thought and leaders among African Americans, but historians are only now beginning to examine more fully the range of black thought and action. The idea of black messianism has assumed that individual black leaders from Frederick Douglass to Martin Luther King, Jr., have spoken for all African

[23]Evelyn Brooks Higginbotham, *Righteous Discontent: The Women's Movement in the Black Baptist Church, 1880–1920* (Cambridge, Mass.: Harvard University Press, 1993); Martha S. Jones, *All Bound Up Together: The Woman Question in African American Public Culture, 1830–1900* (Chapel Hill: University of North Carolina Press, 2007), 2, 9.

[24]Ida Elizabeth Jones and Elizabeth Clark-Lewis, eds., *Emerging Voices and Paradigms: Black Women's Scholarship* (Washington, D.C.: Association of Black Women Historians, 2008); Deborah Gray White, ed., *Telling Histories: Black Women Historians in the Ivory Tower* (Chapel Hill: University of North Carolina Press, 2008).

Americans and have borne responsibility for their deliverance from racial oppression. More than four decades ago, in *Negro Thought in America* (1963), August Meier identified the variety of black ideologies during the age of Booker T. Washington, whom many recognized as the paramount black leader during the late nineteenth and early twentieth centuries.[25]

Recent scholarship on Marcus Garvey and the Universal Negro Improvement Association (UNIA) has probed the class and gender dimensions of the Garvey movement and has shown it to be more than a back-to-Africa movement. Garvey founded UNIA in 1914, and it was the largest mass movement among African Americans until the 1960s. In *Literary Garveyism* (1983), Tony Martin assessed the Garvey phenomenon as an important component of the New Negro Movement and the literary and artistic flowering known as the Harlem Renaissance. The New Negro Movement, which gained prominence after the death of Booker T. Washington in 1915, announced a race conscious and assertive African American determined to gain full citizenship in the United States and respect for African and African American culture throughout the world. Claudrena N. Harold, in *The Rise and Fall of the Garvey Movement in the Urban South* (2007), documented the widespread presence of UNIA chapters throughout the United States, especially in the South; Louisiana, with sixty-four, had the largest number of chapters in the country. Before Harold's book, the Garvey movement had been thought to be primarily a northern urban organization. In *The Veiled Garvey* (2002), Ula Y. Taylor explained how instrumental women were in organizing chapters and writing for Garvey's newspaper, *The Negro World*. Judith Stein, in *The World of Marcus Garvey* (1986), described how Garvey preached middle-class values to improve the status of black people worldwide, but with an emphasis on racial pride and solidarity.[26]

When we turn to African American culture, Nathan Huggins's *Harlem Renaissance* (1971) remains the best study of the period from 1919 to 1929, when the flowering of African American creativity in art, dance, film, literature, and music was at its highest. Huggins placed the Harlem Renaissance within the context of American society and culture and revealed the interdependence of both. *When Harlem Was in Vogue* (1981), by David L. Lewis, explored the lives

---

[25]Kevin K. Gaines, *Uplifting the Race: Black Leadership, Politics, and Culture in the Twentieth Century* (Chapel Hill: University of North Carolina Press, 1996), xii, xvii; August Meier, *Negro Thought in America, 1880–1915: Racial Ideologies in the Age of Booker T. Washington* (Ann Arbor: University of Michigan Press, 1963).

[26]Robert A. Hill, ed., *The Marcus Garvey and Universal Negro Improvement Association Papers*, vols. 1–10 (Berkeley: University of California Press, 1983–2006); Colin Grant, *Negro with a Hat: The Rise and Fall of Marcus Garvey* (New York: Oxford University Press, 2008); Tony Martin, *Literary Garveyism: Garvey, Black Arts, and the Harlem Renaissance* (Dover, Mass.: Majority Press, 1983); Claudrena N. Harold, *The Rise and Fall of the Garvey Movement in the Urban South, 1918–1942* (New York: Routledge, 2007); Ula Y. Taylor, *The Veiled Garvey: The Life and Times of Amy Jacques Garvey* (Chapel Hill: University of North Carolina Press, 2002); Judith Stein, *The World of Marcus Garvey: Race and Class in Modern Society* (Baton Rouge: Louisiana State University Press, 1986).

and significance of those individuals whom Lewis considered the midwives of that Harlem-centered artistic and literary movement. Lewis was more critical of the era than Huggins and questioned the quality of its art and literature, which he argued were treated more like commodities by their white patrons than as a means of racial elevation.[27]

Although New York City with its publishing houses, in particular, was the cultural capital of the United States, recent scholarship has probed creativity during this period among African Americans in Chicago, Philadelphia, and Washington, D.C. Genevieve Fabre and Michel Feith, the editors of *Temples for Tomorrow* (2001), considered the international implications of the Harlem Renaissance for black writers and entertainers who visited and lived in Paris and for black people around the world who read about and were especially influenced by race awareness and pride. Davarian L. Baldwin's *Chicago's New Negroes* (2007) examined cultural vitality outside New York City, the effects of black migration from the South to the North during World War I, and class tensions between newcomers and old settlers. He looked at those topics through the eyes of the black masses who were "more than just the objects of black modernist art and writings . . . but . . . subjects creating and crafting their own ideas that would forever alter the course and shape of the modern world." Within Baldwin's theme of the "consumer marketplace," we witness Chicago's intellectual and cultural vibrancy in art, music, sound recording, and film. It was in the consumer marketplace that the masses came into conversation with traditional intellectuals, who then produced new knowledge.[28]

Just as the issue of class is moving to the fore in African American history, so is the matter of sexuality. For a long time, the black population's emphasis on racial uplift obscured other dynamics within the black community, especially sexuality. A. B. Christa Schwarz, in *Gay Voices of the Harlem Renaissance* (2003), has begun to unpack the layers of racial and sexual themes in the works of Harlem Renaissance writers.[29]

African Americans experienced the Great Depression sooner than the rest of the country, and it lasted longer for them. Nancy J. Weiss, in *Farewell to the Party of Lincoln* (1983), showed how African Americans welcomed the New Deal and shifted their allegiance from the Republican to the Democratic Party in large measure because of New Deal relief efforts. Although African Americans gained some benefits from the New Deal, Harvard Sitkoff, in *A New Deal for Blacks* (1978), made it clear that they did not achieve civil rights legislation, especially

---

[27]Nathan I. Huggins, *Harlem Renaissance* (New York: Oxford University Press, 1971); David L. Lewis, *When Harlem Was in Vogue* (New York: Knopf, 1981).

[28]Genevieve Fabre and Michel Feith, eds., *Temples for Tomorrow: Looking Back at the Harlem Renaissance* (Bloomington: Indiana University Press, 2001); Davarian L. Baldwin, *Chicago's New Negroes: Modernity, the Great Migration, and Black Urban Life* (Chapel Hill: University of North Carolina Press, 2007).

[29]A. B. Christa Schwarz, *Gay Voices of the Harlem Renaissance* (Bloomington: Indiana University Press, 2003).

laws against lynching. Historians have also examined the deleterious effects of the New Deal on African Americans, particularly in compressing the skill level of black workers in relation to their white counterparts. White workers took over many jobs held by black workers during the Great Depression, and New Deal job training programs benefited white more than black labor. Paul E. Mertz, in *New Deal Policy and Southern Rural Poverty* (1978), examined the relief programs of the New Deal, which exacerbated rural poverty. African Americans are still trying to catch up to white Americans who gained economic, educational, and housing advantages through government programs of the New Deal and World War II. In *When Affirmative Action Was White* (2005), Ira Katznelson traces the rise of the white middle class through New Deal job training and the benefits of the GI Bill after World War II, which helped white men and women go to college and purchase homes. African Americans found themselves excluded from job training programs and relegated to domestic and service positions, and because of racial discrimination they had limited access to the benefits of the GI Bill.[30]

Although the National Association for the Advancement of Colored People (NAACP) played a significant role in attacking racial segregation and in securing civil rights for African Americans, primarily through the legal system, the organization was hampered by the thorny problem of economic inequality and the existence of a large black underclass. Founded in 1909, the NAACP sought to have the civil rights of African Americans written into law. Charles F. Kellogg, in *NAACP* (1967), described how the organization scored significant victories, especially through the courts, in voiding grandfather clauses in the South, which had limited the franchise to those individuals, exclusively white, whose grandfathers had voted before the Civil War. The NAACP also successfully challenged the white primary, which excluded black voters from participating in the selection of Democratic Party candidates (itself tantamount to election), gained access for African Americans to graduate and professional schools, and upended the separate-but-equal doctrine. Harvard Sitkoff, in *The Struggle for Black Equality* (1981), and Juan Williams, in *Eyes on the Prize* (1987), explained how the NAACP—together with other civil rights organizations such as the Congress of Racial Equality, organized in 1942; the Southern Christian Leadership Council, formed in 1957; and the Student Nonviolent Coordinating Committee, established in 1960; as well as a coalition of labor and religious groups—achieved important civil rights legislation, especially the Civil Rights Act of 1964, which banned racial discrimination in public accommodations and transportation, the Voting Rights Act of 1965, and the Housing Act of 1968. Harold Cruse, in *Plural*

[30]Nancy J. Weiss, *Farewell to the Party of Lincoln: Black Politics in the Age of FDR* (Princeton, N.J.: Princeton University Press, 1983); Harvard Sitkoff, *A New Deal for Blacks: The Emergence of Civil Rights as a National Issue* (New York: Oxford University Press, 1978); Paul E. Mertz, *New Deal Policy and Southern Rural Poverty* (Baton Rouge: Louisiana State University Press, 1978); Ira Katznelson, *When Affirmative Action Was White: An Untold History of Racial Inequality in Twentieth-Century America* (New York: W. W. Norton, 2005).

But Equal (1987), argued that the civil rights movement was founded on the principle of non-economic liberalism, which pursued legal rather than economic change for African Americans and left them in an unequal position despite gains in civil rights.[31]

Steven F. Lawson and Charles M. Payne, in *Debating the Civil Rights Movement* (1998), examined the extent to which we should emphasize the everyday people who sustained the movement, government actions through civil rights legislation and enforcement, or an appropriate combination of the two. Taylor Branch's trilogy, *Parting the Waters* (1988), *Pillar of Fire* (1998), and *At Canaan's Edge* (2006), covered the civil rights movement and the United States during what Branch called "the King Years." He explored the complex web of connections among civil rights activists, their organizations, and their allies. He equated Martin Luther King, Jr., with America's founders in giving meaning to American democracy and in applying the nation's founding principles to most of her citizens for the first time. Peniel E. Joseph, in *Waiting 'til the Midnight Hour* (2006), asserted that the black power movement built on the dignity that African Americans gained from the civil rights movement and advanced an assertive identity and cultural pride that undergirds African American life today.[32]

The civil rights movement opened more than opportunity for most Americans; it liberated African American history from the constraints of an artificial unity and helped to change the African American narrative at the end of the twentieth century. The story has become more one of looking at black America from the inside out. The triumphs of the civil rights movement made it possible to examine issues such as class, gender, and sexuality, for example, that would have been considered divisive to the struggle for racial equality prior to the 1960s. We can now strip away what Evelyn Brooks Higginbotham, in "African American Women's History and the Metalanguage of Race" (1992), described as a muting of conflict among African Americans that resulted in an uncritical assumption of a monolithic black community. Historians at the beginning of the twenty-first century are giving more attention to what Earl Lewis identified as the multidimensionality of black history. This multidimensional approach to the study of African American history is even more important now because large numbers of

---

[31]Charles F. Kellogg, *NAACP: A History of the National Association for the Advancement of Colored People* (Baltimore: Johns Hopkins University Press, 1967); Harvard Sitkoff, *The Struggle for Black Equality* (New York: Hill and Wang, 1981); Juan Williams, *Eyes on the Prize* (New York: Viking, 1987); Harold Cruse, *Plural But Equal: A Critical Study of Blacks and Minorities and America's Plural Society* (New York: Morrow, 1987), 124–25.

[32]Steven F. Lawson and Charles M. Payne, *Debating the Civil Rights Movement, 1945–1968* (Lanham, Md.: Rowman and Littlefield, 2006); Taylor Branch, *Parting the Waters: America in the King Years, 1954–1963* (New York: Simon & Schuster, 1988); Taylor Branch, *Pillar of Fire: America in the King Years, 1963–1965* (New York: Simon & Schuster, 1998); Taylor Branch, *At Canaan's Edge: America in the King Years, 1965–1968* (New York: Simon & Schuster, 2006); Peniel Joseph, *Waiting 'til the Midnight Hour: A Narrative History of Black Power in America* (New York: Henry Holt, 2006).

people of African ancestry have immigrated to the United States from Africa, the Caribbean, Europe, and Central and South America since the 1960s. Michael Gomez, in *Reversing Sail* (2005), uses the conceptual framework of the African diaspora to study the easy flow of people and ideas, the similarities between the civil rights and decolonization movements, black consciousness, and the international flavor of black music.[33] Although historians have in large measure laid to rest Du Bois's inquiry in 1903 about the role of African Americans in building the United States and placing an indelible imprint on American culture, the issue of African American identity remains a contested area of study for the twenty-first century.

[33] Evelyn Brooks Higginbotham, "African American Women's History and the Metalanguage of Race," *Signs* 17 (Winter 1992): 251–74; Earl Lewis, "To Turn as on a Pivot: Writing African Americans into a History of Overlapping Diasporas," *American Historical Review* 110 (June 1995): 765–87; Michael A. Gomez, *Reversing Sail: A History of the African Diaspora* (New York: Cambridge University Press, 2005).

John Shy and David J. Fitzpatrick

American Military History

For centuries a great deal of written history was the history of wars and battles, but by 1900 professional historians were moving into new fields—economic, intellectual, and social history—and leaving war mostly to the military profession. Military history has never been fully accepted or wholly respectable within the history profession and in colleges and universities. This dubious status is tragic in that it sacrifices the public need to understand war. Though taught in military history courses wherever they exist, war is generally slighted or ignored in the rest of the history curriculum.

From the earliest published histories of English colonial America, authors did not marginalize military events but gave them full attention. The first histories of the Revolutionary War were published soon after the event, and one of the best, by David Ramsay, attempted to analyze the impact of the war on American society. The tradition of full attention to military matters held throughout the nineteenth century, with two of the most celebrated American historians, Francis Parkman and Henry Adams, using war and battles as leitmotifs for their multivolume studies.[1]

One of the earliest hints that the history of war might be in trouble was uttered by Peter Force in 1837. Force was perhaps the greatest-ever collector and publisher of documentary evidence of American history, but in the preface to his never-completed compilation on the American Revolution, he warned that "superficial persons" seemed to think that "the whole history of that Revolution is to be found in the narrative of the [military] campaigns of that War."[2] Force was obviously tired of hearing about Saratoga and Yorktown and sought to redirect

---

[1]David Ramsay, *The History of the American Revolution*, 2 vols., ed. Lester H. Cohen (1789; Indianapolis: The Liberty Fund, 1990), II, Appendix, 625–38. Francis Parkman, *England and France in North America*, 9 vols. (Boston: Little, Brown, 1865–1892), traces the armed struggle for control of North America from the seventeenth century to the final British victory in 1760, with the climactic two volumes of the series entitled *Montcalm and Wolfe* (1884). Henry Adams, *History of the United States of America*, 10 vols. (Boston: Scribner's, 1891–1896), actually deals only with the administrations of Thomas Jefferson and James Madison; much of four volumes is a detailed account of the campaigns and battles of the War of 1812.

[2]Peter Force, *American Archives: A Documentary History of the Origin and Progress of the North American Colonies* (Washington, D.C.: M. St. Clair and Peter Force, 1837), 4th series, I, Preface, 2. Only nine volumes, dealing with the American Revolution, were ever published of the planned series.

attention to the causes and impact of the fight for American independence. His lone voice questioning the centrality of battles and military campaigns to history in general would become a chorus by the early twentieth century.

By 1900 the writing of American military history, despite the warning from Peter Force, appeared to be thriving. Three "little" wars against Britain, Mexico, and Spain dotted the previous century as the American Republic expanded westward to the Pacific and the Rio Grande while hammering the native Indian people into submission. Memoirs and published histories of these conflicts sold well, but the great military events of the age had been the Civil War that had nearly destroyed the Republic and before that the amazing story of the wars of Napoleon. Both the Civil War and Napoleon were given generous attention in the fledging journals of the history profession.[3]

Yet military officers, not professional historians, were the most important historians of war before 1900. Alfred T. Mahan, a Navy captain, and Emory Upton, an Army colonel, wrote pathbreaking studies that established the terms on which much subsequent writing in American military history would be done. Mahan's *The Influence of Sea Power upon History, 1660–1783* (1890) developed a theory of sea power from a close study of British and French naval history in the eighteenth century. From that theory, Mahan argued that a navy's primary responsibility was to establish control of the seas and maintain a nation's sea lines of communications in time of war. He won almost instant fame in every nation with maritime interests or ambitions, including Germany, the United States, and Japan. Before his death in 1881, Emory Upton, a brilliant young officer and Civil War hero, drafted an impassioned history of the military policy of the United States. He argued that military policy since the Revolution had been mishandled by politicians, and he recommended a program of military training in peacetime not unlike that in European states, notably Prussia. Upton's book finally was published in 1904 during the flurry of military reform after the Spanish-American War. Both Mahan and Upton would continue to influence both military thought and the writing of American military history well into the twentieth century, but their books are landmarks in another respect: Each argued vigorously that military history taught lessons that should guide future national strategy.[4] In developing

---

[3]*American Historical Review* started in 1895, *The Mississippi Valley Historical Review* in 1914. A rough count to 1918 shows that each ran at least one article (of about twenty annually) on military history and that a tenth or more of the reviews were of books about some aspect of war.

[4]Alfred Thayer Mahan, *The Influence of Sea Power upon History, 1660–1783* (Boston: Little, Brown, 1890); Emory Upton, *The Military Policy of the United States* (Washington, D.C.: Government Printing Office, 1904). Numerous books have dealt with Mahan's influence; two recent studies are Jon T. Sumida, *Inventing Grand Strategy and Teaching Command: The Classic Works of Alfred Thayer Mahan Reconsidered* (Baltimore: Johns Hopkins University Press, 1997); Sadao Asada, *From Mahan to Pearl Harbor: The Imperial Japanese Navy and the United States* (Annapolis, Md.: Naval Institute Press, 2006). Russell F. Weigley, *Towards an American Army: Military Thought from Washington to Marshall* (New York: Columbia University Press, 1962), emphasized Upton's negative influence in formulating realistic military policy; but Weigley may have misread Upton's work; see David J. Fitzpatrick, "Emory Upton and the Citizen Soldier," *The Journal of Military History* 65 (2001): 355–89.

those lessons, they clearly were attempting to shape national policy, while advocating the interests of their own military services. In doing this, they violated a chief canon of the new professional history and thereby separated their field from mainstream academic history, in which exhaustive research and dispassionate objectivity were key ideals. Even now a great deal of historical writing on war is aimed at deriving applicable lessons.

In 1916, on the eve of America's entry into the First World War, an article appeared in *The Mississippi Valley Historical Review* titled "The Function of Military History."[5] Its author, Arthur L. Conger, was a Harvard graduate and an Army captain who was deeply involved in the effort to apply the standards of professional history to the study of military history within the U.S. Army. His article is a lament for the peculiar difficulty of doing military history because it must serve conflicting constituencies. General readers want exciting stories with heroes and villains, the government rejects criticism of its own military performance, and soldiers demand relevance to their own professional needs. Academic historians expect strict accuracy, critical use of evidence, and an objective viewpoint, although the technical nature of modern warfare requires a level of knowledge that few academic historians can attain. The result, wrote Conger, was a sorry compromise that left the nation ignorant of the nature of war. He had thus identified a key element of a complex problem: In 1916 most military historians saw their work as Mahan and Upton had—guiding the future—while most academic historians wanted only to recapture the past as fully as possible.

The experience of the Great War, 1914–1918, seriously undermined the claim of the military profession to competence, much less to basing its expertise on historical lessons. A growing popular revulsion against *all* war further marginalized military history in the postwar years. Only in its causes did the history of war claim the attention of the professional historians. Military historians had never shown much interest in what caused war, and they did not contest this loss of an important piece of what logically was part of their own subject. But the academic historians' vigorous effort to "revise" the explanation of how nations had blundered into the catastrophic conflict in 1914 strongly influenced the way American historical writing in the 1930s explained America's own great war between 1861 and 1865. Just as Harry Elmer Barnes exposed the alleged foolishness of American entry into European war in 1917, an influential group of revisionist American historians focused on how the United States had blundered into civil war in 1861.[6] They argued that nothing could explain a terrible and

---

[5]A. L. Conger, "The Function of Military History," *Mississippi Valley Historical Review* 3 (1916): 161–71. Carol Reardon, *Soldiers and Scholars: The U.S. Army and the Uses of Military History, 1865–1920* (Lawrence: University Press of Kansas, 1990), is the best account of the troubled relationship between the Army and the historical profession, including Conger's role.

[6]Harry Elmer Barnes, *The Genesis of the World War: An Introduction to the Problem of War Guilt* (New York: Knopf, 1926). Two examples of the many Civil War revisionists are Avery O. Craven, *The Repressible Conflict, 1830–1861* (Baton Rouge: Louisiana State University Press, 1939); and George F. Milton, *The Eve of Conflict: Stephen A. Douglas and the Needless War* (Boston: Houghton Mifflin, 1934).

"needless" war except mass hysteria, the moralization of disagreement, and the failure of political leadership. This further splitting off of the causes of war from the study of war itself pushed military history evermore to the margins of legitimate historical inquiry.

On the eve of World War II, the idea that all war is absurd and avoidable strongly gripped the American imagination, within and outside of the academy. The experience of the Second World War discredited this idea and restored legitimacy to those who made war their study. The first great wave of the restoration began before Pearl Harbor and continued during a long run-up to the centennial of the Civil War in 1961–1965. Journalists, not professional historians or soldiers, led this first wave: Douglas Southall Freeman with multivolume biographies of Robert E. Lee and his lieutenants, followed by Bruce Catton with a trilogy on the Union Army of the Potomac. Allan Nevins, a journalist whose long list of good books in U.S. history earned him a Columbia University professorship, contributed a monumentally researched account of the war to preserve the Union. Scholars praised Nevins, but the history-reading public devoured Freeman and Catton.[7] These three did not alone cause the new enthusiasm for the history of the Civil War, but they surely rode the wave.[8]

Freeman and Catton were neatly paired, South and North, respectively, but in a crucial sense they diverged. Freeman spoke for "the lost cause," a belief that the South fought a noble fight. The lost cause had been sentimentally well established before 1900, reinforced by the revisionist historians of the 1930s, and hugely popularized by Margaret Mitchell's 1936 novel, *Gone with the Wind*.[9] Catton, by contrast, grew up in a household and town imbued with antislavery ideals. As a boy, he heard the stories of Union veterans, and when he began to write history he cast the Civil War as neither avoidable nor needless, but as a deeply moral struggle whose outcome saved the Republic and shaped its future. The abrupt shift away from the lost cause echoed an influential essay by Arthur M. Schlesinger, Jr., who in 1949 had denounced sentimentalism and argued that the Civil War was unavoidable and essential in destroying the evil of slavery.[10]

---

[7]Douglas S. Freeman, *R. E. Lee: A Biography*, 4 vols. (New York: Scribner's, 1934–1935), and *Lee's Lieutenants: A Study in Command*, 3 vols. (New York: Scribner's, 1942–1944); Bruce Catton, *The Army of the Potomac*, 3 vols. (Garden City, N.Y.: Doubleday, 1951–1953); Allan Nevins, *Ordeal of the Union*, 8 vols. (New York: Scribner's, 1947–1971).

[8]Historians and novelists of the Civil War appeared in droves as Americans moved from the Great Depression into World War II. Most of their books were forgettable, but one author, Shelby Foote, after only modest success with *Shiloh: A Novel* (New York: Dial Press, 1952), turned to history with *The Civil War: A Narrative*, 3 vols. (New York: Vintage, 1958–1974), a work notable for its Southern sympathies. Foote later became the voice of the South in the Ken Burns television series on the Civil War and as a celebrity collaborated with the editors of Time-Life to expand his *Narrative* to five volumes (Alexandria, Va.: Time-Life Books, 1998).

[9]See Gary W. Gallagher and Alan T. Nolan, eds., *The Myth of the Lost Cause* (Bloomington: Indiana University Press, 2000).

[10]Arthur M. Schlesinger, Jr., "The Causes of the American Civil War: A Note on Historical Sentimentalism," *Partisan Review* 16 (1949): 969–81.

Catton as well as Nevins clearly shared Schlesinger's position. This changed perspective, coming soon after victory against Nazism and Japanese militarism, owed much to the enduring American memory of the Second World War. It also occurred just when the nation began a long battle within itself over civil rights. But if the experience of 1941–1945 would be the main propellant for a new surge of interest in war and its history, the Civil War centennial was its clearest early manifestation.

The subject of the Civil War generated a vast literature after 1945 and attracted a large group of energetic younger historians who have continued to raise important questions about the war and its impact, as well as to publish high-quality research. Thomas L. Connelly's two-volume history of the Confederate Army of Tennessee altered the habitual focus on Lee and the eastern theater to the war west of the Appalachians. Connelly encouraged historians to see the war as a strategic whole and not just as a series of famous battles in the East. In a later book, *The Marble Man* (1977), Connelly explored the mythical status of Robert E. Lee.[11] With the old paradigm broken, Herman Hattaway and Archer Jones offered a compelling military argument for Union victory and a controversial psychological one for Confederate defeat.[12] These were but a few historians among many who deepened our understanding of the war. Brilliantly synthesizing the results of this work, James McPherson won a Pulitzer Prize in 1989 for his masterful narrative, *Battle Cry of Freedom* (1988).[13] And in the twenty years since then the work has gone on, exploring areas unimagined a generation ago.[14]

Still more profound and enduring than enthusiasm for Civil War history has been the effect on military history of World War II. In March 1942 President Franklin Delano Roosevelt, a serious amateur historian, ordered federal war-related

[11]Thomas L. Connelly, *Army of the Heartland: The Army of Tennessee, 1861–1862* (Baton Rouge: Louisiana State University Press, 1967); *Autumn of Glory: The Army of Tennessee, 1862–1865* (Baton Rouge: Louisiana State University Press, 1971); *The Marble Man: Robert E. Lee and His Image in American Society* (New York: Knopf, 1977).

[12]Herman Hattaway and Archer Jones, *How the North Won: A Military History of the Civil War* (Urbana: University of Illinois Press, 1983); Hattaway and Jones with Richard E. Beringer and William N. Still, Jr., *Why the South Lost the Civil War* (Athens: University of Georgia Press, 1986).

[13]James M. McPherson, *Battle Cry of Freedom: The Civil War Era* (New York: Oxford University Press, 1988), a volume in the distinguished series *The Oxford History of the United States*. Other volumes in this series published to date contain excellent narrative accounts of war: Robert Middlekauf, *The Glorious Cause: The American Revolution, 1763–1789* (revised edition, 2005), and David M. Kennedy, *Freedom from Fear: The American People in Depression and War, 1929–1945* (1999).

[14]David J. Eicher, *The Civil War in Books: An Analytical Bibliography* (Urbana: University of Illinois Press, 1997), is an invaluable guide to the literature prior to its own date of publication. Examples of work on the Civil War pushing well beyond the traditional bounds of military history are William G. Piston, *Lee's Tarnished Lieutenant: James Longstreet and His Place in Southern History* (Athens: University of Georgia Press, 1987); Gary W. Gallagher, *Causes Won, Lost, and Forgotten: How Hollywood and Art Shape What We Know about the Civil War* (Chapel Hill: University of North Carolina Press, 2008); and Drew Gilpin Faust, *The Republic of Suffering: Death and the American Civil War* (New York: Knopf, 2008).

agencies to prepare an objective history of their efforts.[15] Perhaps nothing did more to energize and transform American military history than this one-page directive signed by the president himself. The armed services quickly recruited some of the best scholars from leading universities to carry out the president's order. These were not, with a few exceptions, military historians; they were simply the best available historians, widely respected by their peers. In the spirit of Roosevelt's directive, they were left remarkably free to carry out their work. The results are a monument not simply to military history but to the highest standards of historical scholarship; more than a hundred volumes recount the organization, training, planning, and operations of the armed forces.[16] The eminent Harvard scholar Samuel Eliot Morison, a wartime rear admiral, wrote the fifteen volumes of U.S. naval history. The Princeton early Americanist Wesley Frank Craven and medievalist James L. Cate of the University of Chicago presided over the production of seven large volumes of Air Force history, while Kent Roberts Greenfield of Johns Hopkins, a specialist in European history, oversaw the enormous Army history, planned as more than eighty volumes.[17] The unique role played by General George C. Marshall as de facto senior military adviser to the president gave Army historians access to the record of strategic planning at the highest level, and several volumes go beyond simply Army history to deal with hotly contested issues, including Anglo-American disagreement over operations in the Mediterranean, Soviet pressure to open a second front against Germany, and the priority given to war in the Pacific as well as to Army-Navy conflict in that theater.[18] Most of these

[15]Kent Roberts Greenfield, *The Historian and the Army* (New Brunswick, N.J.: Rutgers University Press, 1954), is an insider's view from the academic leader of the Army's history program.

[16]For those suspicious of all official history as biased, a single volume distilled from the Army project, Kent Roberts Greenfield, ed., *Command Decisions* (New York: Harcourt, Brace, 1959), offers twenty chapters, each focused on a controversial strategic decision, that rebut the charge of bias. The final chapter by Louis Morton, on the decision to drop the atomic bomb, is still cited with respect despite two generations of heated scholarly controversy. Edward M. Coffman, "The Course of Military History in the United States since World War II," *The Journal of Military History* 61 (October 1997): 761–75, offers a more personal account than ours of how the war changed everything.

[17]Kent Roberts Greenfield and Stetson Conn, general eds., *The United States Army in World War II* (Washington, D.C.: Government Printing Office, 1948–). As of 1992, seventy-eight volumes were completed, according to an essential *Reader's Guide*, compiled by R. D. Adamczyk and M. J. MacGregor and published as part of the series. Samuel E. Morison, *History of United States Naval Operations in World War II*, 15 vols. (Boston: Little, Brown, 1947–1962). Wesley Frank Craven and James L. Cate, eds., *The Army Air Forces in World War II*, 7 vols. (Chicago: University of Chicago Press, 1948–1958).

[18]Maurice Matloff and Edwin Snell, *Strategic Planning for Coalition Warfare, 1941–1942* (Washington, D.C.: Government Printing Office, 1953); Matloff, *Strategic Planning for Coalition Warfare, 1943–1944* (Washington, D.C.: Government Printing Office, 1959). Other important volumes dealing with grand strategy include Richard M. Leighton and Robert W. Coakley, *Global Logistics and Strategy, 1940–1943* (Washington, D.C.: Government Printing Office, 1955); Leighton and Coakley, *Global Logistics and Strategy, 1943–1945* (Washington, D.C.: Government Printing Office, 1968); and, on the Pacific, Louis Morton, *Strategy and Command: The First Two Years* (Washington, D.C.: Government Printing Office, 1962). Unfortunately, Morton never completed the second volume.

historians returned to their academic posts after the war and resumed work in their specialties.[19] But they returned to academia with a new understanding of war and respect for its study, an understanding that did not convert all their academic colleagues, but at least contributed to a more tolerant environment for the serious study and teaching of the role of war in American history.

World War II transformed the guild of military historians, and the Civil War centennial gave it a burst of energy, but the Cold War created a new environment, as bewildering as it was energizing, for the historical study of war. Military historians, already notorious for seeking solutions to current and future problems in past wars, soon saw the assertive neighbors of history—political scientists, economists, and sociologists—respond energetically to the same call. Some of the most stimulating historical work on war was done after 1945 by social scientists trying to win the Cold War, and military historians could hardly ignore it. Samuel Stouffer and his colleagues studied the American soldier in the laboratory of the great war just ended, Samuel Huntington developed a challenging prescription for American civil-military relations from his study of the past, Morris Janowitz offered a fascinating picture of the professional military officer, Bernard Brodie, among many others, debated Cold War strategy using history to make his case, and Roberta Wohlstetter applied communications theory to the voluminous reports of congressional hearings on the Pearl Harbor attack to explain why U.S. forces were completely surprised.[20]

In his theory of civil–military relations, Huntington drew on his study of both European and American history to argue that civilian control should not tamper with the inevitably undemocratic, authoritarian, and philosophically conservative bodies that armed forces necessarily must be. Brodie, writing on the nuclear age, dismissed the theories of Jomini, who had influenced the thinking of military professionals and historians since Napoleon, and revived the ideas of Clausewitz, whose reputation had been hurt by fears of Prussian militarism, but who had stressed that all war must be understood in a political framework.[21]

[19]Louis Morton, a star of the Army history project, was an exception; he stayed on for a while after 1945, moved to Dartmouth in 1960, and conceived *The Wars of the United States*, an excellent series that included Russell Weigley's *The American Way of War: A History of United States Military Strategy and Policy* (New York: Macmillan, 1973).

[20]Samuel Stouffer et al., *Studies in Social Psychology in World War II*, 4 vols. (Princeton, N.J.: Princeton University Press, 1949–1950), vols. I and II subtitled *The American Soldier*; Samuel P. Huntington, *The Soldier and the State: The Theory and Politics of Civil-Military Relations* (Cambridge, Mass.: Harvard University Press, 1957); Morris Janowitz, *The Professional Soldier: A Social and Political Portrait* (Glencoe, Ill.: Free Press, 1960); Bernard Brodie, *Strategy in the Missile Age* (Princeton, N.J.: Princeton University Press, 1959); Roberta Wohlstetter, *Pearl Harbor: Warning and Decision* (Stanford, Calif.: Stanford University Press, 1962).

[21]Antoine-Henri Jomini (1779–1869) and Carl von Clausewitz (1780–1831) were veterans of the Napoleonic wars and drew heavily on that experience to write influential theoretical works based on historical study. Jomini sought to derive a few basic principles of universal validity, while Clausewitz strove to deal comprehensively with the phenomenon of war in all its variety. For a century Jomini was the more influential and provided a virtual template for military historians. The victorious wars unifying Germany in 1864, 1866, and 1870 were often attributed in

Janowitz based his typology of professional Army officers on his research in the historical record since about 1900. Stouffer and Wohlstetter, writing on the American soldier and on surprise at Pearl Harbor, respectively, used almost no history and were readily accepted by military historians, while the three historically minded social scientists were welcomed as validating the study of military history but otherwise got a more critical reception.

The contribution and influence of social scientists were complicated and perhaps facilitated by a desultory discussion then going on among military historians about what military history should be. Academic distaste for the traditional focus on battles and campaigns persisted after 1945 and stirred military historians to reconsider the nature of their subject. Influential and controversial journalist S. L. A. Marshall pressed for more, not less, detailed study of armed combat. As head of the Army historical section in wartime Europe, he pushed his research method of immediate collective interviews with soldiers emerging from combat.[22] Eager to use history to win the war, Marshall supported a separate series of "quickie" studies called *American Forces in Action* aimed at helping commanders still fighting the war. Army Air Force historians in particular resisted Marshall's insistence on reconstructing every battle, although the many volumes of the Army series, which recount every major action and most of the minor ones, suggest the extent of Marshall's influence.[23] Admiral Morison, on his own quarterdeck, required no prodding to write the Navy's history battle by battle.

The first serious move in the postwar creation of what was invariably called the "new military history" may be seen as a reaction to Marshall's insistence on combat as the only important subject. A committee of senior Princeton historians (including Craven) oversaw the compilation of a new textbook for teaching military history that displaced combat narrative with chapters on military affairs, especially civil–military relations.[24] This well-intended candidate for a redefinition of military history failed with its test market of undergraduates, who rejected it, as well as in the wider commercial textbook market. Military history without actual warfare could not succeed, and "military affairs" as the answer to the question died an early death.

---

part to the influence of Clausewitz, but not until the Cold War were soldiers and historians willing to tackle the daunting complexity of his theoretical writing. For brief, informed accounts of each man, his writings, and his influence, see Peter Paret, ed., *Makers of Modern Strategy: From Machiavelli to the Nuclear Age* (Princeton, N.J.: Princeton University Press, 1986), chapters 6 and 7.

[22]Marshall is remembered today mainly for one short book, *Men against Fire: The Problem of Battle Command in Future War* (New York: William Morrow, 1947). Allegedly based on hundreds of after-action interviews, the book argues that only a small minority of infantrymen dared fire their weapons in combat. His research has been questioned, but the book led to a radical change in Army training methods.

[23]Personal conversations of John Shy with Wesley Frank Craven, 1957–1966.

[24]Gordon B. Turner, ed., A *History of Military Affairs in Western Society since the Eighteenth Century* (New York: Harcourt, Brace, 1953) was intended to incite this movement away from the "drums and trumpets" of the old military history.

To call what ensued a debate is an exaggeration, yet it was invaluable in at last giving form and focus to the narrowly limited old military history. Most military historians agreed that warfare itself must remain at the core of the subject, but there was also emerging consensus that a viable military history must go beyond the detailed narrative of battles and campaigns to consider the broader context of war. The consensus created a receptive environment for the work of the social scientists.[25] Doubts about the value of all military history did not die, nor did skepticism about capturing in words the chaotic nature of battle, but the appearance in 1976 of John Keegan's *Face of Battle* did much to challenge these negative views. Keegan aroused interest well beyond the circle of military historians for his brilliant re-creation of three English battles—Agincourt 1415, Waterloo 1815, and the first day of the Somme 1916.[26] After Keegan, very few argued that writing the history of the bloodiest side of war was either pointless or impossible. Disagreement, in any case, was less important than the consensus that all aspects of war were the proper field of military history.[27]

The Cold War brought the militarization of American society, a near-continuous sense of crisis—Berlin, Korea, Cuba, Vietnam, and the Middle East—and constant dread of nuclear holocaust.[28] Some military historians

[25]See, for example, Richard H. Kohn, "The Social History of the American Soldier: A Review and Prospectus for Research," *The American Historical Review* 86 (1981): 553–67, which builds on the findings of the Stouffer group in *The American Soldier.*

[26]John Keegan, *The Face of Battle* (London: Jonathan Cape, 1976). Skeptics about battle history included Arthur A. Ekirch, Jr., "Military History: A Civilian Caveat," *Military Affairs* 21 (1957): 49–54; Maury D. Feld, "The Writing of Military History," *Military Affairs* 22 (1958): 38–39; Peter Karsten, "Demilitarizing Military History: Servants of Power and Agents of Understanding," *Military Affairs* 36 (1972): 88–92. The most surprising of the skeptics was Walter Millis, who in *Arms and Men: A Study of American Military History* (New York: Putnam's Sons, 1956) had written a brilliant survey of the ideas underlying military policy since George Washington, only to conclude that all military history before Hiroshima was worthless, even dangerous if taken seriously.

[27]An early, masterful expression of this consensus from a perspective outside the United States is Martin van Creveld, "Thoughts on Military History," *Journal of Contemporary History* 18 (1983): 549–86. It is also a traditional plea for the contemporary utility of military history, a view made familiar by Mahan, Upton, Conger, and S. L. A. Marshall, but one that leaves some military historians (see Millis, in previous note) uneasy.

[28]Korea was for years "the forgotten war," but Allan Millett is changing that; one reviewer has called him a "Korean War power-house." See his *The Korean War* (Lincoln: University of Nebraska Press, 2001) and *The War for Korea, 1945–1950: A House Burning* (Lawrence: University Press of Kansas, 2005), to be followed by a volume on the war itself. Journalists David Halberstam, *The Best and the Brightest* (New York: Random House, 1972), and Neil Sheehan, *A Bright Shining Lie: John Paul Vann and America in Vietnam* (New York: Random House, 1988), won Pulitzer Prizes and left an indelible impression of the Vietnam War, but academic historian George C. Herring has written the best general account, *America's Longest War: The United States and Vietnam, 1950–1975*, 2nd ed. (New York: Knopf, 1986), while Andrew F. Krepinevich, Jr., *The Army and Vietnam* (Baltimore: Johns Hopkins University Press, 1986), and Mark Clodfelter, *The Limits of Air Power: The American Bombing of North Vietnam* (New York:

seemed deaf to the lure of Cold War relevance and, guided by the brief of the new military history, wrote fine, broadly conceived books on old subjects.[29] Others felt the urgency of their times and the pull of contemporary relevance, especially if they worked on subjects close to the present. The American Military Institute, the professional body of military historians, reformed itself in 1990 as The Society for Military History, and its quarterly journal became *The Journal of Military History*. These changes were more than cosmetic, in that they expressed the consensus on what military history ought to be and went far toward healing old rifts between history by and for professional soldiers and history that could meet continuing academic pressure to make military history less militaristic. In effect, by the end of the century, the dynamic changes set in motion by the Second World War had, in the pressure cooker of the Cold War, reached something like resolution. To claim that everyone was satisfied, or that doubts did not persist in a rapidly changing academic environment, would be to claim too much.[30] But never had American military history been in a healthier condition than in the last decade of the twentieth century.

By general agreement, military history today has the study of actual warfare as its indispensable core but requires the inclusion of the political, economic, social, intellectual, and cultural context of war—seen both as determinants of war and warfare and as the realm in which war has its impact. In other words, from warfare itself military history has pushed outward beyond the traditional limits of the field. The works that have pushed outward into context have been

---

Free Press, 1989), are important contributions by (at the time) serving officers. Journalist Rick Atkinson's *Crusade: The Untold Story of the Persian Gulf War* (Boston: Houghton Mifflin, 1993) still stands as the best account of the 1991 war. Herman Kahn, *On Thermonuclear War* (Princeton, N.J.: Princeton University Press, 1960), used modern history freely to frighten all of us.

[29]Outstanding works within the traditional canon are Fred Anderson, *Crucible of War: The Seven Years' War and the Fate of Empire in British North America, 1754–1766* (New York: Knopf, 2000); David Hackett Fischer, *Paul Revere's Ride* (New York: Oxford University Press, 1994) and *Washington's Crossing* (New York: Oxford University Press, 2004); Edward M. Coffman, *The Old Army: A Portrait of the American Army in Peacetime, 1784–1898* (New York: Oxford University Press, 1986), and *The Regulars: The American Army, 1898–1941* (Cambridge, Mass.: Harvard University Press, 2004); Mark Grimsley, *The Hard Hand of War: Union Military Policy toward Southern Civilians, 1861–1865* (New York: Cambridge University Press, 1995).

[30]John A. Lynn worried, in a lecture to the annual meeting of the Society for Military History, that the turn in academic history toward a sociocultural perspective was leaving the typical military historian to play the role of "knuckle-dragging foe of gender studies." See "The Embattled Future of Academic Military History," *The Journal of Military History* 61 (1997): 777–89, quotation from 784. Despite the levity, Lynn seriously proposed that military history should adopt a more sociocultural perspective. Equally witty, and serious, was Roger Spiller's keynote address to the society that military historians were failing to apply their skills to contemporary military issues. See "Military History and Its Fictions," *The Journal of Military History* 70 (2006): 1081–97. That Lynn spent much of his career at the University of Illinois and Spiller at the U.S. Army Command and General Staff College may account for some of the difference between the two arguments.

original and stimulating, of a kind not seen before.[31] At the same time, the best of more traditional studies of warfare display an inclusiveness in their research that yields new insights.[32] Another sign of health has been greater interest in knowing more about both sides, following the example set by the official historians of World War II. The effect has been to restore to military history the dynamic bipolar quality of war so often missed in earlier work, where the enemy often appeared as a foil for the chosen side.[33]

Most other fields of American history have one or more historians who advanced an influential big idea: Frederick Jackson Turner, Charles A. Beard, George F. Kennan, Arthur O. Lovejoy. Military history may be an exception, but it has a candidate: Russell F. Weigley. Weigley began as a historian of the Civil War, but was soon attracted to the history of America at war. After several books dealing with the Army, he produced a lengthy survey of American military history, arguing that out of the experience of the Civil War and the virtual annihilation of the Indian population had come a distinctly national response to war. For Weigley, the American way of war was to use overwhelming force to achieve quick, decisive victory.

For some years, Weigley's *The American Way of War* (1973) held sway, displacing its few competitors and meeting the chronic need for a single volume of American military history. But on close consideration, the general argument and its single overarching explanation of American strategy seemed too simplistic given the diversity of thought within the American military and the variety of

[31]Among the bolder efforts are John W. Dower, *War without Mercy: Race and Power in the Pacific War* (New York: Pantheon, 1986); Michael Sherry, *The Rise of American Air Power: The Creation of Armageddon* (New Haven, Conn.: Yale University Press, 1987), and *In the Shadow of War: The United States since the 1930s* (New Haven, Conn.: Yale University Press, 1995); Joseph T. Glatthaar, *Forged in Battle: The Civil War Alliance of Black Soldiers and White Officers* (New York: Free Press, 1990); George M. Fredrickson, *The Inner Civil War: Northern Intellectuals and the Crisis of the Union* (New York: Harper & Row, 1968); Charles Royster, *A Revolutionary People at War: The Continental Army and American Character* (Chapel Hill: University of North Carolina Press, 1979); Jill Lepore, *The Name of War: King Philip's War and the Origins of American Identity* (New York: Knopf, 1998). Both Roger Spiller, *An Instinct for War: Scenes from the Battlefields of History* (Cambridge, Mass.: Harvard University Press, 2005), and John A. Lynn, *Battle: A History of Culture and Combat* (Boulder, Colo.: Westview Press, 2003), fly well beyond the bounds of American history but deserve inclusion as examples of the most imaginative works of contemporary military history.

[32]For example, David Hackett Fischer, in his books on the "old" subjects of the 1775 outbreak of war in eastern Massachusetts (*Paul Revere's Ride*) and Washington's recrossing of the Delaware in December 1776 (*Washington's Crossing*), provides a new understanding of the nature of social mobilization in 1775 and of the extent and quality of popular resistance to British occupation in New Jersey in early 1777. Both are a result of research that goes beyond the conventional narrative of those military campaigns.

[33]Douglas S. Freeman had rationalized ignoring the other side as preserving the "fog of war" in which all war is conducted. The official historians of World War II had the great advantage of captured enemy records and of interviews with former enemy commanders.

wars actually fought. Critics soon began to question the master narrative of this amiable and highly respected scholar. Today, the criticism has continued, and after his sudden death in 2004 not much is left standing of Weigley's argument except the basic idea and the book's title, recently appropriated by scholars who have a competing idea.[34] Since Weigley, other authors have filled the need for a general survey of American military history that is scholarly and readable, but less dogmatic than *The American Way of War*. Among those alternative perspectives, Allan Millett and Peter Maslowski use recurrent themes—the political nature of military policy, pluralism, geographical isolation, civilian control, growing military professionalism, and industrialization—to guide their narrative, while Fred Anderson and Andrew Cayton build theirs around leading figures from Samuel de Champlain to Colin Powell.[35]

Military historians, like the late comedian Rodney Dangerfield, continue to complain of not getting the respect they surely have earned from their colleagues in the academy, but the field itself is flourishing, ever tempted to instruct the present about the future and ever hobbled within the academy by its embarrassing popularity. War will never be a "normal" subject of study, but since 1945 it has been investigated more responsibly and imaginatively than seemed possible when Captain Conger published his lament in 1916.[36]

[34]Weigley, *The American Way of War*. Brian Linn published the first comprehensive critique in "The American Way of War Revisited," *The Journal of Military History* 66 (October 2002): 501–33, arguing that the "tradition" was far more pragmatic than Weigley had argued; a response from Professor Weigley appears on pp. 531–33 of the journal. Linn's critique was based on research done for his *The Echo of Battle: The Army's Way of War* (Cambridge, Mass.: Harvard University Press, 2007).

[35]Allan R. Millett and Peter Maslowski, *For the Common Defense: A Military History of the United States of America*, rev. ed. (New York: Free Press, 1994); Fred Anderson and Andrew Cayton, *The Dominion of War: Empire and Liberty in North America, 1500–2000* (New York: Viking, 2005). Though it is only in part concerned with the United States and engages heartily in guessing the future, Paul Kennedy, *Rise and Fall of the Great Powers: Economic Change and Military Conflict from 1500 to 2000* (New York: Random House, 1987), deserves a place on the shelf of any American military historian.

[36]Valuable guides to the study of military history are John W. Chambers, II, et al., eds., *The Oxford Companion to American Military History* (New York: Oxford University Press, 1999), and John E. Jessup, Jr., and Robert W. Coakley, eds., *A Guide to the Study and Use of Military History* (Washington, D.C.: Center of Military History, U.S. Army, 1979).

CHRISTOPHER L. TOMLINS

Expanding Boundaries: A Century of Legal History

Over the last hundred years, legal history has overcome its early constraints and has realized much of its imaginative potential. The field was late-blooming. Considered "as an area of study with the sense of its own intellectual integrity and with an organized institutional structure to promote it," American legal history did not exist before the 1970s.[1] Its growth since has been rapid. In the early twenty-first century, legal history is an important and vigorous presence within the disciplines both of law and of history in the United States.

The course of scholarly production in legal history over the last century has generated a considerable volume of knowledge. What distinguishes the legal historical knowledge of 2007 from that of 1907 other than quantity? The question is complicated because legal history has been tied to the professionalization of two distinct disciplines—law and history. Before the 1970s, legal history developed almost exclusively within law scholarship.[2] Since then its development has been marked by the contrasting, sometimes contradictory, demands and needs of both. As we survey legal history's expansion, we must consider the relative influence of both forms of knowledge in directing its course.

Lawyers are present-minded, largely focused on matters of immediate consequence. But if law is to have authority it must have credible claims to legitimacy. At the beginning of the twentieth century, what was known as "historical jurisprudence" answered that requirement. Historical jurisprudence was not a form of history but a theory of law. Its adherents argued that law's origins, hence its legitimacy, lay in long-established custom. Legal norms, rules, and procedures had developed over time, had been refined by jurists, and had finally been confirmed by systematic inquiry into legal texts designed to identify uniformities and restate them as principles. This was the foundation on which Harvard Law School Dean Christopher Columbus Langdell (1826–1906) built much of his innovative case method of law teaching.

---

[1] Stanley Katz, "The Problem of a Colonial Legal History," in Jack P. Greene and J. R. Pole, eds., *Colonial British America: Essays in the New History of the Early Modern Era* (Baltimore: Johns Hopkins University Press, 1984), 466.

[2] "It was the law professors who wrote legal history, not historians." David Rothman, "The Promise of Legal History," *Reviews in American History* 2 (March 1974): 17.

Historical jurisprudence did not last much beyond the turn of the century. In the United States it was put out of business by Roscoe Pound, one of Langdell's most important successors at Harvard and a dominant figure in his era's legal scholarship. Pound pointed to a troubling discrepancy between textual law in books and the social expression of law in action. For much of the nineteenth century (the "formative era," as Pound would later dub it), American law had avoided this discrepancy through lively innovation. But, said Pound, by the end of the century the tightening grip of outdated ideas and self-referential principles had caused innovation to cease. "Kindred branches of learning"—philosophy, political science, economics, and sociology—had long since begun to adopt "the economic and social interpretation" of life. Pound thought it crucial that law in the Progressive Era likewise disengage itself from the past and turn its attention to "the facts of human conduct" in the present. Social science (those "kindred disciplines") would identify the facts. Law would then go to work to make "law in the books such that the law in action can conform to it."[3]

Pound's sociological jurisprudence is often thought of as a forerunner of the critiques of law developed in the 1920s by legal realist scholars who derided judicial reliance on self-referential principles to decide social conflicts instead of engaging in investigation of the social problems themselves. In fact, Pound was ambivalent about the realist critique, and in the 1930s, as the New Deal's huge investment in administrative process threatened to swamp adjudicative law, his ambivalence turned to outright condemnation. Always careful to protect the sphere of legal expertise, Pound turned to history for support by writing an account of the formative era of American law that gave all the credit for the nineteenth century's innovative capacities to the era's jurists. American law, Pound argued, possessed its own independent core of historical continuity, encapsulated in a legal tradition originally received from England and transmitted through generations of lawyers and judges tempered by training and practice. This "taught legal tradition" had produced effective adaptation to social needs. It was "much more significant in our legal history than the economic conditions of time and place."[4]

Pound's *Formative Era* (1938) was not particularly good history, but it was the only attempt at a general synthetic account of the development of American law to appear before the 1950s. Better legal historians than Pound would slowly gather at Columbia—Julius Goebel joining the law school in 1925, followed

---

[3]Roscoe Pound, "Law in Books and Law in Action," *American Law Review* 44 (1910): 22, 24–30, 35–36.

[4]Roscoe Pound, *The Formative Era of American Law* (Boston: Little, Brown, 1938), 82–83. Historians like Oscar and Mary Flug Handlin and Richard B. Morris would later return the compliment by writing histories that provided the New Deal with a legal pedigree. See Oscar Handlin and Mary Flug Handlin, *Commonwealth: A Study of the Role of Government in the American Economy: Massachusetts, 1774–1861* (New York: New York University Press, 1947); Richard B. Morris, *Government and Labor in Early America* (New York: Columbia University Press, 1946).

many years later by Joseph H. Smith. Richard B. Morris joined the history department in 1946.[5] A few others, outside the legal academy, engaged sporadically in forms of legal-historical research: in the 1920s the Wisconsin institutional economist John R. Commons, much later the Harvard intellectual historian Perry Miller.[6] Still, in the 1930s and for considerable time thereafter, legal historians were few and far between.[7] In a tiny field almost entirely confined to one or two East Coast law schools, Pound cast a big shadow. No one directly challenged his account of the formative era before James Willard Hurst of the University of Wisconsin Law School in the 1950s, followed by Morton Horwitz of Harvard Law School in the 1970s. Between them, Hurst and Horwitz would completely redefine American legal history.

Willard Hurst began to create his own very distinctive approach to legal history in the late 1930s.[8] His starting point, like the young Pound's, was the relationship between law and social processes. There the resemblance ended. Pound had proposed his sociological jurisprudence more as a strategy for legal reform than as an investigation of law as a subject. Hurst taught law as an aspect of society, and his history followed on, the goal always to understand the "interplay of law and social growth."[9] In that interplay Hurst's historical research revealed a causality that completely undermined Pound. "In the interaction of law and American life the law was *passive*, acted upon by other social forces, more often than acting upon them."[10]

Hurst's signature account of the formative era is *Law and the Conditions of Freedom in the Nineteenth Century United States* (1956). The book found American law originating not in a taught tradition emanating from the other side of the Atlantic but sprouting in the rich democratic sod of the Midwest, not from the actions of wise jurists but from those of ordinary citizens such as "Jason Lothrop—Baptist minister, schoolteacher, boarding house proprietor, and civic leader." Ordinary people made law in Hurst's formative era. They did so pragmatically, hardly pausing to construct any lasting framework "except in areas which [Americans] saw most directly contributing to the release of private energy and the increase of private options." With the grandeur of constitution-making

---

[5]All were best known for their work in the legal history of the colonial and early national periods, stressing English background and American beginnings.

[6]John R. Commons, *Legal Foundations of Capitalism* (New York: Macmillan, 1924); Perry Miller, *The Life of the Mind in America, from the Revolution to the Civil War* (New York: Harcourt, Brace, 1965).

[7]In 1931 Karl Llewellyn, "Book Review," *Columbia Law Review* 31 (1931): 732, thought the field "near empty." Looking back, Willard Hurst observed that in the 1930s there had been at most "three or four practicing legal historians" in the entire United States. Hendrik Hartog, "Snakes in Ireland: A Conversation with Willard Hurst," *Law and History Review* 12 (Fall 1994): 385.

[8]Hurst began co-teaching the Law in Society course with Dean Lloyd K. Garrison soon after arriving at Wisconsin Law School in 1937.

[9]William J. Novak, "Law, Capitalism, and the Liberal State: The Historical Sociology of James Willard Hurst," *Law and History Review* 18 (Spring 2000): 97, 99, 100.

[10]James Willard Hurst, *The Growth of American Law: The Lawmakers* (Boston: Little, Brown, 1950), 4 [emphasis added].

out of the way, "The nineteenth century was prepared to treat law more casually, as an instrument to be used whenever it looked as if it would be useful."[11]

Hurst is famous for the self-interest he saw exhibited in American law. But self-interest had a context—a relatively homogenous national consciousness, or what 1950s historians called "consensus." For Hurst, consensus on values meant that struggles to advance one's interests could occur without escalating into conflicts that could rupture the social system. Law, he emphasized, was the key arena where the jockeying took place and where the actual tasks of "order[ing] social relations" were performed. The goal was balance, so that "particular blocs could not run roughshod over other interests in society." Still, the possibility of balance was perennially undercut by Americans' preoccupation "with the economy as a field for private adventure," which bred indifference to the creation of efficient public institutions and left law open to the influence of special interests.[12]

Pound's taught legal tradition had represented law as hermetic, invulnerable to externalities. For Hurst, history's job was not to participate in myth-making. It was to assess objectively how legal institutions had performed in fields of public policy.[13] That Hurst's law and society perspective stimulated completely new kinds of legal-historical research can be seen simply from the titles of the first books to follow his lead: *Law and Locomotives: The Impact of the Railroad on Wisconsin Law in the Nineteenth Century* (1958), by Robert S. Hunt; *The Business of a Trial Court: 100 Years of Cases: A Census of the Actions and Special Proceedings in the Circuit Court for Chippewa County, Wisconsin, 1855–1954* (1959), by Francis W. Laurent; *Insurance and Public Policy: A Study in the Legal Implementation of Social and Economic Public Policy, Based on Wisconsin Records, 1835–1959* (1960), by Spencer Kimball; *Water Purity, a Study in Legal Control of Natural Resources* (1961), by Earl Finbar Murphy; *Law and Mineral Wealth: The Legal Profile of the Wisconsin Mining Industry* (1962), by James A. Lake; and *Contract Law in America: A Social and Economic Case Study* (1965), by Lawrence M. Friedman.[14]

By unpacking the interactions of American law, market capitalism, national consciousness, and the state from the early nineteenth to the early twentieth centuries, Hurst's law and society perspective established the agenda for modern American legal history.[15] In 1971, no less an observer than Supreme Court Justice

[11]James Willard Hurst, *Law and the Conditions of Freedom in the Nineteenth Century United States* (Madison: University of Wisconsin Press, 1956), 3, 5, 10; James Willard Hurst, *Law and Social Order in the United States* (Ithaca, N.Y.: Cornell University Press, 1977), 23–24. See also James Willard Hurst, *Law and Social Process in United States History* (Ann Arbor: University of Michigan Law School, 1960).

[12]Hurst, *Growth of American Law*, 439, 440, 444.

[13]Hurst "wrote his books as background briefs for present-day lawmakers." Robert W. Gordon, "Hurst Recaptured," *Law and History Review* 18 (Spring 2000): 172.

[14]All were published by the University of Wisconsin Press (Madison) except Hunt's *Law and Locomotives*, which was published by the State Historical Society of Wisconsin (Madison).

[15]Robert W. Gordon, "Willard Hurst and the Common Law Tradition in American Legal Historiography," *Law and Society Review* 10 (1975); Harry N. Scheiber, "At the Borderland of Law and Economic History: The Contributions of Willard Hurst," *American Historical Review* 75 (February 1970).

Byron White credited Hurst for bringing about a turn in legal research in general from the "narrow study of judicial doctrine" to "the ties between law and society." Justice White's praise appeared to come with an approving echo from historians, for it was included in his introduction to *Law in American History*, published in 1971 for Harvard's Charles Warren Center.[16] But appearances deceive. *Law in American History* was no endorsement of the law and society perspective. Hurst wrote the keynote essay, but virtually all the remaining essays eschewed Hurst's approach for the old law school tradition of court-centered legal-doctrinal analysis rewritten largely from the perspective of intellectual and institutional history. *Law in American History* incidentally confirmed that legal history remained rare in history departments. More than half the authors were based in law schools or political science departments.[17]

Still, the book was greeted warmly in history journals as "an extremely important step in the revival of the long neglected practice of legal history in this country."[18] No author in the volume would be more important to that revival than Morton Horwitz, whose essay, "The Emergence of an Instrumental Conception of American Law, 1780–1820," foreshadowed his remarkable 1977 book, *The Transformation of American Law*.

A junior member of the Harvard law faculty in the early 1970s, Horwitz's attention—as the young Hurst's had been—was focused on the old enemy, Roscoe Pound, and his "taught legal tradition."[19] But for Horwitz, doctrine, not Hurst's social process, lay at the heart of legal history. The very centrality of doctrine explained the absence of professional historians: The prospect of having to confront law's technicalities always left them "paralyzed with fear."[20] Still, what kept historians away from legal history was not Horwitz's concern. His goal was to write a new kind of doctrinal legal history that would reject the practice of uncovering beginnings, finding continuities, and celebrating intact traditions that justified "the world as it is" but that instead would explore how legal doctrine had helped to change the world as it had been.[21] Nor did Horwitz accept Hurst's contention that law was engaged in realizing the goals of a shared national consciousness. The disproportionate accrual of benefits to entrepreneurial and commercial groups during the formative era left him skeptical of histories that

[16]Byron R. White, "Introduction," in Donald Fleming and Bernard Bailyn, eds., *Law in American History* (Boston: Little, Brown, 1971), vi.

[17]What most of the authors had in common were Harvard Ph.D.'s either in history (three) or government/political science (three).

[18]Martin Shapiro and Barbara Shapiro, "Interdisciplinary Aspects of American Legal History," *Journal of Interdisciplinary History* 4 (Spring 1974): 611.

[19]This, of course, returned the emphasis of legal history right to the battlefield of legal doctrine and ideas that Hurst had labored to minimize. Morton J. Horwitz, "The Conservative Tradition in the Writing of American Legal History," *American Journal of Legal History* 17 (1973).

[20]The only unparalyzed historian Horwitz could name was Leonard W. Levy, on the strength of his *The Law of the Commonwealth and Chief Justice Shaw* (Cambridge, Mass.: Harvard University Press, 1957), 275.

[21]Horwitz, "Conservative Tradition," 275, 281.

represented legal innovations as pragmatic responses to consensual social needs. *Transformation* was instead a story of how legal elites used their command of the legal system "to enable emergent entrepreneurial and commercial groups to win a disproportionate share of wealth and power in American society."[22]

The Horwitz thesis, as *Transformation*'s argument came to be known, provoked strong reactions. Legal academics spent much of the following decade excoriating the book.[23] Historians treated *Transformation* with greater respect, dwelling less on the details of its doctrinal arguments than on its account of law's socioeconomic effects. The disparity in reaction notwithstanding, *Transformation* was hugely influential on both sides of the aisle. Among historians it brought legal history into the field of professional vision with far greater immediacy than Hurst had ever managed. Hurst was never much of a stylist. He wrote dense and abstract books, each of which tended to repeat the same core contentions. It took "translators" like Lawrence Friedman and his *A History of American Law* (1973) to make the essentials of the Hurstian approach accessible to a wide audience.[24] Horwitz's doctrinal argumentation was not much easier for the uninitiated, but it came accompanied by strong causal statements and conclusions that appealed to historians convinced by the 1970s that social inequality and skewed distributions of wealth and resources were deeply embedded in the structure of American society. It was really in *Transformation*'s wake that American legal history took off in history departments. Never again would legal history be written only by law professors.

In the law schools, *Transformation* did not begin a new scholarly trend (apart from Horwitz-denial) so much as influence an existing one. Horwitz himself was identified with the critical legal studies movement (more widely known as CLS), a radical group with a following among law school academics. Some of CLS's leading lights developed an approach to legal history they called, not surprisingly, "critical legal history." Briefly interested in Hurst's social-legal approach, critical legal historians soon turned their attention to *Transformation*'s deep immersion in the intellectual history of legal doctrine. But by the early 1980s its exponents had given up on the claim—so interesting to historians—that the study of law in historical context revealed causal relationships between legal rules and socioeconomic outcomes.[25] Critical legal historians were instead

---

[22]Morton J. Horwitz, *The Transformation of American Law: 1780–1860* (Cambridge, Mass.: Harvard University Press, 1977), xvi.

[23]See, for example, John Phillip Reid, "A Plot Too Doctrinaire," *Texas Law Review* 55 (1977).

[24]Lawrence Friedman, *A History of American Law* (New York: Simon & Schuster, 1973; 2nd ed. 1985; 3rd revised ed. 2005). For another comprehensive single-volume history influenced by Hurst's perspectives, see Kermit Hall, *The Magic Mirror: Law in American History* (New York: Oxford University Press, 1989). For an early monograph "translating" Hurst for historians, see Stanley I. Kutler, *Privilege and Creative Destruction: The Charles River Bridge Case* (Philadelphia: J. B. Lippincott, 1971).

[25]So had Horwitz, as the different tenor of his sequel volume, *The Transformation of American Law, 1870–1960: The Crisis of Legal Orthodoxy* (New York: Oxford University Press, 1992), indicated.

increasingly dedicated to the proposition that *no* determinative relationship existed between legal rules and social and economic outcomes. In 1984 Stanford law professor Robert W. Gordon summed up critical legal history's shift in a historiographical essay appropriately entitled "Critical Legal Histories." Gordon identified a category of scholarship that he labeled "evolutionary functionalism" that purported to include literally every form of post-Enlightenment social-historical explanation from Marx and Weber to Hurst and Horwitz. What united all these thinkers was their embrace of some form of causal relationship between law and society. Gordon then tossed the entire august company out the window in favor of the theory of legal indeterminacy mapped through doctrinal history by converting all "legal historiography" to "the intellectual history of the rise and fall of paradigm structures of thought."[26]

In the 1980s and 1990s, legal history's takeoff in history departments and the furious battles over history in the law schools stimulated a rising tide of books and articles that explored more and more of the U.S. legal system from an increasing plurality of perspectives. Inside the law schools the doctrinal turn remained highly influential. Outside, the emphasis was much more on attempts to refine causal arguments. For all the density of Hurst's prose, the general law and society perspective that he had championed still proved attractive to the growing numbers of young scholars being trained in legal history *as historians.* David Konig was one of the first historians to follow a law and society tack in his research on judicial institutions and dispute settlement in early America— *Law and Society in Puritan Massachusetts: Essex County, 1629–1692* (1979). William Offutt followed along some years later with *Of "Good Laws" and "Good Men": Law and Society in the Delaware Valley, 1680–1710* (1995). Students of Harry Scheiber also embraced Hurst's law and society perspective in research whose subjects hearkened back to the wave of Hurst-influenced scholarship that appeared in the late 1950s and early 1960s, notably Arthur McEvoy in *The Fisherman's Problem: Ecology and Law in the California Fisheries, 1850–1980* (1986) and Victoria Saker Woeste, *The Farmer's Benevolent Trust: Law and Agricultural Cooperation in Industrial America, 1865–1945* (1998). Another of U.S. legal history's great mentors, Morton Keller of Brandeis, taught his students a critical appreciation for Hurst while encouraging them to develop legal history's orientation to questions of governance and state capacity. Hendrik Hartog's *Public Property and Private Power: The Corporation of the City of New York in American Law, 1730–1870* (1983) is one fine example, Michael Grossberg's *Governing the Hearth: Law and the Family in Nineteenth-Century America* (1985) another. Some years later another of Keller's students, William J. Novak, published *The People's Welfare: Law and Regulation in Nineteenth-Century America* (1996). One of the most important books in the field in the 1990s, *The People's Welfare* convincingly challenged the long-standing assumption that

[26]Robert W. Gordon, "Critical Legal Histories," *Stanford Law Review* 36 (1984): 116.

the United States had historically been dedicated to a weak (laissez-faire) form of governance.[27]

In many cases, well-established forms of historical practice suggested directions for legal history. Historians had always been adept at biography. Kent Newmyer's *Supreme Court Justice Joseph Story: Statesman of the Old Republic* (1985) was an outstanding demonstration of the application of the craft to legal history. Michael Willrich's brilliant *City of Courts: Socializing Justice in Progressive Era Chicago* (2003) showed how legal history might ally itself with urban history. Histories of lawyers and legal education, of law firms and of lawyers' professional activities all showed how historians could mobilize political and intellectual history, and the history of institutions and organizations, in conjunction with legal history — apparent in, for example, Jean V. Matthews's *Rufus Choate: The Law and Civic Virtue* (1980), William LaPiana's *Logic and Experience: The Origin of Modern American Legal Education* (1994), William G. Thomas's *Lawyering for the Railroad: Business, Law, and Power in the New South* (1999), and Kenneth Lipartito and Joseph Pratt's *Baker and Botts in the Development of Modern Houston* (1991).[28]

As the field continued to expand, new standpoints and new subject matter moved into focus. The dominance of social history in U.S. history departments meant that most legal historians were trained in social history's methods and perspectives. As social historians turned to class, race, and gender as categories of analysis, so too did legal historians.[29] In *From Bondage to Contract: Wage Labor,*

[27]David Thomas Konig, *Law and Society in Puritan Massachusetts: Essex County, 1629–1692* (Chapel Hill: University of North Carolina Press, 1979); William M. Offutt, *Of "Good Laws" and "Good Men": Law and Society in the Delaware Valley, 1680–1710* (Urbana: University of Illinois Press, 1995); Arthur F. McEvoy, *The Fisherman's Problem: Ecology and Law in the California Fisheries, 1850–1980* (Cambridge and New York: Cambridge University Press, 1986); Victoria Saker Woeste, *The Farmer's Benevolent Trust: Law and Agricultural Cooperation in Industrial America, 1865–1945* (Chapel Hill: University of North Carolina Press, 1998); Hendrik Hartog, *Public Property and Private Power: The Corporation of the City of New York in American Law, 1730–1870* (Chapel Hill: University of North Carolina Press, 1983); Michael Grossberg, *Governing the Hearth: Law and the Family in Nineteenth-Century America* (Chapel Hill: University of North Carolina Press, 1985); William J. Novak, *The People's Welfare: Law and Regulation in Nineteenth-Century America* (Chapel Hill: University of North Carolina Press, 1996).

[28]R. Kent Newmyer, *Supreme Court Justice Joseph Story: Statesman of the Old Republic* (Chapel Hill: University of North Carolina Press, 1985); Michael Willrich, *City of Courts: Socializing Justice in Progressive Era Chicago* (Cambridge and New York: Cambridge University Press, 2003); Jean V. Matthews, *Rufus Choate: The Law and Civic Virtue* (Philadelphia: Temple University Press, 1980); William P. LaPiana, *Logic and Experience: The Origin of Modern American Legal Education* (New York: Oxford University Press, 1994); William G. Thomas, *Lawyering for the Railroad: Business, Law, and Power in the New South* (Baton Rouge: Louisiana State University Press, 1999); Kenneth Lipartito and Joseph Pratt, *Baker and Botts in the Development of Modern Houston* (Austin: University of Texas Press, 1991).

[29]These developments are discussed, with examples, in Barbara Welke, "Willard Hurst and the Archipelago of American Legal Historiography," *Law and History Review* 18 (Spring 2000).

Marriage, and the Market in the Age of Slave Emancipation (1998), Amy Dru Stanley combined gender with race and class perspectives to produce an outstanding account of nineteenth-century contract ideology. Three years later Barbara Welke joined gender to race in her equally outstanding study of the railroad revolution's impact on the law of accidental injury, nervous shock, and racial segregation, *Recasting American Liberty: Gender, Race, Law and the Railroad Revolution, 1865–1920* (2001). Gender and sex became the richest of these new areas of legal history research, extending to all periods of U.S. history in books like Cornelia Dayton's *Women before the Bar: Gender, Law, and Society in Connecticut, 1639–1789* (1995), Nancy Isenberg's *Sex and Citizenship in Antebellum America* (1998), and Leslie Reagan's *When Abortion Was a Crime: Women, Medicine, and Law in the United States, 1867–1973* (1997). Others, like Peter Bardaglio in *Reconstructing the Household: Families, Sex, and the Law in the Nineteenth-Century South* (1995), Nancy Cott in *Public Vows: A History of Marriage and the Nation* (2000), and Hendrik Hartog in *Man and Wife in America: A History* (2000), brought gender to bear on the legal history of marriage and the family. Still others, notably Michael Grossberg in *A Judgment for Solomon: The d'Hauteville Case and Legal Experience in Antebellum America* (1996), used gender and marital experience to explore American legal culture.[30] Currently a wave of new work on sexuality is building at the intersection of legal and cultural history.[31]

Legal historians have also been making major contributions to areas of U.S. history that have been investigated in depth over the years but without research that touches on their legal significance. Since the early 1980s, for example, slavery has received detailed attention, both in its relatively familiar constitutional aspect—for example, Paul W. Finkelman, *An Imperfect Union: Slavery, Federalism, and Comity* (1981)—and its much less familiar common-law

[30]Amy Dru Stanley, *From Bondage to Contract: Wage Labor, Marriage, and the Market in the Age of Slave Emancipation* (Cambridge and New York: Cambridge University Press, 1998); Barbara Young Welke, *Recasting American Liberty: Gender, Race, Law and the Railroad Revolution, 1865–1920* (Cambridge and New York: Cambridge University Press, 2001); Cornelia Hughes Dayton, *Women before the Bar: Gender, Law, and Society in Connecticut, 1639–1789* (Chapel Hill: University of North Carolina Press, 1995); Nancy Isenberg, *Sex and Citizenship in Antebellum America* (Chapel Hill: University of North Carolina Press, 1998); Leslie Reagan, *When Abortion Was a Crime: Women, Medicine, and Law in the United States, 1867–1973* (Berkeley: University of California Press, 1997); Peter W. Bardaglio, *Reconstructing the Household: Families, Sex, and the Law in the Nineteenth-Century South* (Chapel Hill: University of North Carolina Press, 1995); Nancy F. Cott, *Public Vows: A History of Marriage and the Nation* (Cambridge, Mass.: Harvard University Press, 2000); Hendrik Hartog, *Man and Wife in America: A History* (Cambridge, Mass.: Harvard University Press, 2000); Michael Grossberg, *A Judgment for Solomon: The d'Hauteville Case and Legal Experience in Antebellum America* (Cambridge and New York: Cambridge University Press, 1996).

[31]See Margot Canaday, "Heterosexuality as a Legal Regime," in Michael Grossberg and Christopher Tomlins, eds., *The Cambridge History of Law in America* (Cambridge and New York: Cambridge University Press, 2008), vol. 3.

aspects—notably Thomas D. Morris's *Southern Slavery and the Law, 1619–1860* (1996) and Ariela Gross's *Double Character: Slavery and Mastery in the Antebellum Southern Courtroom* (2000).[32] Labor history, likewise, has been greatly augmented by research in legal history,[33] while the history of the colonial era has also seen considerable renewed participation from legal historians.[34] Hardy perennials in the field, such as the history of the Supreme Court, have flourished as volume after volume of the definitive Oliver Wendell Holmes Devise *History of the Supreme Court of the United States* have been published[35] and as the *Documentary History* of the Court's first decade has been completed.[36] The recent upsurge of interest in the history of American Indians has also had its counterpart among legal historians.[37]

The more legal history has been written outside the law schools, the more it has developed a standpoint that calls in question the self-referential tendencies of law within the law schools. Some legal scholars have responded by dismissing

[32]Paul W. Finkelman, *An Imperfect Union: Slavery, Federalism, and Comity* (Chapel Hill: University of North Carolina Press, 1981); Thomas D. Morris, *Southern Slavery and the Law, 1619–1860* (Chapel Hill: University of North Carolina Press, 1996); Ariela Gross, *Double Character: Slavery and Mastery in the Antebellum Southern Courtroom* (Princeton, N.J.: Princeton University Press, 2000).

[33]Christopher L. Tomlins, *The State and the Unions: Labor Relations, Law, and the Organized Labor Movement in the United States, 1880–1960* (New York and Cambridge: Cambridge University Press, 1985), and *Law, Labor, and Ideology in the Early American Republic* (Cambridge and New York: Cambridge University Press, 1993); William E. Forbath, *Law and the Shaping of the American Labor Movement* (Cambridge, Mass.: Harvard University Press, 1991); Karen Orren, *Belated Feudalism: Labor, the Law, and Liberal Development in the United States* (New York and Cambridge: Cambridge University Press, 1991); Robert J. Steinfeld, *Coercion, Contract, and Free Labor in the Nineteenth Century* (Cambridge and New York: Cambridge University Press, 2001).

[34]For example, Bruce H. Mann, *Neighbors and Strangers: Law and Community in Early Connecticut* (Chapel Hill: University of North Carolina Press, 1987); Christopher L. Tomlins and Bruce Mann, eds., *The Many Legalities of Early America* (Chapel Hill: University of North Carolina Press, 2001); Holly Brewer, *By Birth or Consent: Children, Law, and the Anglo-American Revolution in Authority* (Chapel Hill: University of North Carolina Press, 2005); Mary Sarah Bilder, *The Transatlantic Constitution: Colonial Legal Culture and the Empire* (Cambridge, Mass.: Harvard University Press, 2004); Daniel J. Hulsebosch, *Constituting Empire: New York and the Transformation of Constitutionalism in the Atlantic World, 1664–1830* (Chapel Hill: University of North Carolina Press, 2005).

[35]The most recent is volume 12, William M. Wiecek, *The Birth of the Modern Constitution: The United States Supreme Court, 1941–1953* (New York and Cambridge: Cambridge University Press, 2006).

[36]Maeva Marcus et al., eds., *The Documentary History of the Supreme Court of the United States, 1789–1800*, 8 vols. (New York: Columbia University Press, 1986–2007).

[37]For example, Blue Clark, *Lone Wolf v. Hitchcock: Treaty Rights and Indian Law at the End of the Nineteenth Century* (Lincoln: University of Nebraska Press, 1994); Stuart Banner, *How the Indians Lost Their Land: Law and Power on the Frontier* (Cambridge, Mass.: Harvard University Press, 2005).

any legal history that did not resemble what lawyers would write.[38] This was predictable; the reaction occurs whenever a historian wanders onto legal terrain. Willard Hurst had thought that laymen undertaking research on law would always require "lawmen" to guide them so as to avoid ignorant errors. Critical legal historians like Horwitz and Gordon dropped similar hints. Horwitz wondered whether historians were capable of dealing with doctrine. Gordon found elaborate reconstructions of formal mandarin legality (what critical legal historians did) far more exciting than "the grimy details" of how ruling classes ruled (what historians did).[39]

But times have changed. Before the 1970s virtually no one outside the law schools wrote legal history. In the early years of the twenty-first century that is far from the case. Perhaps for that very reason, in 1997 Gordon flung wide the doors of critical legal history to "*any* approach to the past . . . that inverts or scrambles familiar narratives of stasis, recovery or progress; *anything* that advances rival perspectives . . . alternative trajectories . . . [or] unsettles the familiar strategies that we use to tame the past in order to normalize the present." In Gordon's view, "Virtually all history as practiced by modern historians" qualified.[40]

Opening the domain of law to any and all history has proven to be an extremely productive conjunction of disciplines. If society is, as Roberto Unger has put it, "a human artifact," law is surely one of the most potent technologies through which inventive activity is pursued.[41] Legal historians have taken that insight and applied it in myriad realms of economic, social, and cultural action. As they do so, they have moved from Hurst's perception of law as a function of society to one of law's relative autonomy, from law as a mechanism or forum of social mediation to one of active creation. In terms I have used in my own work, legal history has moved from recording manifestations of the rule of law to actively investigating how law rules. Today's legal historians do not think of law as a dependent variable responding to external circumstance, nor as one social institution among many. Rather law is a key agency through which power is exercised.

---

[38]Robert A. Ferguson of Columbia Law School, for example, argues that the best legal history is written by lawyers or those who can think like lawyers and pays proper attention to "hard-edged peculiarities and concrete particularities of legal doctrine and legal procedure." Ferguson, "Book Review," *William and Mary Quarterly* 59 (January 2002).

[39]Robert W. Gordon, "The Past as Authority and as Social Critic: Stabilizing and Destabilizing Functions of History in Legal Argument," in Terrence J. McDonald, ed., *The Historic Turn in the Human Sciences* (Ann Arbor: University of Michigan Press, 1996), 360. For an outstanding combination of mandarin legality with grimy details, see John Witt, *The Accidental Republic: Crippled Workingmen, Destitute Widows, and the Remaking of American Law* (Cambridge, Mass.: Harvard University Press, 2004).

[40]Robert W. Gordon, "Foreword: The Arrival of Critical Historicism," *Stanford Law Review* 49 (May 1997): 1024.

[41]Roberto Mangabeira Unger, *Social Theory: Its Situation and Task* (Cambridge and New York: Cambridge University Press), 1987, 1.

The yield at the intersection of law and history has been immense.[42] Of course, one must acknowledge that when any disciplinary conjunction takes place, each discipline brings its limitations along with its insights. Law's limitation is its tendency to self-referentiality. History's limitations lie in its tendency to frustrate attempts to understand the present through the past by insisting on their separation. As one leading historian puts it, "It is the people of the 1780s, not the people of 2006, that the historian is interested in."[43] Because law is a discipline whose understanding of the present is often founded on unexamined assumptions about the legal past, history's promise for law lies in replacing unexamined assumptions with properly researched inquiry. But its actual utility lies in bringing that better-understood legal past into an improved conjunction with law's present. If historians resist the legitimacy of that objective, legal history's development will be stunted.

A field so young as American legal history needs room to grow. It cannot afford constraints on its imagination. Fortunately, since its late-1970s takeoff, legal history has managed to embrace the best tendencies of its two parents while avoiding the worst. As an organized field of study it has avoided hierarchy, it has been receptive to newcomers, and on the whole it has proven refreshingly free of dogmatic statements of what legal history should be. The result has been a proliferation of scholarship of astonishing variety. In the early twenty-first century, what appeared not so long ago the driest of subjects—arcane, antiquarian, and inward-looking—has become one of the most exciting and expansive of scholarly enterprises.

[42]For the most complete synthesis and bibliographic survey of American legal history as it stands in the early twenty-first century, see Grossberg and Tomlins, eds., *The Cambridge History of Law in America*, 3 vols.

[43]Gordon S. Wood, in reply to Calvin H. Johnson, *New York Review of Books* 53 (May 11, 2006).

Mark A. Noll

American Religious History, 1907–2007

At the start of the twentieth century American religious history meant primarily church history, and church history meant primarily the institutional and intellectual histories of English-language Protestant churches.[1] Authors who studied the main Protestant denominations took for granted that the aggregate of their stories constituted the nation's religious history. In the last decade of the nineteenth century, an impressive American Church History series exemplified the state of the art. The lead editor was Philip Schaff, one of the era's genuine polymaths, who directed the series from Union Theological Seminary in New York City. Ten of the thirteen volumes were given over to individual Protestant bodies, with 80 percent of that coverage devoted to churches of British origin and 20 percent to Protestant churches with roots on the European continent. At the time the series was published, Roman Catholics had become the most numerous religious body in the country, Jews were mounting increasingly successful efforts at ending readings from the King James Version of the Bible in the nation's public schools, and the strongly Mormon population of Utah was for the first time winning the right to send a Mormon to the U.S. Senate. Yet non-Protestant coverage in the series was limited to one volume on the Catholics and very brief mention of Mormons, Jews, and "others" in two general volumes.[2]

The series was, thus, a refined extension of the best earlier treatments of the subject, like Robert Baird's *Religion in America* (1844), which had introduced the

---

[1]An outstanding summary of historiographical changes during the twentieth century is Catherine A. Brekus, "Interpreting American Religion," in William L. Barney, ed., *A Companion to 19th-Century America* (Oxford: Blackwell, 2001), 317–33. Unusually helpful interim reports are provided in Harry S. Stout and D. G. Hart, eds., *New Directions in American Religious History* (New York: Oxford University Press, 1997), especially Stout and Robert M. Taylor, Jr., "Studies of Religion in American Society: The State of the Art," 15–47; and in John F. Wilson, *Religion and the American Nation: Historiography and History* (Athens: University of Georgia Press, 2003). For fuller bibliographical coverage of the immense literature that is sampled below, see Edwin S. Gaustad and Mark A. Noll, eds., *A Documentary History of Religion in America*, 2 vols. (Grand Rapids, Mich.: Eerdmans, 2003): vol. I, 89–91, 190–93, 292–94, 402–4, 514–26, 597–99; vol. II, 84–86, 188–91, 298–301, 436–38, 569–73, 740–46.

[2]The two general volumes were the first, Henry K. Carroll, *The Religious Forces of the United States, Enumerated, Classified, and Described on the Basis of the Government Census of 1890* (New York: Christian Literature, 1896), and the last, Leonard Woolsey Bacon, *A History of American Christianity* (New York: Christian Literature, 1897).

unexpected flourishing of American Protestant churches to Europeans on the eve of the first meeting of the Evangelical Alliance in London in 1846, and Daniel Dorchester's *Christianity in the United States from the First Settlement Down to the Present Time* (1890), which a few decades later stressed the vitality of America's voluntary religious organizations and the enduring threats of social decay (found mostly in cities) and coercive religion (identified mostly with Catholicism).[3] For most of the series authors, as for these earlier landmarks, religion in America was the story of how Protestant traditions had flowered in the American environment by adding a creative can-do spirit in coping with the frontier, an energetic embrace of voluntary organization stimulated by the separation of church and state, and an emphasis on the individual keyed both to Protestant belief in the priesthood of all believers and the principles of liberal democracy. The negative reference point for this historiographical tradition was Roman Catholicism, which seemed to embody the worst aspects of lifeless traditionalism, stultifying hierarchy, and anti-American authoritarianism.

The American Church History series was an effort linked to the founding in 1888 of the American Society of Church History (ASCH), one of the many projects begun by Philip Schaff.[4] Schaff hoped that the new society would combine elements of modern scientific history, especially high standards of research, with traditional Christian edification. Five years after Schaff's death in 1893, the ASCH became a constituent member of the American Historical Association (AHA), itself founded in 1884. If this move revealed some weakening of Schaff's conception of a specifically Christian purpose for historical research, it nonetheless maintained the perspective of progressive Protestantism that lay behind the church history series.

In fact, the church historians working with Schaff were exercising less and less control over the American past. Neither their interpretation of American Protestantism as uniting the best of the Reformation with the best of American democracy nor their view of American history as guided by Protestant principles carried much weight with the emerging leadership of professional academic history. Instead, a variety of this-worldly perspectives dominated history as practiced in colleges and universities: the frontier as the defining national experience (Frederick Jackson Turner), diplomacy studied with standards imitating the sciences (Henry Adams), government understood as developing through constitutional change (J. Franklin Jameson), and society studied through application of the emerging social sciences (James Harvey Robinson). Amateurs like Theodore

---

[3]Robert Baird, *Religion in America: Or an Account of the Origin, Relation to the State, and Present Condition of the Evangelical Churches in the United States. With Notices of the Unevangelical Denominations* (New York: Harper and Brothers, 1844); Daniel Dorchester, *Christianity in the United States from the First Settlement Down to the Present Time* (New York: Phillips and Hunt, 1888).

[4]For excellent treatment, see Henry Warner Bowden, *Church History in an Age of Science: Historiographical Patterns in the United States, 1876–1918* (Chapel Hill: University of North Carolina Press, 1971).

Roosevelt and Woodrow Wilson (presidents of the AHA in 1912 and 1924, respectively) might retain much of the church historians' belief concerning the importance of providence in the American past, but not those who set the course for college and university historical study.

Even further from the concerns of the leading professionals was the substantial historiography that had developed among Roman Catholics, but in a parallel universe. By the early twentieth century, Catholics also practiced the same sophisticated exploration of archives, the same scientific ordering of primary sources, and the same offering of historical research in service to their religion. Like Schaff's church history series, John Gilmary Shea's four-volume *A History of the Catholic Church within the Limits of the United States* exemplified these enhanced professional standards.[5] Soon the establishment of the *Catholic Historical Review* (1915), the creation of the American Catholic Historical Association (1919), and the publication of breakthrough studies like Gerald Shaughnessy's *Has the Immigrant Kept the Faith?* (1925) testified to both new levels of expertise and new skill at charting the effects of American experience on traditional Catholic faith.[6] Yet even more than the work done by Protestants in the ASCH, this Catholic historiography remained of little interest to the arbiters of the nation's new professional history.

In the late 1920s and early 1930s, American religious history turned a corner when a few scholars from the nation's premier secular institutions began a far-reaching reassessment of New England Puritanism. Where the Protestant church historians had shown how the churches embodied the finest American ideals, this new strand of scholars stressed instead how the churches had contributed to the self-defining of America. It also challenged the picture prevailing in advanced academic circles of Puritanism as a barrier to enlightened civilization. That picture had been articulated in influential works like Vernon Louis Parrington's *Main Currents in American Thought* (1927), where Puritanism appeared as a narrow-minded, persecuting scholasticism that needed to be overthrown before a liberated society could emerge.[7]

Against this prevailing view, Samuel Eliot Morison offered a dissent when in *Builders of the Bay Colony* (1930) he pictured the early Puritans as humane, resourceful path makers whose intellectual achievements were especially significant. Morison went on to document those achievements in a notable series of sympathetic books on the early history of Harvard College.[8] Perry Miller, a younger Harvard professor, became the most important voice for recovering the Puritans when in rapid succession he published a study of the early Puritans'

---

[5]John Gilmary Shea, *A History of the Catholic Church within the Limits of the United States, from the First Attempted Colonization to the Present Time* (New York: J. G. Shea, 1886).

[6]Gerald Shaughnessy, *Has the Immigrant Kept the Faith? A Study of Immigration and Catholic Growth in the United States, 1790–1920* (New York: Macmillan, 1925).

[7]Vernon Louis Parrington, *Main Currents in American Thought: An Interpretation of American Literature from the Beginnings to 1920* (New York: Harcourt, Brace, 1927).

[8]Samuel Eliot Morison, *Builders of the Bay Colony* (Boston: Houghton Mifflin, 1930); *The Founding of Harvard College* (Cambridge, Mass.: Harvard University Press, 1935); *Harvard College in the Seventeenth Century* (Cambridge, Mass.: Harvard University Press, 1936).

ecclesiastical innovations, coedited a substantial anthology of Puritan writing, and brought out a dense account of Puritan theology.[9] Morison and Miller were not writing church history keyed to internal questions of religious thought, liturgy, or belief as such. Rather, their sympathetic studies were calling for new respect for the Puritans' willingness to acknowledge the deeply seated character of human evil, for their concern about the ever-present dangers of cultural hypocrisy, and for their attention to the fragility of well-ordered civilization. This reassessment of the Puritans was sustained by an able corps of students, many of them trained at Harvard, and then in turn by students of these students. At the forefront of a rapidly expanding number of such scholars was Edmund S. Morgan, whose 1944 book on domestic life and whose 1958 biography of Massachusetts's early governor, John Winthrop, set high standards for readability, research, and empathy.[10]

Beyond the mere recovery of the Puritans, several of these historians, with Miller in the lead, advanced the argument that better understanding of the Puritans led to a better grasp of the essential American character as a whole. This interpretation was hardly unprecedented, since the importance of religion for national (or group) identity had been a main theme in classic studies like Alexis de Tocqueville's *Democracy in America* (1835–1840) and W. E. B. Du Bois's *The Souls of Black Folk* (1903).[11] But Perry Miller's postwar writing made these claims with new force, especially in a 1949 biography of Jonathan Edwards and a widely read book of essays from 1956.[12]

The doorway opened by Miller and similar historians also facilitated more complicated moves among church historians. First came a deepening and then somewhat later a broadening that complicated the simple narratives of Protestant-guided social ascent. Joseph Haroutunian, who was one of the first Americans to promote the European neoorthodox theology of Karl Barth and Emil Brunner, illustrated the deepening when in 1932 he published a study of eighteenth-century theology that interpreted adjustment to the democratic individualism of Revolutionary America as decline.[13] In 1937 H. Richard Niebuhr added further complexity with his programmatic account of religion throughout American history in which every ameliorating step toward progress and self-fulfillment was matched by a backward step toward superficiality and

---

[9]Perry G. Miller, *Orthodoxy in Massachusetts, 1630–1650: A Genetic Study* (Cambridge, Mass.: Harvard University Press, 1933); edited with Thomas Herbert Johnson, *The Puritans* (New York: American Book Co., 1938); *The New England Mind: The Seventeenth Century* (New York: Macmillan, 1939).

[10]Edmund S. Morgan, *The Puritan Family: Essays on Religion and Domestic Relations in Seventeenth-Century New England* (Boston: Trustees of the Public Library, 1944); *The Puritan Dilemma: The Story of John Winthrop* (Boston: Little, Brown, 1958).

[11]Alexis de Tocqueville, *Democracy in America* (London: Saunders and Otley, 1835–1840); W. E. B. Du Bois, *The Souls of Black Folk: Essays and Sketches* (Chicago: A. C. McClurg, 1903).

[12]Perry G. Miller, *Jonathan Edwards* (New York: W. Sloane Associates, 1949); *Errand into the Wilderness* (Cambridge, Mass.: Harvard University Press, 1956).

[13]Joseph Haroutunian, *Piety versus Moralism: The Passing of the New England Theology* (New York: Henry Holt, 1932).

self-delusion.[14] More than a decade before Miller's biography of Jonathan Edwards, Niebuhr joined Haroutunian in commending Edwards expressly for the content of his religious convictions. The transition of Edwards from a repellent curiosity to an intellectual icon was under way.

A second development in the wake of the opening created by Perry Miller and others moved attention away from intellectual elites of the seventeenth and mid-eighteenth centuries to popular Protestants of the late-eighteenth and nineteenth centuries. Timothy Smith propelled this move in 1957 with an argument for the socially progressive character of nineteenth-century revivalism, which the era's secular historical establishment had routinely treated as rank enthusiasm.[15] Soon thereafter, in a series of provocative essays, Sidney Mead suggested that every supposedly enlightened move in the American founding had been supported by Protestant sectarians, and every supposedly religious advance in the new nation had benefited from some form of political enlightenment.[16]

In 1964 Henry F. May took note of these changes in a much-cited tour d'horizon entitled "The Recovery of American Religious History." He began with a bold claim: "For the study and understanding of American culture, the recovery of American religious history may well be the most important achievement of the last thirty years."[17] May rested his case in part on empirical evidence—that religion had been very important for many Americans throughout all of American history, that neoorthodox theology from a traumatized Europe had inspired at least some American scholars to reengage Christian teachings, and that a postwar revival of religion showed the continuing relevance of religious concerns to American historical understanding. He also highlighted academic developments, from the willingness of leaders in the field like Arthur M. Schlesinger, Sr., at Harvard to guide graduate students like Timothy Smith in pursuing religious subjects to the impact that Perry Miller had exerted in convincing some other historians to take religious thought seriously. May also pointed to the ferment among Catholic scholars arising from Monsignor John Tracy Ellis's "American Catholics and the Intellectual Life" that was pushing some Catholic historians to broader engagement with the historical profession as a whole.[18]

May's own career exemplified what his article described as a trend. In 1949 he published *Protestant Churches in Industrial America*, which had begun life as a dissertation under Harvard's Schlesinger. It anticipated the future by choice of

---

[14]H. Richard Niebuhr, *The Kingdom of God in America* (Chicago: Willett, Clark, 1937).

[15]Timothy L. Smith, *Revivalism and Social Reform in Mid-Nineteenth-Century America* (New York: Abingdon, 1957).

[16]Sidney Earl Mead, *The Lively Experiment: The Shaping of Christianity in America* (New York: Harper and Row, 1963).

[17]Henry F. May, "The Recovery of American Religious History," *American Historical Review* 70 (1964): 79–92; quotation from May, *Ideas, Faiths and Feelings: Essays on American Intellectual and Religious History, 1952–1982* (New York: Oxford University Press, 1983), 67.

[18]John Tracy Ellis, "American Catholics and the Intellectual Life," *Thought* 30 (1955): 351–88, and *American Catholics and the Intellectual Life* (Chicago: Heritage Foundation, 1956).

subject, but not so much by treatment, since in the book religion was important for how it affected (or in this case, mostly did not affect) the main economic changes of the Progressive Era. More than a quarter century later, May published *The Enlightenment in America*, a book marked by closer attention to the importance of religious convictions for secular ideas, the importance of secular presuppositions for religious belief, and the enduring but often ambiguous syntheses that resulted.[19] The difference of this interpretive scheme from that used in the earlier book reflected the way that mature consideration of religious ideas, viewed as both acting and acted upon, had entered into the main narratives of American history.

One last element in May's 1964 essay was prescient. After suggesting that the battle was mostly won to treat religious ideas and institutions as fully important, he noted a growing interest in researching the social roles of religion among non-elites. May had caught the beginnings of a great surge. American religious history felt the shocks of the 1950s and 1960s as much as any other subfield of the discipline. When the civil rights movement and, shortly thereafter, the New Christian Right brought sharply focused religion back into politics, it finished off whatever remained of the notion that a diffuse civilizing aura of mainstream Protestantism defined the national religious past. The Immigrant and Nationality Act of 1965, with the proliferation of religions from elsewhere that swiftly followed, further stimulated scholarship on groups that had been perceived as inconsequential. In addition, strident arguments over "whose America, after all?" — elites versus the rest, female versus male, rich versus poor versus middle class, white versus black versus brown, newcomers versus old stock — energized hitherto neglected historical questions for increasingly diverse cadres of able scholars eager to propose answers. Convincing assaults on an ideal of history as a dispassionate, objective social science in service to the unquestioned national good made some religious historians just as alert as their peers to how perspective, paradigms, partiality, and power influenced historical writing.

Into the 1960s, the writing of religious history had followed an evolutionary path — from progressive national Protestantism to a more secular progressive nationalism. While explicitly Christian interpretations mostly faded away in this process, much else remained the same — a focus on New England Puritanism as the foundation; a prejudice against Roman Catholicism; a concentration on the male leaders of national organizations centered on the East Coast; a relegation of women, African Americans, and religions of non-British origin to the sidelines; and a predisposition to define religion in intellectual and institutional terms. The tumults of the last half-century in both society and the academy derailed this evolutionary progression. Wholesale questioning of a national story defined by the centrality of progressive Protestants was matched by the deflation of idealistic claims for the nation, except for its ability to guarantee an equal-access playing field. The result for religious history was a startling burst of energy combined with a bewildering loss of cohesion.

[19]Henry F. May, *Protestant Churches and Industrial America* (New York: Harper, 1949), and *The Enlightenment in America* (New York: Oxford University Press, 1976).

In the wake of the recovery of religious history documented by Henry May, the pluralization of the subfield took place in full professional view. From the 1960s, religious subjects were increasingly accepted for Ph.D. dissertations at virtually all graduate schools; articles on religious subjects proliferated in many journals; and a growing number of history departments joined religion departments, religious colleges, and theological seminaries in employing specialists in American religious history. For their part, academic historians expressed wildly diverging judgments about the social benefits or harm of individual religious beliefs and practices. Yet unlike the period before 1960, the importance of religion as a necessary theme for understanding the American past was now a given.

By the mid-1960s, the best university presses and commercial publishers had begun to issue a growing number of professionally reviewed and even prize-winning books on Jews, Catholics, revivalists, infidels, southern religion, black religion, slavery and religion—all subjects that professional historians had once neglected.[20] New methods soon became almost as evident as new subjects. For example, Anthony F. C. Wallace promoted ethnological methods for studying religion and offered an extended case study of Native Americans, who were themselves receiving fresh attention from professional historians. In a much-used volume, Edwin S. Gaustad literally put religion on the map with his *Historical Atlas of Religion in America*.[21]

Soon religious history was enriched by being connected with research on employment cycles, marriage and childbearing patterns, income disparities, outmigration, local political tension, and literacy rates. Such ways of contextualizing religion were first used for colonial New England, but quickly began the process that displaced Puritanism—and a stress on leader-driven intellectual history—as central to religious history as a whole.[22]

---

[20]In this and the following notes, I cite only a fraction of the great number of possible examples. For these subjects, see Nathan Glazer, *American Judaism* (Chicago: University of Chicago Press, 1957); John Courtney Murray, *We Hold These Truths: Catholic Reflections on the American Proposition* (New York: Sheed and Ward, 1960); William G. McLoughlin, *Modern Revivalism: Charles Grandison Finney to Billy Graham* (New York: Ronald, 1959); Martin E. Marty, *The Infidel* (Cleveland: Meridian, 1961); James Silver, *Confederate Morale and Church Propaganda* (Tuscaloosa, Ala.: Confederate Publishing, 1957); E. Franklin Frazier, *The Negro Church in America* (New York: Schocken, 1963); Donald G. Mathews, *Slavery and Methodism: A Chapter in American Morality, 1780–1845* (Princeton, N.J.: Princeton University Press, 1965).

[21]Anthony F. C. Wallace, *Religion: An Anthropological View* (New York: Random House, 1966); Wallace Steen and Sheila C. Steen, *The Death and Rebirth of the Seneca* (New York: Knopf, 1969); Edwin S. Gaustad, *Historical Atlas of Religion in America* (New York: Harper and Row, 1962).

[22]Pathbreaking books included Richard L. Bushman, *From Puritan to Yankee: Character and the Social Order in Connecticut, 1690–1765* (Cambridge, Mass.: Harvard University Press, 1967); John Demos, *A Little Commonwealth: Family Life in Plymouth Colony* (New York: Oxford University Press, 1970); Philip J. Greven, *Four Generations: Population, Land, and Family in Colonial Andover, Massachusetts* (Ithaca, N.Y.: Cornell University Press, 1970); Paul S. Boyer and Stephen Nissenbaum, *Salem Possessed: The Social Origins of Witchcraft* (Cambridge, Mass.: Harvard University Press, 1974).

Once started, the diffusion of subject matter and method expanded to take in Mormons, sects, immigrants, political reactionaries, Pentecostals, healing evangelists, the Eastern Orthodox, missionaries, Native Americans, practitioners of metaphysical religions, Hispanics, civil rights activists, and an ever-widening range of European-origin Protestants and Catholics.[23] Scholarship on women and religion exploded with intense interest in domestic lives, reform, ecclesiastical and public institutions, missionary service, and more.[24] The same was true for African American subjects, where *The Autobiography of Malcolm X* both dramatized hitherto neglected realities in black churches and introduced Islam as an American subject. For academic study of African American religion, Albert Raboteau's 1978 *Slave Religion* was an especially effective stimulation, with its careful exploration of interpretive cruxes, like the degree of African survival in African American faiths, and its marshalling of evidence for the self-directing character of antebellum black Christianity.[25] Raboteau's work and much of the scholarship on women bore the mark of new attention to religion as a symbol system, ideology as a reflection of social relationships, and ritual as a marker to social order that reflected a major theoretical boost from Clifford Geertz's *The Interpretation of Cultures* (1973).[26]

[23]Examples include Leonard Arrington and Davis Britton, *The Mormon Experience: A History of the Latter-Day Saints* (New York: Knopf, 1979); Ronald L. Numbers, *Prophetess of Health: A Study of Ellen G. White* (New York: Harper and Row, 1976); Stephan Thernstrom, ed., *Harvard Encyclopedia of Ethnic Groups* (Cambridge, Mass.: Harvard University Press, 1980); Leo P. Ribuffo, *The Old Christian Right: The Protestant Far Right from the Great Depression to the Cold War* (Philadelphia: Temple University Press, 1983); Robert Mapes Anderson, *Vision of the Disinherited: The Making of American Pentecostalism* (New York: Oxford University Press, 1979); David Edwin Harrell, *All Things Are Possible: The Healing and Charismatic Revival in Modern America* (Bloomington: Indiana University Press, 1975); John King Fairbank, ed., *The Missionary Enterprise: China and America* (Cambridge, Mass.: Harvard University Press, 1974); William G. McLoughlin, *Cherokees and Missionaries, 1783–1839* (New Haven, Conn.: Yale University Press, 1984); Robert S. Ellwood, *Alternative Altars: Unconventional and Eastern Spirituality in America* (Chicago: University of Chicago Press, 1979); David J. Garrow, *Bearing the Cross: Martin Luther King, Jr., and the Southern Christian Leadership Conference* (New York: W. Morrow, 1986). For scholarship on Eastern Orthodoxy and American Hispanics, see Thernstrom, *Harvard Encyclopedia*.

[24]Examples include Barbara Welter, "The Feminization of American Religion, 1800–1860," in *Dimity Convictions: The American Woman in the Nineteenth Century* (Athens: Ohio University Press, 1976); Ann Douglas, *The Feminization of American Culture* (New York: Knopf, 1977); Ruth Bordin, *Women and Temperance: The Quest for Power and Liberty, 1873–1900* (Philadelphia: Temple University Press, 1981); Barbara Leslie Epstein, *The Politics of Domesticity: Women, Evangelism, and Temperance* (Middletown, Conn.: Wesleyan University Press, 1981); and as an early summation, Rosemary Radford Ruether and Rosemary Skinner Keller, eds., *Women and Religion in America*, 3 vols. (San Francisco: Harper and Row, 1981–1986).

[25]Malcolm X (with Alex Haley), *The Autobiography of Malcolm X* (New York: Grove Press, 1965); Albert J. Raboteau, *Slave Religion: The "Invisible Institution" in the Antebellum South* (New York: Oxford University Press, 1978).

[26]Clifford Geertz, *The Interpretation of Cultures* (New York: Basic Books, 1973).

Yet in the rush that almost overnight created vast new domains for religious history, older emphases retained surprising strength. Widely read books continued to appear on Christian theological movements like Protestant modernism and fundamentalism and on the meaning of religion for the meaning of America.[27] A particularly fruitful line of investigation, which continues to expand into the present, linked American developments to what transpired across the Atlantic.[28] Two masterful syntheses also testified to the flexibility of older paradigms. In 1972 Sydney Ahlstrom published *A Religious History of the American People*, which remains the most important text for American religion understood in terms of intellectual, theological, denominational, and public life. While Ahlstrom's title gestured toward the new emphasis on history from the bottom up, his plot featured elite theologians, influential institutions, and mainstream cultural presuppositions, but with an even-handed patience that has not been bettered. Twelve years later Martin Marty's *Pilgrims in Their Own Land* displayed many of Ahlstrom's same skills while reprising much of the Protestant-dominated history Ahlstrom had told so well (1984).[29] Yet, proportionately considered, Marty gave more coverage to Catholics, Eastern Orthodox, African Americans, Jews, and women; he shifted attention away from the East to the West, Midwest, and South; and he took for granted that American religion was essentially a pluralistic story from the beginning.

A number of exemplary books published in 1985 revealed a subdiscipline in the midst of rapid maturation, but also rapid diversification. Thus, in that one year appeared the most influential application yet published of diachronic ethnographical research on the religious practices of non-elites, one of the most impressive intellectual histories of elite thinkers since the heyday of Perry Miller, an effective plea to factor religion into the nation's climactic event, a pathbreaking documentary record of the nation's most important minority, an unusually adept attention to religious dynamics combined with conventional American history applied to a homegrown American religion, an effective demonstration of the close interconnections between missionary history and women's history, and the first volume in what remains probably the best history of an American denominational tradition.[30]

[27]William Hutchison, *The Modernist Impulse in American Protestantism* (Cambridge, Mass.: Harvard University Press, 1976); George Marsden, *Fundamentalism and American Culture: The Shaping of Twentieth-Century Evangelicalism, 1870–1925* (New York: Oxford University Press, 1980); Robert Handy, *A Christian America: Protestant Hopes and Historical Realities* (New York: Oxford University Press, 1971).

[28]Robert Handy, *A History of the Churches in the United States and Canada* (New York: Oxford University Press, 1977); Richard Carwardine, *Transatlantic Revivalism: Popular Evangelicalism in Britain and America, 1790–1865* (Westport, Conn.: Greenwood, 1978).

[29]Sydney E. Ahlstrom, *A Religious History of the American People* (New Haven, Conn.: Yale University Press, 1972); Martin E. Marty, *Pilgrims in Their Own Land: 500 Years of Religion in America* (Boston: Little, Brown, 1984).

[30]Robert A. Orsi, *The Madonna of 115th Street: Faith and Community in Italian Harlem, 1880–1950* (New Haven, Conn.: Yale University Press, 1985); Bruce Kuklick, *Churchmen and*

In the decades since 1985, the tide has rolled on, with religion figuring prominently in scholarship on politics, war, cultural conflict, democratization, economic life, international relations, and more.[31] The recent political prominence of Protestant evangelicals, fundamentalists, and Pentecostals has been matched by a new set of authoritative historical accounts.[32] The ordinary practices of ordinary people have become the focus for methodological reorientation, extended research, and detailed case studies.[33] First-rate biographies abound for figures famous as religious leaders (Joseph Smith, Harriet Beecher Stowe, Woodrow Wilson, Aimee Semple McPherson, Oral Roberts, Bishop Fulton Sheen, Billy Graham), for those where religion might be unexpected (Thomas Jefferson, W. E. B. Du Bois, Theodore Roosevelt), and for a few where religion has been a source of perennial contestation (Abraham Lincoln).[34] Major books on theology,

---

Philosophers: From Jonathan Edwards to John Dewey (New Haven, Conn.: Yale University Press, 1985); C. C. Goen, *Broken Churches, Broken Nation: Denominational Schisms and the Coming of the American Civil War* (Macon, Ga.: Mercer University Press, 1985); Milton C. Sernett, *Afro-American Religious History: A Documentary Witness* (Durham, N.C.: Duke University Press, 1985); Jan Shipps, *Mormonism: The Story of a New Religious Tradition* (Urbana: University of Illinois Press, 1985); Patricia Ruth Hill, *The World Their Household: The American Woman's Foreign Mission Movement and Cultural Transformation, 1870–1920* (Ann Arbor: University of Michigan Press, 1985); Richard K. MacMaster, *Land, Piety, Peoplehood: The Establishment of Mennonite Communities in America, 1683–1790*, vol. 1; Theron Schlabach, ed., *The Mennonite Experience in America* (Scottdale, Pa.: Herald Press, 1985).

[31] Richard Carwardine, *Evangelicals and Politics in Antebellum America* (New Haven, Conn.: Yale University Press, 1993); Harry S. Stout, *Upon the Altar of the Nation: A Moral History of the Civil War* (New York: Viking, 2006); Robert Wuthnow, *The Restructuring of American Religion: Society and Faith since World War II* (Princeton, N.J.: Princeton University Press, 1988); Nathan O. Hatch, *The Democratization of American Christianity* (New Haven, Conn.: Yale University Press, 1989); Leigh Eric Smith, *Consumer Rites: The Buying and Selling of American Holidays* (Princeton, N.J.: Princeton University Press, 1995); Peter D'Agostino, *Rome in America: Transnational Catholic Ideology from the Risorgimento to Fascism* (Chapel Hill: University of North Carolina Press, 2004).

[32] Joel A. Carpenter, *Revive Us Again: The Reawakening of American Fundamentalism* (New York: Oxford University Press, 1997); Grant Wacker, *Heaven Below: Early Pentecostals and American Culture* (Cambridge, Mass.: Harvard University Press, 2001).

[33] Ann Taves, *The Household of Faith: Roman Catholic Devotions in Mid-Nineteenth-Century America* (Notre Dame, Ind.: University of Notre Dame Press, 1986); Colleen McDannell, *The Christian Home in Victorian America, 1840–1900* (Bloomington: Indiana University Press, 1986); David D. Hall, *Worlds of Wonder, Days of Judgment: Popular Religious Belief in Early New England* (New York: Knopf, 1989); David D. Hall, ed., *Lived Religion in America: Toward a History of Practices* (Princeton, N.J.: Princeton University Press, 1997); Laurie Maffley-Kipp, Leigh Eric Schmidt, and Marc Valeri, eds., *Practicing Protestants: Histories of Christian Life in America, 1630–1965* (Baltimore: Johns Hopkins University Press, 2006).

[34] Richard L. Bushman, *Joseph Smith: Rough Stone Rolling* (New York: Knopf, 2005); Joan D. Hedrick, *Harriet Beecher Stowe: A Life* (New York: Oxford University Press, 1994); John M. Mulder, *Woodrow Wilson: The Years of Preparation* (Princeton, N.J.: Princeton University Press, 1978); Edith W. Blumhofer, *Aimee Semple McPherson: Everybody's Sister* (Grand Rapids, Mich.: Eerdmans, 1993); David Edwin Harrell, *Oral Roberts: An American Life* (Bloomington: Indiana University Press, 1985); Thomas C. Reeves, *America's Bishop: The Life and Times of*

theologians, specific theological subjects like providence, Jewish-Christian relations, and shifting American perceptions of Jesus testify to the staying power of
traditional subjects.[35] It is the same with major publishing projects like *The Works
of Jonathan Edwards* from Yale University Press, which Perry Miller started in the
1950s; only a few of its twenty-six total volumes had been brought out until the
pace picked up after 1990.[36]

If this surge of scholarship has resulted from flinging open the gates of what
counts as respectable historical endeavor, it has also led to conflicting streams of
interpretation. Thus, general arguments resting on specialized monographs have
both hailed the recent past as a new era of post-Christian pluralism and shown it
to be noteworthy primarily for the new multiethnic character of the nation's overwhelming Christian majority.[37] Major studies have also queried long-standing
assumptions about the progressive character of American liberal democracy by
highlighting persistent strands of retrogressive anti-Catholicism.[38] The remarkable thing, however, is not that such conflicts of interpretation exist, but that in
the profusion of new scholarship there have been so relatively few of them. This

---

Fulton J. Sheen (San Francisco: Encounter, 2001); William C. Martin, *A Prophet with Honor:
The Billy Graham Story* (New York: W. Morrow, 1991); Edwin S. Gaustad, *Sworn on the Altar of
God: A Religious Biography of Thomas Jefferson* (Grand Rapids, Mich.: Eerdmans, 1996);
Edward J. Blum, *W. E. B. Du Bois: American Prophet* (Philadelphia: University of Pennsylvania
Press, 2007); Joshua David Hawley, *Theodore Roosevelt: Preacher of Righteousness* (New Haven,
Conn.: Yale University Press, 2008); Allen Guelzo, *Abraham Lincoln: Redeemer President* (Grand
Rapids, Mich.: Eerdmans, 1999); Richard Carwardine, *Lincoln: A Life of Purpose and Power*
(New York: Knopf, 2003); Stewart Winger, *Lincoln, Religion, and Romantic Cultural Politics*
(DeKalb: Northern Illinois University Press, 2003).

[35]E. Brooks Holifield, *Theology in America: Christian Thought from the Age of the Puritans
to the Civil War* (New Haven, Conn.: Yale University Press, 2003); Mark A. Noll, *America's
God: From Jonathan Edwards to Abraham Lincoln* (New York: Oxford University Press, 2002);
Nicholas Guyatt, *Providence and the Invention of the United States, 1607–1876* (New York:
Cambridge University Press, 2007); Naomi Cohen, *Jews in Christian America: In Pursuit of
Religious Equality* (New York: Oxford University Press, 1992); Stephen R. Prothero, *American
Jesus: How the Son of God Became a National Icon* (New York: Farrar, Straus and Giroux,
2003); Richard Wightman Fox, *Jesus in America: Personal Savior, Cultural Hero, National
Obsession* (San Francisco: HarperSanFrancisco, 2004).

[36]Harry S. Stout et al., eds., *The Works of Jonathan Edwards*, 26 vols. (New Haven, Conn.:
Yale University Press, 1957–2008).

[37]See Diana Eck, *A New Religious America: How a "Christian Country" Has Now Become
the World's Most Religiously Diverse Nation* (San Francisco: HarperSanFrancisco, 2001); as
compared to R. Stephen Warner and Judith G. Witner, eds., *Gatherings in Diaspora: Religious
Communities and the New Immigration* (Philadelphia: Temple University Press, 1998); and
Warner, "The De-Europeanization of American Christianity," in *A Church of Our Own: Dises-
tablishment and Diversity in American Religion* (New Brunswick, N.J.: Rutgers University
Press, 2005), 257–62.

[38]See especially Philip Hamburger, *The Separation of Church and State: A Theologically
Liberal, Anti-Catholic, and American Principle* (Chicago: University of Chicago Press, 2002);
John T. McGreevy, *Catholicism and American Freedom* (New York: W. W. Norton, 2003).

fact speaks to the absence of dominant ruling convictions that, with the exception of the commitment to tolerance, now prevails in the American academy. One measure of the distance traveled in the last century is provided by noting the religious histories that in recent years have been awarded the Bancroft prize, given annually by Columbia University to the best books in all of American history. The first of these volumes was a cultural and ethnographic study of Mormon eschatology (John L. Brooke, *The Refiner's Fire: The Making of Mormon Cosmology, 1644–1844* [1994], awarded 1995); the second a social history of family, gender, power, and disorder stimulated by the Baptist and Methodist movements that rose so suddenly in the early nineteenth century (Christine Leigh Heyrman, *Southern Cross: The Beginnings of the Bible Belt* [1997], awarded 1998); the third a cultural and intellectual biography of Jonathan Edwards (George M. Marsden, *Jonathan Edwards: A Life* [2003], awarded 2004); and the fourth a bi-community study of black and white religion on a Georgia plantation (Erskine Clarke, *Dwelling Place: A Plantation Epic* [2005], awarded 2006).[39] Taken together, the four award winners present a complex picture of traditional institutional leaders and traditional high theology alongside social tensions, marginal outsiders, and protean religious belief. By no means do these books point to a single grand narrative, but they do suggest the field's current vitality.[40]

But has the rise of religious history affected the discipline and social consciousness the way that the discipline and social consciousness have affected religious history? For general accounts of American history, the efflorescence of religious history has clearly shaped narratives carrying the story through the Civil War and covering the era of civil rights reform.[41] For the postbellum period and much of the twentieth century, however, the integration of religion into general histories remains a serious problem. Both the multiplying diversity of individual faiths and the preeminence of social, economic, and political perspectives have made it difficult to incorporate religion, in all its American diversity, into overarching historical narratives.[42] In addition, despite the profusion of solid

[39]John L. Brooke, *The Refiner's Fire: The Making of Mormon Cosmology, 1644–1844* (New York: Cambridge University Press, 1994); Christine Leigh Heyrman, *Southern Cross: The Beginnings of the Bible Belt* (New York: Knopf, 1997); George M. Marsden, *Jonathan Edwards: A Life* (New Haven, Conn.: Yale University Press, 2003); Erskine Clarke, *Dwelling Place: A Plantation Epic* (New Haven, Conn.: Yale University Press, 2005).

[40]On the absence of grand narratives as a good thing, see Thomas Tweed, ed., *Retelling U.S. Religious History* (Berkeley: University of California Press, 1997); on that same situation as a challenge, see Catherine A. Brekus, ed., *The Religious History of American Women: Reimagining the Past* (Chapel Hill: University of North Carolina Press, 2007).

[41]As outstanding examples, see Orville Vernon Burton, *The Age of Lincoln* (New York: Hill and Wang, 2007); Daniel Walker Howe, *What Hath God Wrought: The Transformation of America, 1815–1848* (New York: Oxford University Press, 2007); Taylor Branch, *America in the King Years*, 3 vols. (New York: Simon & Schuster, 1988–2006).

[42]See especially Jon Butler, "Jack-in-the-Box Faith: The Religion Problem in Modern American History," *Journal of American History* 90 (2003): 1357–78.

scholarship, general textbooks that comprehend religion in every age and aspect of American history are still a rarity.[43]

A more difficult question is whether religion as a point of view—as a claim about transcendence or the ultimate meaning of existence—has exerted an influence on academic historians. Sales of books that describe God's special ways with the United States do reach stratospheric heights, but historiographically credible attempts to reveal a divine meaning for American history are extremely rare and almost completely unnoticed in colleges and universities.[44] Historians from many faiths and of no faith have exploited the open historiographical landscape of the recent past to carry out fair-minded studies of many religious traditions. Using conventional historical methods to defend one such tradition as the only or best truth is something quite different. A wide range of scholarship—some of it from religious historians, more from philosophers and historians of science—has mostly overcome crudely reductionist accounts of religion. The most prevalent alternative to either an older-style church-centered providential history or a new-style secular functionalism has, however, remained a cautious reserve about ultimate questions rather than a new paradigm for transcendent interpretation.

The division of specialists in American religious history among history departments, departments of religious studies, and religiously defined colleges and seminaries adds complexity. In actuality, interests and methods stereotyped as religious studies (ethnographic, comparative, phenomenological, recent), history (public, intellectual, political, colonial/antebellum), and church history (ecclesiastical, dogmatic, normative, universal) have never been neatly apportioned among these distinct institutional settings. Yet the rise of religious studies and the continuing strength of church history increase the difficulty in charting a single course for American religion in general historical accounts.

The extraordinary proliferation of religious history in recent decades, with countless expert monographs presenting the compelling stories of an ever-expanding circle of groups practicing an ever-expanding variety of religions, requires assessment from multiple directions. For historians of religion in America, it is in many ways the best of times—with more good scholarship on more religious topics than Phillip Schaff or Perry Miller could ever have imagined. Yet by largely avoiding larger questions about what the religions in religious history ultimately mean, the recent flourishing of religious history may not be doing everything as well as it was done in the generations of Miller and Schaff.

---

[43]An exception is David Edwin Harrell, Jr., Edwin S. Gaustad, John B. Boles, Sally Foreman Griffith, Randall M. Miller, and Randall B. Woods, *Unto a Good Land: A History of the American People* (Grand Rapids, Mich.: Eerdmans, 2005).

[44]Two examples of strong religion and solid historiography are Donald J. D'Elia, *The Spirits of '76: A Catholic Inquiry* (Front Royal, Va.: Christendom, 1983); Steven J. Keillor, *This Rebellious House: American History and the Truth of Christianity* (Downers Grove, Ill.: InterVarsity, 1996).

Susan D. Ware

Century of Struggle: The History of Women's History

Few fields of American history have grown as dramatically as that of women's history over the past century. Courses in women's history taught by specialists who have trained in the field are now standard in most colleges and universities; many schools also offer interdisciplinary women's studies programs. Historians continue to produce a wide range of scholarship on issues of women and gender. American history survey texts that once relegated their coverage of women to luminaries such as Abigail Adams, Harriet Beecher Stowe, Sojourner Truth, and Eleanor Roosevelt now include full discussions of major topics and viewpoints in women's history as an integrated part of the general narrative. Despite ongoing controversy about how American history should be taught, historical scholarship will never return to the days when women were totally absent from history books or broader historical narratives.[1]

Although the revival of feminism in the 1970s dramatically spurred interest in uncovering women's contributions to the past, women's history did not start from scratch in that decade. Women's history itself has a history, which, in turn, has influenced how the field developed, what kinds of questions were asked at various times, and how the field interacted with larger trends of American history in general.[2] One of the most vibrant elements about the field of women's history is its determination to avoid complacency. According to Linda Gordon, whose pioneering work in the 1970s on the history of the birth control movement helped spur development of the field, women's historians have been "continuously self-critical of our generalizations."[3] To revisit some of those earlier generalizations and to examine how questions have been recast and deepened over time provides a good introduction to the field as a whole.

[1]Adapted from Susan Ware, "Introduction," in Sheridan Harvey, Janice E. Ruth, Barbara Orbach Natanson, Sara Day, and Evelyn Sinclair, eds., American Women: A Library of Congress Guide for the Study of Women's History and Culture in the United States (Washington, D.C.: Government Printing Office, 2001).

[2]Jacqueline Goggin, "Challenging Sexual Discrimination in the Historical Profession: Women Historians and the American Historical Association, 1890–1940," American Historical Review 97 (June 1992): 769–802; Julie Des Jardins, Women and the Historical Enterprise in America: Gender, Race, and the Politics of Memory, 1880–1945 (Chapel Hill: University of North Carolina Press, 2003); Bonnie G. Smith, The Gender of History: Men, Women, and Historical Practice (Cambridge, Mass.: Harvard University Press, 1998).

[3]Linda Gordon, U.S. Women's History (Washington, D.C.: American Historical Association, 1997), 5.

Some of the earliest work in American women's history dates to the late nineteenth century. Usually produced by amateur historians, works such as Alice Morse Earle's *Colonial Dames and Good Wives* (1895) are often referred to as "compensatory" or "contributory" history because they focused on previously unknown or neglected contributions that women had made to various aspects of the American experience. Many of these early historical works were biographies of famous women, often authors, First Ladies, or women otherwise defined by their relationship to prominent men, a focus that became less dominant as the field matured. Not terribly sophisticated methodologically, but often written in a lively and accessible style, these early attempts to put women into history were nevertheless important for showing that plentiful materials and resources existed to write about women's lives and their contributions to American life.[4]

As certain American women, primarily those of the white middle class, gained access to higher education and professional training in the late nineteenth and early twentieth centuries, the range of scholarship about women expanded, although it remained on the margins of how American history in general was taught and conceptualized. A pioneering work of early scholarship was Lucy Maynard Salmon's *Domestic Service* (1897), which treated household labor as a subject worthy of historical attention. (Salmon also influenced the discipline of history by teaching several generations of Vassar students, including Caroline F. Ware, an early practitioner of social history in the 1920s and 1930s.) Arthur M. Schlesinger, Sr., included a chapter on "The Role of Women in American History" in his *New Viewpoints in American History* (1922), but the *American Historical Review* and the *Mississippi Valley Historical Review*, the nation's leading historical journals, published only three articles on women before 1940, none by a woman historian.[5] Elisabeth Anthony Dexter's *Colonial Women of Affairs* (1924) and Julia Cherry Spruill's *Women's Life and Work in the Southern Colonies* (1938) were among the handful of published works in women's history in those decades.[6]

The situation of women in the historical profession actually declined in the 1940s and 1950s, but that did not stop scholars from publishing influential works of women's history. Mary Beard's *Woman as Force in History* (1946) challenged the view of women as marginal or unimportant to history by demonstrating that women had always played active roles in society and public life. Eleanor Flexner offered a meticulously researched narrative of the women's rights movement from Seneca Falls through the winning of suffrage in *Century of Struggle* (1959). When women's history as an academic discipline began to grow dramatically in the 1970s, all these pioneering books, along with feminist classics such as Simone

[4]Alice Morse Earle, *Colonial Dames and Good Wives* (Boston: Houghton Mifflin, 1895).

[5]Lucy Maynard Salmon, *Domestic Service* (New York: Macmillan, 1897); Arthur M. Schlesinger, *New Viewpoints in American History* (New York: Macmillan, 1922); Goggin, "Challenging Sexual Discrimination in the Historical Profession," 781.

[6]Elisabeth Anthony Dexter, *Colonial Women of Affairs* (Boston: Houghton Mifflin, 1924); Julia Cherry Spruill, *Women's Life and Work in the Southern Colonies* (Chapel Hill: University of North Carolina Press, 1938).

de Beauvoir's *The Second Sex* (published in France in 1949 and available in trans-
lation in the United States in 1953), became highly influential texts.[7]

Various factors came together in the 1960s and 1970s to fuel the growth of
women's history: the waves of social protest set in motion by the civil rights movement in the 1950s; the revival of feminism as a national issue, sparked in part by
Betty Friedan's *The Feminine Mystique* (1963); the emergence of the women's liberation movement separate from antiwar activism and student protest; and demographic changes in women's lives, including higher workforce participation and
widening access to higher education. A critical influence on the emergence of
women's history was the new focus on social history in scholarly research and
teaching. Social history studied the lives of ordinary Americans and their communities, workplaces, family lives, and recreation, and thus challenged historians' traditional focus on wars and diplomacy, presidents and politics summed up
in the phrase "dead white men." Emboldened by the revival of feminism and
motivated by the sweeping changes going on in their own lives, many female
scholars (and a few male colleagues) began actively asking new and different
questions about history. As historian Linda Kerber noted aptly, "Activists are hun-
gry for their history."[8] Professors who had been trained in traditional fields such
as diplomatic history (Blanche Wiesen Cook) and Russian history (Linda Gordon) switched their research interests to American women's history, training
themselves as they went. So new—and to some departments and university
administrators, so threatening—were the first courses in women's history that
offering one felt like a revolutionary act.

In this exciting and creative time for women's history in the 1970s, much of
the early research focused on the concept of separate spheres in mid-nineteenth-
century America, that is, the way in which women's lives were directed toward
the familial and private whereas men inhabited the wider world of politics, work,
and public life. Although much of this early work interpreted separate spheres as
an example of the oppression of women, works like Nancy Cott's *The Bonds of
Womanhood* (1977) offered a competing, and at times simultaneous, emphasis on
the empowerment and autonomy women could enjoy in a world where, in Carroll Smith-Rosenberg's often-quoted phrase, "men made but a shadowy appearance."[9] This balancing act between emphasizing victimization and oppression

[7]Mary Beard, *Woman as Force in History* (New York: Macmillan, 1946); Eleanor Flexner,
Century of Struggle: The Woman's Rights Movement in the United States (Cambridge, Mass.:
Harvard University Press, 1959); Simone de Beauvoir, *The Second Sex*, trans. and ed. H. M.
Parshley (New York: Knopf, 1953).

[8]Linda K. Kerber, "Gender," in Anthony Molho and Gordon Wood, eds., *Imagined Histories: American Historians Interpret the Past* (Princeton, N.J.: Princeton University Press, 1998), 41.

[9]Barbara Welter, "The Cult of True Womanhood," *American Quarterly* 18 (1966): 151–74;
Nancy Cott, *The Bonds of Womanhood: "Woman's Sphere" in New England, 1780–1835* (New
Haven, Conn.: Yale University Press, 1977); Carroll Smith-Rosenberg, "The Female World of
Love and Ritual: Relations between Women in Nineteenth-Century America," *Signs: Journal
of Women in Culture and Society* 1 (Autumn 1975): 1–29.

on the one hand and women's agency and activism on the other continues to shape the field today.

Exciting as this outpouring of new research was, the limitations of the separate spheres paradigm soon became apparent, one of many instances in which women's history has shown its ability to criticize itself and move beyond working generalizations or discard them entirely. African American scholars pointed out that the separate spheres concept had little relevance to the lives of black women, for whom restriction to a domestic sphere was virtually negated by institutions like slavery or the need to seek paid employment outside the home. Scholars who studied working-class or immigrant women made the same point. The separate spheres model also depended on sources from New England, with less relevance for the South and, especially, the West. Furthermore, it began to dawn on scholars that white middle-class women might have as much or more in common with men of their own social and economic class than with other women. Scholars also demonstrated that the line between public and private was much more fluid than nineteenth-century prescriptive literature (that is, sermons and etiquette books prescribing women's proper behavior) initially suggested.[10]

The dethroning of the concept of separate spheres with its emphasis on the universality of women's experience and its replacement by a recognition of difference (the diversity of women's experiences, not their commonality) was well under way by the early 1980s. No longer was it enough to use the term *women*; scholars had to be clear about which women. Women were divided by a range of factors that included race, class, ethnicity, religion, geography, age, sexual orientation, and so forth. Historians also increasingly addressed conflicts among women and the unequal power dynamics shaping relations between women: mistresses on southern plantations and their female slaves; white professional women whose careers were made possible by cheap domestic help, usually black or minority women; and white native-born social workers and their working-class and immigrant clients. Suddenly it became much harder to make generalizations about the category of *woman*.[11] Difference has continued to be one of the most important organizing concepts of women's history. Another new trend in the 1980s was the growing acceptance of the concept of *gender*, a term that was virtually nonexistent in 1970s scholarship. *Gender* refers to the historical and cultural constructions of roles assigned to the biological differences and attributes of men and women. If someone did a keyword search of women's history scholarship of the past twenty-five years, *gender* would probably rival *women* as the most frequently cited word. Joan Scott's enormously influential 1986 article, "Gender:

[10]Nancy Hewitt, "Beyond the Search for Sisterhood: American Women's History in the 1990s," in Ellen Carol DuBois and Vicki L. Ruiz, eds., *Unequal Sisters: A Multicultural Reader in U.S. Women's History*, 3rd ed. (New York: Routledge, 2005). See also Hewitt, *Women's Activism and Social Change: Rochester, New York, 1822–1872* (Ithaca, N.Y.: Cornell University Press, 1984).

[11]The first edition of Ruiz and DuBois, *Unequal Sisters*, which appeared in 1990, played an important role here.

A Useful Tool of Historical Analysis," played a key role here.[12] Another way to date this shift is to examine the number of books that began to use the word in their titles, such as Ruth Milkman's *Gender at Work: The Dynamics of Job Segregation by Sex during World War II* (1987).[13] Because all historical actors have a gender, practically any historical question or topic from diplomacy to leisure to state policy can, hypothetically, be subjected to a gender analysis.[14] In addition, gender analysis has spurred new scholarship on the construction of masculinity and the way men's roles at work, as members of families, and in popular culture have changed over time.[15]

In the 1990s, in addition to widening attention to the intersections of race, class, and gender, practitioners of women's history and gender studies took what has been called a "linguistic turn." Spurred in part by writings of French scholars such as Jacques Derrida and especially Michel Foucault, American historians began to analyze more deeply questions of language and discourse, that is, the ways in which underlying power structures and inequalities were forged and maintained in words, speech, and other representations. Literary criticism and cultural analysis challenged the authenticity of texts by showing that experience and identity were never simple or unchanging. For example, categories such as "heterosexual" and "homosexual" were shown to be historically constructed, not innate or immutable, with the emergence of heterosexual identity (as well as other sexual orientations) a fairly recent development.[16]

One of the most far-reaching items on the women's history agenda is the continued questioning of the meaning of *whiteness*. Too often in the literature of women's history, white women have appeared as raceless, their experiences shaped entirely by gender. In contrast, African American women and other women of color have been viewed primarily in terms of their race, to the exclusion of factors such as class and gender. Yet historians now realize that everyone

[12]Joan Wallach Scott, "Gender: A Useful Tool of Historical Analysis," *American Historical Review* 91 (December 1986): 1053–75.

[13]Ruth Milkman, *Gender at Work: The Dynamics of Job Segregation by Sex during World War II* (Urbana: University of Illinois Press, 1987).

[14]Laura Wexler, *Tender Violence: Domestic Visions in an Age of U.S. Imperialism* (Chapel Hill: University of North Carolina Press, 2000); Kristin L. Hoganson, *Fighting for American Manhood: How Gender Politics Provoked the Spanish-American and Philippine-American Wars* (New Haven, Conn.: Yale University Press, 1998).

[15]E. Anthony Rotundo, *American Manhood: Transformations in Masculinity from the Revolution to the Modern Era* (New York: Basic Books, 1993); Gail Bederman, *Manliness and Civilization: A Cultural History of Gender and Race in the United States, 1880–1917* (Chicago: University of Chicago Press, 1995).

[16]Michel Foucault, *The History of Sexuality*, vol. I: *An Introduction* (New York: Vintage, 1978); John D'Emilio and Estelle Freedman, *Intimate Matters: A History of Sexuality in America* (New York: Harper and Row, 1988); Joanne Meyerowitz, *How Sex Changed: A History of Transsexuality in the United States* (Cambridge, Mass.: Harvard University Press, 2002).

has ethnicity and race, that whiteness is as much a racial identity as being black or Latina.[17]

A multicultural approach, that is, one that recognizes difference and diversity in women's experiences, has been at the center of scholarship on women and race since the 1990s. One of the important contributions of this approach is that it moves the field of history beyond the old framework of seeing race matters solely in terms of black and white. Here the contributions of historians of the American West such as Susan Armitage, Sarah Deutsch, and Peggy Pascoe have been especially important because the people and events they are studying fail to fit neatly into anything resembling a biracial dichotomy. Where would that dichotomy leave Native American women, Latinas, and Asian women, who often existed side by side with black and Anglo women in western communities? What happens when members of these groups intermarry? This widened field of vision encourages women's historians to put issues of diversity in race, class, and gender relationships at the heart of all questions under inquiry. This insight, of course, applies to the study of men as well.[18]

One of the greatest accomplishments of women's history over the past three decades has been the rich outpouring of scholarship on African American women's history. This research, on everything from education to suffrage to work to slavery to music, has brought the enormous contributions made by African American women to their communities and to the country at large into the historical record.[19] Evelyn Brooks Higginbotham analyzed black women's roles in the Baptist church, Hazel Carby surveyed the emergence of African American novelists, and bell hooks examined feminist theory. Especially pathbreaking was the publication in 1993 of *Black Women in America: An Historical Encyclopedia*, edited by Darlene Clark Hine, Elsa Barkley Brown, and Roslyn Terborg-Penn.[20]

---

[17]David R. Roediger, *The Wages of Whiteness: Race and the Making of the American Working Class* (New York: Verso, 1991); Karen Anderson, *Changing Women: A History of Racial Ethnic Women in Modern America* (New York: Oxford University Press, 1996); Ruth Frankenberg, *White Women, Race Matters: The Social Construction of Whiteness* (Minneapolis: University of Minnesota Press, 1993).

[18]Susan Armitage and Elizabeth Jameson, eds., *The Women's West* (Norman: University of Oklahoma Press, 1987), and *Writing the Range: Race, Class, and Culture in the Women's West* (Norman: University of Oklahoma Press, 1997); Nancy Shoemaker, ed., *Negotiators of Change: Historical Perspectives on Native American Women* (New York: Routledge, 1995); Sarah Deutsch, *No Separate Refuge: Culture, Class, and Gender on the Anglo-Hispanic Frontier in the American Southwest, 1880–1940* (New York: Oxford University Press, 1987); Peggy Pascoe, *Relations of Rescue* (New York: Oxford University Press, 1990); Theda Perdue, ed., *Sifters: Native American Women's Lives* (New York: Oxford University Press, 2001).

[19]Darlene Clark Hine and Kathleen Thompson, *A Shining Thread of Hope: The History of Black Women in America* (New York: Broadway Books, 1998); Paula Giddings, *When and Where I Enter: The Impact of Black Women on Race and Sex in America* (New York: William Morrow, 1984); Deborah Gray White, *Too Heavy a Load: Black Women in Defense of Themselves, 1894–1994* (New York: W. W. Norton, 1999).

[20]Evelyn Brooks Higginbotham, *Righteous Discontent: The Women's Movement in the Black Baptist Church, 1880–1920* (Cambridge, Mass.: Harvard University Press, 1993); Hazel

Research on Asian American women, Latinas, Puerto Rican women, and immigrants from Caribbean and South American countries has also begun in earnest, but because the fields are much newer and the number of practitioners smaller, they have not yet had the impact on scholarship in women's history that the historiography on African American women has.[21] From these fields and the fruitful scholarship being done on the American West, practitioners of women's history have begun to utilize concepts like borderlands, intercultural borders, frontiers, and contact zones, terms that describe situations where two (or more) cultures meet accompanied by a consciousness of ambiguity, constant flux, multiple identities, and divided loyalties.[22] Vicki Ruiz's 2006 presidential address to the Organization of American Historians entitled "Nuestra America: Latino History as U.S. History" reflects this new approach.[23]

Contemporary women's historical scholarship also revisits topics that had once seemed settled or fully explored by asking different questions and using new approaches. An excellent example is the woman suffrage movement. Documentation of the history of women's suffrage began in 1881 during the movement itself, with the compilation of the multivolume *History of Woman Suffrage* by Elizabeth Cady Stanton, Susan B. Anthony, and Matilda Joslyn Gage, an important if flawed source because it focused on only one wing of the movement while ignoring the contributions of the other.[24] Flexner's *Century of Struggle* brought the story of woman suffrage to a new generation of readers, and the early women's rights movement became the focus of some of the most influential early works in women's history, such as Gerda Lerner's *The Grimke Sisters from South Carolina: Rebels against Slavery* (1967), Anne Firor Scott's *The Southern Lady: From*

Carby, *Reconstructing Womanhood: The Emergence of the Afro-American Woman Novelist* (New York: Oxford University Press, 1987); bell hooks, *Feminist Theory: From Margin to Center* (Boston: South End Press, 1994); Darlene Clark Hine, Elsa Barkley Brown, and Roslyn Terborg-Penn, eds., *Black Women in America: An Historical Encyclopedia* (Brooklyn, N.Y.: Carlson Publishing, 1993).

[21]Vicki Ruiz, *From Out of the Shadows: Mexican Women in Twentieth-Century America* (New York: Oxford University Press, 1998); Judy Yung, *Unbound Feet: A Social History of Chinese Women in San Francisco* (Berkeley: University of California Press, 1995); Huping Ling, *Surviving on the Gold Mountain: A History of Chinese American Women and Their Lives* (Albany: State University of New York Press, 1998); Shirley Hune and Gail Nomura, eds., *Asian/Pacific Islander American Women: A Historical Anthology* (New York: New York University Press, 2003); Mae Ngai, *Impossible Subjects: Illegal Aliens and the Making of Modern America* (Princeton, N.J.: Princeton University Press, 2004); Laura Briggs, *Reproducing Empire: Race, Sex, and U.S. Imperialism in Puerto Rico* (Berkeley: University of California Press, 2002).

[22]Gloria Anzaldua, *Borderlands/La Frontera: The New Mestiza* (San Francisco: Aunt Lute Books, 1987); Ramon A. Gutierrez, *When Jesus Came, the Corn Mothers Went Away: Marriage, Sexuality, and Power in New Mexico, 1500–1846* (Stanford, Calif.: Stanford University Press, 1991).

[23]Vicki Ruiz, "Nuestra America: Latino History as U.S. History," *Journal of American History* 93 (December 2006): 655–72.

[24]Elizabeth Cady Stanton, Susan B. Anthony, and Matilda Joslyn Gage, eds., *History of Woman Suffrage* (New York: Fowler and Wells, 1881).

Pedestal to Politics, 1830–1930 (1970), and Ellen Carol DuBois's *Feminism and Suffrage: The Emergence of an Independent Women's Movement in America, 1848–1869* (1978).[25] Interest in suffrage has ebbed and flowed, but it has risen recently as historians probe more deeply into the embedded racism of much of the suffragists' ideology and leadership strategies, both in the United States and internationally. A topic that once seemed to be mainly about winning the vote now presents a window on issues such as racism, imperialism, and power.[26]

The growing interest in suffrage is also part of a resurgence of interest in political history. In the early days of women's history, inspired largely by the dramatic growth of social history, most attention focused on the lives of ordinary women, with political elites or prominent women given a lower priority. Partly as a by-product of moving beyond the separate spheres paradigm, historians began to realize that women had been much more involved in public life than previously suspected. They may not have been voters or held political office, but they influenced public policy nonetheless, through voluntary associations, churches and charities, family connections, and even participation in public demonstrations and crowd actions. Any former notions of women as nonpolitical have gone by the wayside. To put it another way, women's history has helped broaden the definition of what is political in ways that have been productive not only for research on women and gender but also for the field of American political history.[27]

As part of a new attention to the making of public policy and how public authority is forged, women's historians have also turned a more critical eye to areas like the growth of the state, especially state policies affecting women and children such as welfare laws. As another example of how topics in women's history continue to grow and deepen as they are revisited by new generations of scholars, early work on the New Deal in the 1930s focused on the contributions that an elite band of women—primarily white but also including the prominent African American Mary McLeod Bethune—made to the formulation of New Deal policies.[28] Building on that basis, later studies asked harder questions. It was

[25]Gerda Lerner, *The Grimke Sisters from South Carolina: Rebels against Slavery* (Boston: Houghton Mifflin, 1967); Anne Firor Scott, *The Southern Lady: From Pedestal to Politics, 1830–1930* (Chicago: University of Chicago Press, 1970); Ellen Carol DuBois, *Feminism and Suffrage: The Emergence of an Independent Women's Movement in America, 1848–1869* (Ithaca, N.Y.: Cornell University Press, 1978).

[26]Louise Michele Newman, *White Women's Rights: The Racial Origins of Feminism in the United States* (New York: Oxford University Press, 1999); Bonnie S. Anderson, *Joyous Greetings: The First International Women's Movement, 1830–1860* (New York: Oxford University Press, 2000); Rebecca J. Mead, *How the Vote Was Won: Woman Suffrage in the Western United States, 1868–1914* (New York: New York University Press, 2004).

[27]Rebecca Edwards, *Angels in the Machinery: Gender in American Party Politics from the Civil War to the Progressive Era* (New York: Oxford University Press, 1997); Catherine Allgor, *Parlor Politics: In Which the Ladies of Washington Help Build a City and a Government* (Charlottesville: University Press of Virginia, 2000); Melanie Gustafson, Kristie Miller, and Elizabeth Perry, eds., *We Have Come to Stay: American Women and Political Parties, 1880–1960* (Albuquerque: University of New Mexico Press, 1999).

[28]Susan Ware, *Beyond Suffrage: Women in the New Deal* (Cambridge, Mass.: Harvard University Press, 1981).

no longer enough to know that women administrators were active in a New Deal network; historians wanted to determine how the attitudes of those women affected the policies that they were developing and administering. In the case of Social Security, first passed in 1935, the law was written from the very conservative premise that men were breadwinners, women were wives, and any system of old-age insurance should be built on that dichotomy. As historians such as Alice Kessler-Harris and Robyn Muncy have shown, women administrators accepted this deeply gendered conceptualization and perpetuated it, despite the fact that their own lives often diverged from the model.[29]

Another field to which women's history has increasingly turned in recent years is biography. Of course, biographies of famous women, like those of men, have been standard fare since the nineteenth century, but in the excitement of the rediscovery of women's history in the 1960s and 1970s and the ascendancy of social history, biographies of well-known and influential women were fairly uncommon. (Gerda Lerner's book on the Grimke sisters and Kathryn Kish Sklar's 1973 biography of Catharine Beecher are noteworthy exceptions, as was the groundbreaking publication in 1971 of the three-volume *Notable American Women, 1607–1950: A Biographical Dictionary*, edited by Edward T. James, Janet Wilson James, and Paul S. Boyer.)[30] Yet historians remained intrigued by biography because it gave them a window into many aspects of women's lives, be they ordinary (like Martha Ballard in Laurel Thatcher Ulrich's *A Midwife's Tale* [1990]) or extraordinary (like Eleanor Roosevelt as portrayed in Blanche Wiesen Cook's volumes).[31] Especially important to the field of biography as a whole has been the insistence of feminist scholars that attention must always be paid to the interplay between the personal and the professional in forging an interpretation of a subject's overall significance.[32] This insight, first developed to draw attention to the private constraints under which many female historical figures labored as they pioneered in the public realm, is also helpful

[29]Alice Kessler-Harris, *In Pursuit of Equity: Women, Men, and the Quest for Economic Citizenship in 20th-Century America* (New York: Oxford University Press, 2001); Robyn Muncy, *Creating a Female Dominion in American Reform, 1890–1930* (New York: Oxford University Press, 1991).

[30]Kathryn Kish Sklar, *Catharine Beecher: A Study in American Domesticity* (New Haven, Conn.: Yale University Press, 1973); Edward T. James, Janet Wilson James, and Paul S. Boyer, eds., *Notable American Women, 1607–1950: A Biographical Dictionary* (Cambridge, Mass.: Harvard University Press, 1971). See also the subsequent volumes: Barbara Sicherman and Carol Hurd Green, eds., *Notable American Women: The Modern Period* (Cambridge, Mass.: Harvard University Press, 1980), and Susan Ware and Stacy Braukman, eds., *Notable American Women: Completing the Twentieth Century* (Cambridge, Mass.: Harvard University Press, 2004).

[31]Laurel Thatcher Ulrich, *A Midwife's Tale: The Life of Martha Ballard, Based on Her Diary, 1785–1812* (New York: Knopf, 1990); Blanche Wiesen Cook, *Eleanor Roosevelt, Vol. I, 1884–1933* (New York: Viking, 1992), and *Eleanor Roosevelt, Vol. II, 1933–1938* (New York: Viking, 1999). See also Susan Ware, *Still Missing: Amelia Earhart and the Search for Modern Feminism* (New York: W. W. Norton, 1993).

[32]Sara Alpern, Joyce Antler, Elizabeth Perry, and Ingrid Scobie, eds., *The Challenge of Feminist Biography: Writing the Lives of Modern American Women* (Urbana: University of Illinois Press, 1992).

in understanding men's lives, as Kathleen Dalton showed in her biography of Theodore Roosevelt.[33]

One of the strongest continuities of women's history scholarship, stretching back to Progressive Era investigations of conditions of women's industrial work such as Margaret Byington's *Homestead: The Households of a Mill Town* (1910) and Katherine Anthony's *Mothers Who Must Earn* (1914), is its focus on women's work, and this emphasis is alive and well.[34] "Women have always worked" is a generalization that truly does stand up to scrutiny, and historians such as Alice Kessler-Harris, Dorothy Sue Cobble, Ava Baron, and Eileen Boris have documented the range of working women's lives, from industrial work to labor organizing to the significant theoretical recognition that women's unpaid domestic labor is critical to (and usually undercounted in) the wider economy. Also of interest have been the sectors of the economy where women traditionally have clustered: domestic service, waitressing, teaching, nursing, clerical work, librarianship, social work, and the like. How these occupations became typed as female and why they have stayed that way, despite monumental changes in the meaning of work and in the realities of women's lives, are questions that still tantalize historians.[35]

Another question that has been a constant on the women's history agenda from its early days concerns women and social change. Starting with Mary Beard's *Women's Work in Municipalities* (1915), historians have documented the wide variety of women's contributions to their communities and to public life. Through voluntary associations, religious groups, professional organizations, activist groups, and other forums, women have often been in the forefront of movements for social change, not always as leaders, but certainly behind the scenes.[36] But this activism has not been confined to liberal or progressive women.

[33]Kathleen Dalton, *Theodore Roosevelt: A Strenuous Life* (New York: Knopf, 2002).

[34]Margaret Byington, *Homestead: The Households of a Mill Town* (1910, reprinted New York: Arno, 1969); Katherine Anthony, *Mothers Who Must Earn* (New York: Survey Associates, 1914).

[35]General surveys include Alice Kessler-Harris, *Out to Work: A History of Wage-Earning Women in the United States* (New York: Oxford University Press, 1982); Jacqueline Jones, *American Work: Black and White Labor since 1600* (New York: W. W. Norton, 1998); Susan Strasser, *Never Done: A History of American Housework* (New York: Pantheon, 1982); Eileen Boris, *Home to Work: Motherhood and the Politics of Industrial Homework in the United States* (New York: Cambridge University Press, 1994); Ava Baron, ed., *Work Engendered: Toward a New History of American Labor* (Ithaca, N.Y.: Cornell University Press, 1991); Dorothy Sue Cobble, *The Other Women's Movement: Workplace Justice and Social Rights in Modern America* (Princeton, N.J.: Princeton University Press, 2004).

[36]Mary Ritter Beard, *Woman's Work in Municipalities* (New York: D. Appleton and Company, 1915); Anne Firor Scott, *Natural Allies: Women's Associations in American History* (Urbana: University of Illinois Press, 1991); Glenna Matthews, *The Rise of Public Woman: Woman's Power and Woman's Place in the United States, 1630–1970* (New York: Oxford University Press, 1992); Evelyn Brooks Higginbotham, *Righteous Discontent: The Women's Movement in the Black Baptist Church, 1880–1920* (Cambridge, Mass.: Harvard University Press, 1993); Karen J. Blair, *The Clubwoman as Feminist: True Womanhood Redefined, 1868–1914* (New York: Holmes and Meier, 1980).

Much exciting new research is being done on conservative women and their political agendas. Examples include women in the Ku Klux Klan in the 1920s, the mothers' movement against war in the 1930s, women in the Republican Party, and biographies of conservative activists such as Phyllis Schlafly.[37]

As historians increasingly aim to situate United States history within a global context, historians of American women are also venturing beyond national borders. Historians such as Leila Rupp and Ellen Carol DuBois, who have studied the interactions between American women's organizations and their foreign equivalents, have often been struck by how deeply and unconsciously women who consider themselves feminists will hold up the Western model as the only one for the advancement of women. Women's historians are also rethinking topics like migration and labor in a global framework. As historians document the extensive contact that American women have always had beyond national borders and how in turn international trends influenced domestic events, they show one direction that women's history will likely take in the future.[38]

One hundred years ago women were marginal figures in the field of history. Now they have moved from margin to center, as witnessed by the number of women's historians who have been elected to the prestigious position of president of the Organization of American Historians.[39] The ability to prod the historical profession to look at history in new ways, and with a much wider array of historical actors, is one of the most important contributions that women's history has made, and continues to make, to the writing and teaching of American history. With such a successful track record, the next century should be less of a struggle.

[37]Kathleen Blee, *Women of the Klan: Racism and Gender in the 1920s* (Berkeley: University of California Press, 1991); Glen Jeansonne, *Women of the Far Right: The Mothers' Movement and World War II* (Chicago: University of Chicago Press, 1996); Catherine E. Rymph, *Republican Women: Feminism and Conservatism from Suffrage through the Rise of the New Right* (Chapel Hill: University of North Carolina Press, 2006); Donald T. Critchlow, *Phyllis Schlafly and Grassroots Conservatism: A Woman's Crusade* (Princeton, N.J.: Princeton University Press, 2005).

[38]Leila J. Rupp, *Worlds of Women: The Making of an International Women's Movement* (Princeton, N.J.: Princeton University Press, 1997); Ellen Carol DuBois, *Harriot Stanton Blatch and the Winning of Woman Suffrage* (New Haven, Conn.: Yale University Press, 1997); Ann Stoler, *Haunted by Empire: Geographies of Intimacy in North American History* (Durham, N.C.: Duke University Press, 2006); Catherine Ceniza Choy, *Empires of Care: Nursing and Migration in Filipino American History* (Durham, N.C.: Duke University Press, 2003); Donna R. Gabaccia and Vicki L. Ruiz, eds., *American Dreaming, Global Realities: Re-Thinking U.S. Immigration History* (Urbana: University of Illinois Press, 2006).

[39]Gerda Lerner was elected in 1981, followed by Anne Firor Scott, Mary Frances Berry, Joyce Appleby, Linda Kerber, Darline Clark Hine, Jacqueline Dowd Hall, Vicki Ruiz, and Nell Irvin Painter. A forerunner from an earlier generation was Louise Kellogg, who served as president in the year 1930–1931.

Donald Worster

The Rise of Environmental History

Today's headlines tell of melting ice caps, devastating earthquakes and hurricanes, the diminished carrying capacity of the planet's soils and waters, and the high price of energy, all reminders of the vital role the natural world plays in human affairs and the potential for humans to damage the systems that support life and community. The growing awareness that there is an environmental component to almost everything we do has given rise to a new perspective on the past. As a result, in 1975 scholars organized the American Society for Environmental History, which has been followed by similar societies in Europe and Latin America.[1] All have attempted to expand the purview of history to include the long, tangled relationship humans have had with the natural world. That relationship has not always been in an unhealthy state, but trying to understand how it has changed over time has acquired a global and historical urgency that it did not have a hundred years ago.

This new environmental history seems destined to become more central to our understanding of the past as the twenty-first century unrolls, but its roots are hardly shallow; they go deeper into the past than the first Earth Day in 1970 or the 1997 Kyoto treaty on climate change. In fact, they go all the way back to 1908, when President Theodore Roosevelt reinterpreted the past in his opening address to a conference of governors called to drive home the need for conservation, which he called "the gravest problem of today." He argued that, since colonial times, resource issues had been at the heart of American development: "The Constitution of the United States . . . grew in large part out of the necessity for united action in the wise use of one of our natural resources"—namely, waterways such as the Potomac, Chesapeake, and Mississippi. America's extraordinary rise to prosperity and power, Roosevelt stated, owed much to a fortunate abundance of natural resources, an abundance that he warned was fast disappearing. Future scarcity would bring profound changes to the country unless the government

[1]A broad overview of the field, with extensive bibliography, can be found in Carolyn Merchant, *American Environmental History* (New York: Columbia University Press, 2007). The American Society for Environmental History publishes the quarterly journal *Environmental History*, while the European Society for Environmental History is supported by the journal *Environment and History*. Another new group, the Sociedade Latino-americana e Caribenha de História Ambiental (SOLCHA), now meets annually.

began, in the words of Supreme Court Justice Oliver Wendell Holmes, Jr., "to protect the atmosphere, the water, and the forests within its territory."[2]

No professional historian was present at that governors' conference, but the University of Wisconsin's Frederick Jackson Turner would have been an obvious candidate to include. In his 1892 essay "Problems in American History," Turner had pointed to westward expansion—"this ever retreating frontier of free land"— as the dominant theme in the country's history. He also called for merging the history of Earth and its myriad life-forms with the history of humankind. "Little has yet been done toward investigating the part played by the environment in determining the lines of our development. . . . When the geologist, the meteorologist, the biologist, and the historian shall go hand in hand in this study, they will see how largely American history has been determined by natural conditions."[3] Turner was no rigid determinist. But in contrast to most of his academic colleagues, he believed that ideals and institutions are not the product of humankind's unfettered imagination but emerge out of material conditions that humans did not make. Thus, the professional historian Turner and the amateur historian Roosevelt agreed on the need for an environmental perspective on the past.

Before the midpoint of the twentieth century, despite Turner's high standing in historical circles, such ideas made little impact on the conventional wisdom among historians. History had long been conceived as the study of human affairs, mainly political, divorced from nature and free of all connection with the natural sciences. Any challenges to those suppositions had to come from mavericks writing on the profession's margins. From the 1930s to the mid-1950s two scholars of the Great Plains, Walter Prescott Webb and James Malin, were almost alone in writing history from an environmental perspective. Webb, in his book *The Great Plains* (1931), asked "what happened in American civilization when in its westward progress it emerged from the woods and essayed life on the Plains," where increasing aridity posed unfamiliar challenges? Malin, beginning in the late 1940s, was the first historian to acknowledge the science of ecology, which studies the interactions of plants and animals in their geophysical settings, and to define history as part of that ecology, a study of human adaptation to a shifting environment.[4]

Those beginnings in Turner's frontierism and Roosevelt's conservationism did not have much impact on the prevailing view of historians that history is "past politics," but eventually they led to a subset of political history focused on the making of environmental policy. In 1959 Harvard University Press published Samuel Hays's *Conservation and the Gospel of Efficiency*, a study of the origins of

[2]Opening Address by the President, *Proceedings of a Conference of Governors, May 13–15, 1908* (Washington, D.C.: Government Printing Office, 1909), 3–12.

[3]Frederick Jackson Turner, "Problems in American History" (1892), reprinted in Ray Allen Billington, ed., *Frontier and Section: Selected Essays of Frederick Jackson Turner* (Englewood Cliffs, N.J.: Prentice-Hall, 1961), 30.

[4]Walter Prescott Webb, *The Great Plains* (Boston: Ginn, 1931); James Malin, "Ecology and History" (1950), reprinted in Robert P. Swierenga, ed., *History and Ecology: Studies of the Grassland* (Lincoln: University of Nebraska Press, 1984), 105–11.

the modern movement to conserve such natural resources as forests, water, and the public rangelands. In contrast to interpretations arguing that conservation began as a popular democratic uprising against corporate interests, Hays argued that conservation was a project on the part of scientific elites to achieve planned economic development. Far from being a product of the western grassroots, conservation came from the East and reflected a more urban, post-frontier society. Whatever the merits of Hays's interpretation, the next generation or two would build on his landmark book a full-blown history of "the environmental management state."[5]

A different outgrowth of the frontier school of history, one little concerned with building bridges to ecology or examining the role of science in environmental policies, was a series of works appearing in post–World War II era intellectual and cultural history that became classic texts in American studies. The texts looked to nature and the land as keys to the nation's imaginative life and cultural exceptionalism. Perry Miller, widely known as a historian of Puritanism, traced that religion's development as it confronted the New World wilderness and its transmutation into a highly spiritualized celebration of America as "nature's nation." Henry Nash Smith's study of western mythology, *Virgin Land* (1950), emphasized how powerful an influence "the physical fact of the continent" had on people's imaginations, a theme that David Potter, in *People of Plenty* (1954), Leo Marx, in *The Machine in the Garden* (1967), and Roderick Nash, in *Wilderness and the American Mind* (1973), expanded into an eco-interpretation of national culture. Nature for all these historians was a social construct, an idea whose meaning could change radically over time, but they also regarded nature as an independent material force that left an imprint on literature and popular thinking as well as on institutions and politics.[6]

---

[5]Samuel P. Hays, *Conservation and the Gospel of Efficiency: The Progressive Conservation Movement, 1890–1920* (Cambridge, Mass.: Harvard University Press, 1959). Hays's graduate-school adviser was Frederick Merk, who had been Turner's student. The phrase "environmental management state" comes from Adam Rome, "Review Essay: Environmental Perspectives on Modern America," *Environmental History* 7 (April 2002): 304. Recent important works on this subject include Paul Hirt, *A Conspiracy of Optimism: Management of the National Forests since World War Two* (Lincoln: University of Nebraska Press, 1994); David Stradling, *Smokestacks and Progressives: Environmentalists, Engineers, and Air Quality in America, 1881–1951* (Baltimore: Johns Hopkins University Press, 1999); Kendrick Clements, *Hoover, Conservation, and Consumerism: Engineering the Good Life* (Lawrence: University Press of Kansas, 2000); Karen Merrill, *Public Lands and Political Meaning: Ranchers, the Government, and the Property between Them* (Berkeley: University of California Press, 2002).

[6]Perry Miller, *Errand into the Wilderness* (Cambridge, Mass.: Harvard University Press, 1956), and *Nature's Nation* (Cambridge, Mass.: Harvard University Press, 1967); Henry Nash Smith, *Virgin Land: The American West as Symbol and Myth* (Cambridge, Mass.: Harvard University Press, 1950); David Potter, *People of Plenty: Economic Abundance and the American Character* (Chicago: University of Chicago Press, 1954); Leo Marx, *The Machine in the Garden: Technology and the Pastoral Ideal in America* (New York: Oxford University Press, 1967); Roderick Nash, *Wilderness and the American Mind* (New Haven, Conn.: Yale University Press, 1973) and subsequent editions.

Marginal or mainstream, those early environmental approaches to American history were nearly buried by the early 1970s as historians turned away from politics to embrace the new social history, with the rallying cry of "race, class, and gender." The only issue that mattered, many argued, was the struggle between oppressors and oppressed, not the one between humans and nature. Yet national and world events were pushing scholars once more to take the natural world seriously. Scientists such as Rachel Carson, Paul Ehrlich, Barry Commoner, and Edward O. Wilson pointed to a set of global environmental concerns: not only the older problem of resource scarcity caused by runaway economic growth but also a newer problem of runaway technology that was making the earth into an artificial habitat untested for evolutionary fitness. Conservation became environmentalism, and the new targets were man-made threats to the health of all organisms.[7] In *Silent Spring* (1962) Carson warned of a "chemical barrage" that "has been hurled against the fabric of life."[8] She wrote against pesticides, radioactivity, and air and water pollutants that were endangering the planet's livability. Worries about those toxic substances joined with fears of nuclear annihilation, land degradation, and mass species extinction to redraw the boundaries of historical research. The study of the human past, some historians once more began to argue, should not limit itself merely to social relations; it should also try to address the winds of economic and technological change and their impact on the natural world. This shift of perspective would be nothing less than revolutionary.

Environmental history in the United States thus emerged out of long-established public concerns and owed much to scientists' playing the role of social reformers. Above all, it began as a study of the relationship between *ecology*, a shorthand term for all the natural systems that have evolved on Earth, and *economy*, the ways in which societies try to turn nature into consumable products, beginning with basic nutrition and expanding to an infinite list of modern "wants."

This ecology-economy model was one I followed in two books: *Dust Bowl* (1979), a study of the effects of commercial agriculture on the Southern Plains, and *Rivers of Empire* (1985), which dealt with the role of capital and the state in developing water resources in the arid West. Both books owed much to Webb, Malin, and Hays, but they were conceived in a more critical era and reflect the

---

[7]The exact meanings of such labels as "conservation," "preservation," and "environmentalism" are not easy to pin down. *Conservation* often refers to the prudent use of natural resources and *preservation* to protecting wild and beautiful places from exploitation. But preservationists sometimes call themselves conservationists, too. *Environmentalism*, in its post–World War II meaning, evokes a sense of man-made threats to health and life from pollution, nuclear weapons, overpopulation, or resource depletion.

[8]Rachel Carson, *Silent Spring* (Boston: Houghton Mifflin, 1962), 297. See also Paul Ehrlich, *The Population Bomb* (New York: Ballantine Books, 1968); Barry Commoner, *The Closing Circle: Nature, Man and Technology* (New York: Knopf, 1971); E. O. Wilson, ed., *Biodiversity* (Washington, D.C.: National Academy Press, 1986). On the transition from conservation to environmentalism, see Samuel P. Hays, *Beauty, Health, and Permanence: Environmental Politics in the United States, 1955–1985* (New York: Cambridge University Press, 1987), 13–40.

fact that so many development projects around the world had gone awry. William Cronon's best-selling *Changes in the Land* (1983) and *Nature's Metropolis* (1991) are also studies of how modern capital has tried to reorganize natural systems — New England invaded by resource-hungry colonists, midwestern prairies and Great Lakes forests plowed up and cut down during the nineteenth century — into what Cronon called "second nature," a landscape redesigned for economic rationality. A similar focus on the conflict between economy and ecology can be found in Arthur McEvoy's *The Fisherman's Problem* (1986), on the collapse of California's riverine and oceanic fisheries; Carolyn Merchant's *Ecological Revolutions* (1989), which presents a theory of revolutions in land use; and Theodore Steinberg's *Nature Incorporated* (1991), on the role of nature in industrialization, and *Down to Earth* (2002), a comprehensive reinterpretation of American history from the perspective of ecology and political economy.[9]

That ecology and economy can exist harmoniously on the North American continent, in what moderns call "sustainable development," is a more recent theme among environmental historians, a response to objections that environmental history is concerned with disaster and decline only. Brian Donahue's *The Great Meadow* (2004), a richly detailed and carefully mapped study of the successful adaptation of English farming to Concord, Massachusetts, offers one such example of sustainable land use in the premarket colonial era. Geoff Cunfer, in his *On the Great Plains* (2005), makes a similar claim of successful ecological adaptation for a modern market-based agricultural economy.[10]

Most environmental historians of the United States, however, have turned to non-European premodern societies for lessons in sustainability. Such societies include those created by Native Americans before European contact. Indians, over more than ten thousand years of presence on the continent, provide many compelling examples of alternative ways of living on the land. What began as a tendency to idealize Indian relations with nature, however, has increasingly become a darker tale of Indians' mass extinction of ancient megafauna, persistent precontact warfare over resources, wholesale burning of vegetation, and surprisingly ready accommodation to market incentives. No longer do all the indigenous

---

[9]Donald Worster, *Dust Bowl: The Southern Plains in the 1930s* (New York: Oxford University Press, 1979), and *Rivers of Empire: Water, Aridity, and the Growth of the American West* (New York: Pantheon, 1985); William Cronon, *Changes in the Land: Indians, Colonists, and the Ecology of New England* (New York: Hill and Wang, 1983), and *Nature's Metropolis: Chicago and the Great West* (New York: W. W. Norton, 1991); Carolyn Merchant, *Ecological Revolutions: Nature, Gender, and Science in New England* (Chapel Hill: University of North Carolina Press, 1989); Arthur McEvoy, *The Fisherman's Problem: Ecology and Law in California Fisheries, 1850–1980* (New York: Cambridge University Press, 1986); Theodore Steinberg, *Nature Incorporated: Industrialization and the Waters of New England* (New York: Cambridge University Press, 1991), and *Down to Earth: Nature's Role in American History* (New York: Oxford University Press, 2002, 2009).

[10]Brian Donahue, *The Great Meadow: Farmers and the Land in Colonial Massachusetts* (New Haven, Conn.: Yale University Press, 2004); Geoff Cunfer, *On the Great Plains: Agriculture and Environment* (College Station: Texas A&M University Press, 2005).

ways of getting a living seem so wonderfully sustainable. Richard White's admiring study of Indian tribes' resistance to an invasive Euro-American economy (*The Roots of Dependency* [1983]) has been significantly qualified by Dan Flores, Elliott West, and Shepherd Krech, whose Indians seem less skilled managers of the environment and more like the rest of humanity.[11]

No one has done more than White to bridge the gap separating the new social history from the environmental field.[12] In his provocative 1995 essay, "Are You an Environmentalist or Do You Work for a Living?" he accused white environmentalists, past and present, of a lack of sympathy and respect for working people. He particularly became the critic of preservationists, whose project of saving wild lands, endangered species, and national parks seemed to him misguided or nostalgic. This widely admired historian was intent on purging history of the wrong kind of environmentalism and bringing environmental history more into line with the moral agenda of social history, where "justice" (a notoriously spacious word) trumped all other values.[13]

White's critique of environmentalism raised important philosophical questions that historians as much as the public in general have debated: Does nature present any independent value or exhibit any autonomy beyond humans, and

[11]Richard White, *The Roots of Dependency: Subsistence, Environment, and Social Change among the Choctaws, Pawnees, and Navajos* (Lincoln: University of Nebraska Press, 1983); Dan Flores, "Bison Ecology and Bison Diplomacy" (1991), reprinted in *The Natural West: Environmental History in the Great Plains and Rocky Mountains* (Norman: University of Oklahoma Press, 2001), 50–70; Elliott West, *The Way West: Essays on the Central Plains* (Albuquerque: University of New Mexico Press, 1995), 13–50; Shepherd Krech, *The Ecological Indian: Myth and History* (New York: W. W. Norton, 1999). For a non–North American example of a sustainable society, see Robert Netting, *Balancing on an Alp: Ecological Change and Continuity in a Swiss Mountain Community* (New York: Cambridge University Press, 1981). Also see Mark Elvin, "Three Thousand Years of Unsustainable Growth: China's Environment from Archaic Times to the Present," *East Asia History* 6 (November 1993): 7–46.

[12]The integration of cultural, social, and environmental history has also engaged a few southern historians, most notably Jack Temple Kirby, whose personalized, story-rich *Mockingbird Song: Ecological Landscapes of the South* (Chapel Hill: University of North Carolina Press, 2006) suggests a new model for regional studies.

[13]Richard White, "'Are You an Environmentalist or Do You Work for a Living?'" in William Cronon, ed., *Uncommon Ground: Toward Reinventing Nature* (New York: W. W. Norton, 1995), 171–85. See also William Cronon, "The Trouble with Wilderness; or, Getting Back to the Wrong Nature," in ibid., 69–90. For other works debunking preservationists, see Karl Jacoby, *Crimes against Nature: Squatters, Poachers, Thieves, and the Hidden History of American Conservation* (Berkeley: University of California Press, 2001); Mark Spence, *Dispossessing the Wilderness: Indian Removal and the Making of the National Parks* (New York: Oxford University Press, 1999); Louis Warren, *The Hunter's Game: Poachers and Conservationists in Twentieth-Century America* (New Haven, Conn.: Yale University Press, 1997). For a more sympathetic analysis, see Paul Sutter, *Driven Wild: How the Fight against Automobiles Launched the Modern Wilderness Movement* (Seattle: University of Washington Press, 2002). Melissa Leach and Cathy Green have provided a useful overview of another link with social history: "Gender and Environmental History: From Representation of Women and Nature to Gender Analysis of Ecology and Politics," *Environment and History* 3 (October 1997): 343–70.

where and how should we try to protect that nature from exploitation? Can science provide a reliable description of the natural order, or is the idea of nature merely a fleeting reflection of the many cultures and subcultures that pass before us? Most environmentalists, whether laymen or scientists, have said emphatically yes to the need to protect the integrity of nature and yes to relying on scientific guidance in doing so. In contrast, it was not always clear what White and other critics wanted in the way of environmental policies or historical reinterpretations. Did they regard the setting aside of national parks or wildlife refuges as a mistake to be remedied? Did they believe that preserved lands should be given back to the Indians or opened to native hunting, corporate mining, or oil drilling? Would they dismiss science altogether as an authority in environmental debates and treat it as merely another form of cultural imperialism? What was clear was that a number of historians were unwilling to distinguish between what is "natural" and what is "artificial." How far back into the continent's history do we have to go, they asked, to find a "pristine" nature free of human influence? Has not the continent everywhere been an "artifact" since humans first arrived here?

In writing about the Columbia River, White did not deny that "a state of nature" had existed before the arrival of humans; he allowed that the river had been radically rearranged by technology. But he insisted that such man-made interventions as dams, fish hatcheries, cities, and pulp mills should now be considered part of the river itself, which he identified as a hybrid environment, an "organic machine."[14] Few if any historians would disagree that a line cannot easily be drawn between nature and culture, but not all were convinced that calling a man-made structure like Bonneville Dam a work of nature made it so. Whether White's "hybrid" metaphor was fertile or was as sterile as a mule, whether it offered a way out of that ancient conundrum, what is nature and what is not, are questions that have not been settled, and there is no consensus in environmental history on what nature refers to or who is best qualified to define it.

This was mainly a debate over the politics of environmentalism, the kind of values dispute that historians of Jeffersonian America or the Cold War or labor–management relations will quickly recognize. What it demonstrated on the positive side was how important the discourse about nature had been in the nation's past and how much more animated it had become in recent years. The debate sent historians back to look at early conservationists, whom they discovered had held surprisingly complicated attitudes toward nature, technology, capitalism, religion, gender, ethnicity, and social class. That complexity of thinking had intensified with the emergence of modern environmentalism and had been aided by

---

[14]Richard White, *The Organic Machine: The Remaking of the Columbia River* (New York: Hill and Wang, 1995), 110. See also his review essay, "From Wilderness to Hybrid Landscapes: The Cultural Turn in Environmental History," *Historian* 66 (2004): 557–64; Mark Fiege, *Irrigated Eden: The Making of an Agricultural Landscape in the American West* (Seattle: University of Washington Press, 1999); Douglas Sackman, *Orange Empire: California and the Fruits of Eden* (Berkeley: University of California Press, 2005).

historians' asking what environmentalism's moral vision should be, what it means to be human or natural, and which environments need attention.[15]

Among the environments recently drawing attention from environmental historians have been the city and the suburb. Scholars have discovered that cities are not only a significant force in how all lands, even the most remote wilderness areas, are used or preserved, but that they also are places where nature continues to exercise at least a modicum of power (for example, Hurricane Katrina's devastation of New Orleans) and continues to maintain an ineradicable presence. Nature is more than a distant prairie or woodland; nature includes the air and water that flow in and around our habitations, the fossil fuels that keep our cities humming, and all those plants, animals, and microorganisms that have found urban niches of their own. Scholars like Kathleen Brosnan, Andrew Hurley, Martin Melosi, Adam Rome, Joel Tarr, Ari Kelman, and Craig Colton have broadened our thinking about the human–nature interface and have demonstrated that human settlements, like human economies, are collective entities that must feed and excrete. In that metabolic process cities, like farms or factories, show their embeddedness in nature, if they are not nature itself.[16]

So many philosophical debates and competing themes may suggest a general state of confusion among environmental historians, but that would be too harsh a reading. Environmental history has been open to dissent and exploration, but it has consistently pursued a mission of bringing the material reality of the natural world into the study of the human past. Without such a mission, the new field of study would soon have vanished. Its most innovative work has not been telling stories of what nature has meant to people or exploring the political history of environmentalism. Nor has environmental history aspired to become a neatly circumscribed or esoteric subspecialty stuck out on the edges of the professional mainstream. Instead, it has sought nothing less than to put the study of history on a new foundation.

---

[15]Examples of recent biographies that have given us a far more nuanced view of the conservation and environmentalist tradition include Linda Lear, *Rachel Carson: Witness for Nature* (New York: Henry Holt, 1997); David Lowenthal, *George Perkins Marsh: Prophet of Conservation* (Seattle: University of Washington Press, 2000); Char Miller, *Gifford Pinchot and the Making of Modern Environmentalism* (Washington, D.C.: Island Press, 2001); Donald Worster, *A River Running West: The Life of John Wesley Powell* (New York: Oxford University Press, 2001).

[16]Kathleen Brosnan, *Uniting Mountain and Plain: Cities, Law, and Environmental Change along the Front Range* (Albuquerque: University of New Mexico Press, 2002); Andrew Hurley, *Environmental Inequalities: Class, Race, and Industrial Pollution in Gary, Indiana, 1945–1980* (Chapel Hill: University of North Carolina Press, 1995); Martin Melosi, *Garbage in the Cities: Refuse, Reform, and the Environment* (Pittsburgh: University of Pittsburgh Press, 2005); Adam Rome, *The Bulldozer in the Countryside: Suburban Sprawl and the Rise of American Environmentalism* (New York: Cambridge University Press, 2001); Joel Tarr, *The Search for the Ultimate Sink: Urban Pollution in Historical Perspective* (Akron, Ohio: University of Akron Press, 1996); Ari Kelman, *A River and Its City: The Nature of Landscape in New Orleans* (Berkeley: University of California Press, 2003); Craig Colton, *An Unnatural Metropolis: Wresting New Orleans from Nature* (Baton Rouge: Louisiana State University Press, 2005).

Fulfilling that mission requires historians to keep on building bridges to the natural sciences. Now that postmodernism's effort to dethrone the sciences has begun to fade, science appears more than ever to be an indispensable ally for understanding past as well as present environmental change. The theories and methods of the natural sciences are, to be sure, not perfectly reliable, and to some extent they fall and rise with fashion and cultural influence. But, as many environmental historians have long recognized, the sciences offer vast funds of useful knowledge, and increasingly scientists demonstrate a capacity not only to explain the vicissitudes of climate, the evolution of organisms, and the genetic basis of human behavior, but also to suggest new insights into the social dimensions of those physical realities, as Carson, Commoner, and Ehrlich did in their influential works.

The literature of environmental history includes plenty of examples of science-based and science-literate work. For example, Alfred Crosby's *Ecological Imperialism* (1986), which drew on the ecology of species invasions, conflict, and struggle, has radically changed the way we understand the coming of Europeans to the New World. Stephen Pyne's many erudite volumes on the history of fire and fire-made landscapes, natural and anthropogenic, have given us a deeper awareness of the dynamic history of the planet. John McNeill, in *Something New Under the Sun* (2000), has combed through the scientific literature to assemble a comprehensive measure of the ecological changes experienced in the twentieth century, including increases in lead and carbon dioxide emissions and decreases in cropland and forest cover. On a smaller scale, Nancy Langston's study of forest management and mismanagement in the Pacific Northwest's Blue Mountains draws heavily on the sciences. Like Crosby, Pyne, and McNeill, Langston ignores conventional political units that have so monopolized the historian's attention and lets nature suggest the terrain. Taken together, these scientifically informed historians demonstrate that there are other scales and other boundaries—local, regional, continental, or global—worthy of consideration, scales that may altogether ignore the nation-state and its constricting hold over our conceptualization of the past.[17]

[17]Alfred Crosby, *Ecological Imperialism: The Biological Expansion of Europe, 900–1900* (New York: Cambridge University Press, 1986); Stephen Pyne, *Fire: A Brief History* (Seattle: University of Washington Press, 2001), and *Awful Splendour: A Fire History of Canada* (Vancouver, Canada: UBC Press, 2007); John McNeill, *Something New under the Sun: An Environmental History of the Twentieth-Century World* (New York: W. W. Norton, 2000); Nancy Langston, *Forest Dreams, Forest Nightmares: The Paradox of Old Growth in the Inland West* (Seattle: University of Washington Press, 1995). Langston's essay, "People and Nature," in the textbook *Ecology* by Stanley Dodson, Timothy Allen, Stephen Carpenter, Anthony Ives, Robert Jeanne, James Kitchell, and Monica Turner (New York: Oxford University Press, 1998), 25–76, is a fine example of integrating science and history. For examples of scientists venturing into history, see Emily W. B. Russell, *People and the Land through Time: Linking Ecology and History* (New Haven, Conn.: Yale University Press, 1997); David R. Foster and John D. Aber, eds., *Forests in Time: The Environmental Consequences of 1,000 Years of Change in New England* (New Haven, Conn.: Yale University Press, 2004); Jared Diamond, *Guns, Germs, and Steel: The Fates of Human Societies* (New York: W. W. Norton, 1997), and *Collapse: How Societies Choose to Fail or Succeed* (New York: Viking, 2005).

As part of that renewed embrace of science, environmental historians have most recently gravitated toward disease, health, and evolution as unifying concepts in the field. Health is never simply a concept free of cultural perceptions and understandings, and its history has stimulated important new work on how Americans have thought about their own health and the health of places they inhabited.[18] At the same time, health can be measured by rigorous scientific methods for human populations and for grasslands, oceans, and the biosphere. Health and sickness are polarities that govern nature as well as society. They lead us to conceive of human history as part and parcel of the natural world, netted together by a long evolutionary past.

Thus, environmental historians have arrived at a point of rediscovering what the wildlife ecologist Aldo Leopold understood back in the 1940s when he looked at the sometimes ravaged American landscape and what Rachel Carson understood a decade or two later when she sat down to write about pesticides: The health of people and land are intertwined, in the past as they are today. Health, Leopold wrote, is the capacity of an organism for "internal self renewal." Its opposite, sickness or disease, is a decline in that capacity. Conservation "is our effort to understand and preserve this capacity."[19] This is a broader definition of conservation than Theodore Roosevelt had in mind; it moves us beyond the role of resources in national development and puts humans directly and intimately within their surroundings. Environmental history is still growing, exploring, and debating what it offers in the way of a new perspective on the past. But that turn toward a broad, comprehensive study of the health of people intertwined with that of land is an important development. It is leading a new generation of historians to look at the land–people nexus in ways that Frederick Jackson Turner never quite grasped.

[18]Conevery Bolton Valencius, *The Health of the Country: How American Settlers Understood Themselves and Their Land* (New York: Basic Books, 2002); Linda Nash, *Inescapable Ecologies: A History of Environment, Disease, and Knowledge* (Berkeley: University of California Press, 2006). For a wide-ranging discussion of this theme, see Greg Mitman, "In Search of Health: Landscape and Disease in American Environmental History," *Environmental History* 10 (April 2005): 184–210.

[19]Aldo Leopold, *Sand County Almanac* (New York: Oxford University Press, 1949), 221.

Alan M. Kraut

A Century of Scholarship in American Immigration and Ethnic History

Ship manifests for April 17, 1907, indicate that 11,747 newcomers passed through the Great Hall of New York's Ellis Island, making that day the single busiest in the sixty-two-year history of the nation's flagship immigration depot. More than 1.3 million newcomers arrived on America's shores that year. Over a million of them were processed on Ellis Island alone. Immigrants coming from southern and eastern Europe, parts of Asia, and Latin America arrived by steamship. Others came by rail; many Mexicans and Canadians walked across the border. Unlike today, when Mexicans, Chinese, Indians, and Pakistanis dominate the flow, the leading donor nations in 1907 were Austria-Hungary, Italy, and Russia. Between 1880 and the early 1920s, approximately 23.5 million newcomers entered the country. A half-century earlier, between 1840 and 1860, 4.5 million newcomers had arrived, mostly Irish, Germans, and Scandinavians. Already a nation of nations, the United States was becoming more so each year.

The United States was being peopled by the other nations of the world, but those who chose to write the history of the country in the nineteenth and early twentieth centuries wrote as little of the immigrant as they did of the slave or laborer or of women. Historians in the nineteenth century, George Bancroft and Francis Parkman, for example, saw all foreign-born people who were not of English heritage like themselves as minor threads in the fabric of the American experience. They viewed the English, French, Dutch, and Spanish as settlers, not immigrants.[1] When later generations of American historians such as Herbert Baxter Adams considered the promise of America, he attributed it to the superiority of earlier white arrivals, especially those of "Teutonic" heritage. Tracing American democracy to the tribes of the great German forests, Adams was apprehensive about whether arrivals who did not share that heritage were capable of appreciating and preserving democracy.[2]

---

[1]George Bancroft, *History of the United States, from the Discovery of the American Continent*, 10 vols. (Boston: Little, Brown, 1834–1875); Francis Parkman, *The Works of Francis Parkman*, 16 vols. (New York: Charles Scribner's Sons, 1915). Not until the end of the twentieth century would slaves be acknowledged as "forced migrants."

[2]Herbert Baxter Adams, "The Germanic Origin of New England Towns. With Notes on Cooperation in University Work," *Johns Hopkins University Studies*, 1st ser., 2 (1882): 1.

If historian Adams was dismissive of late-nineteenth-century newcomers, social scientists such as Robert Park, Louis Wirth, William I. Thomas, and Florian Znaniecki at the University of Chicago were not.[3] These members of the Chicago School brought the insights of sociology, economics, political science, and anthropology to the study of immigrants. They understood immigration as a voluntary movement of peoples from a donor society to a host society in a single linear direction, and a perspective on such movement derived only from the host society. This definition remained in vogue with later scholars, including historians. The writings that emerged from Chicago intellectually nourished the social work of Progressive urban reformers such as Jane Addams, Lillian Wald, and Jacob Riis, who saw understanding migration and migrants as a first step to integrating the newcomers into American society and culture.

In 1912, sociologist Peter Roberts advocated rapid incorporation of newcomers. He wrote, "I believe in the immigrant. He has in him the making of an American, provided a sympathetic hand guides him and smoothes the path which leads to assimilation."[4] Others vehemently disagreed. Two years later, Wisconsin sociologist E. A. Ross concluded that "subcommon" immigrants arriving in the United States might sap the vitality of the American population. He deplored the arrival of the 10 to 20 percent whom he observed to be "hirsute, low-browed, big-faced persons of obviously low mentality."[5] Nor was Ross exceptional in his views. Madison Grant's *The Passing of the Great Race* (1916) synthesized many nativist arguments into a masterful and popular volume on the superiority of heredity over environmental factors in shaping mankind.[6]

Franz Boas, a German Jewish immigrant who taught anthropology at Columbia University, refuted such arguments. Because the slope of the cranium had often been regarded as a reliable indicator of race, Boas measured the skulls of second-generation immigrants and discovered that many no longer physically resembled their parents. Boas concluded that nutrition and other aspects of living conditions determined these "racial characteristics" more than heredity did.[7]

[3]Louis Wirth, *The Ghetto* (Chicago: University of Chicago Press, 1928); Robert E. Park and Herbert A. Miller, *Old World Traits Transplanted* (New York: Harper, 1921); William I. Thomas and Florian Znaniecki, *The Polish Peasant in Europe and America: Monograph of an Immigrant Group*, 5 vols. (Boston: Gorham Press, 1918–1920).

[4]Peter Roberts, *The New Immigration: A Study of the Industrial and Social Life of Southeastern Europeans in America* (New York: Macmillan, 1912).

[5]Edward Alsworth Ross, *The Old World and the New: The Significance of Past and Present Immigration to the American People* (New York: Century, 1914), 285.

[6]Madison Grant, *The Passing of the Great Race* (New York: Charles Scribner's Sons, 1916), 18.

[7]Franz Boas, *The Mind of Primitive Man* (New York: Macmillan, 1911), and "Changes in Bodily Form of Descendants of Immigrants," in *Reports of the Immigration Commission*, 61st Cong., 2nd sess., Senate Document No. 208 (Washington, D.C.: Government Printing Office, 1911), vol. 38.

The importance of environment had long been fundamental to historians' thought. Renowned for his frontier thesis, Frederick Jackson Turner believed in the power of the American environment to transform newcomers. Turner observed, "In the crucible of the frontier the immigrants were Americanized, liberated, and fused into a mixed race, English in neither nationality nor characteristics."[8] On the frontier, migrants, domestic and foreign-born, would vote for representatives and craft constitutions. Moreover, Turner hailed the western frontier as a homogenizer. He believed that the diversity of stocks "with their different habits, morals, and religious doctrines and ideals . . . led to cross-fertilization and the evolution of a profoundly modified society."[9] Turner himself never conducted serious historical studies of immigration. His treatment of ethnic minorities, often appearing in the popular press, was seasoned with commonplace stereotypes and bromides. Italians were to him "quick-witted and supple in morals." Jews he regarded as "thrifty to disgracefulness, while their ability to drive a bargain amounts to genius."[10]

Turner's graduate student, Marcus Lee Hansen, the Wisconsin-born child of a Danish father and a Norwegian mother, was inspired to study immigration by his mentor's confidence in the formative power of the American environment. Hansen believed that newcomers could be readily incorporated into American society to the benefit of both arrivals and hosts.[11] Among Hansen's many scholarly contributions was his observation about how the foreign-born and their descendants related to their immigrant heritage. He observed, "What the son wishes to forget the grandson wishes to remember."[12] Immigrants' children would embrace assimilation, but newcomers' curious grandchildren, comfortable in their American identity, would seek knowledge of the family's roots.[13]

Hansen was hardly alone in his desire to explore immigration's role in American history. In the interwar years, after the highly restrictive Johnson-Reed

[8]Frederick Jackson Turner, "The Significance of the Frontier in American History," in Ray Allen Billington, ed., *Frontier and Section, Selected Essays of Frederick Jackson Turner* (Englewood Cliffs, N.J.: Prentice-Hall, 1961), 51.

[9]Frederick Jackson Turner, *The United States, 1830–1850: The Nation and Its Sections* (New York: P. Smith, 1935), 286.

[10]Quoted in Ray Allen Billington, *Frederick Jackson Turner: Historian, Scholar, Teacher* (New York: Oxford University Press, 1973), 171.

[11]Hansen's *Atlantic Migration, 1607–1860* (Cambridge, Mass.: Harvard University Press, 1940) was published posthumously in 1940 and was awarded the 1941 Pulitzer Prize for history. A second volume, *The Immigrant in American History* (Cambridge, Mass.: Harvard University Press, 1940), was also published posthumously in 1940.

[12]Marcus Lee Hansen, "Who Shall Inherit America?" *Interpreter Releases* 14 (July 1937): 231.

[13]An excellent discussion of Hansen and his contribution to understanding generational differences among newcomers is Peter Kivisto and Dag Blanck, eds., *American Immigrants and Their Generations: Studies and Commentaries on the Hansen Thesis after Fifty Years* (Urbana: University of Illinois Press, 1990).

Immigration Act of 1924 mandated a quota system to curb immigration from southern and eastern Europe, other scholars of northern European parentage also penned works on immigration. These included volumes by George M. Stephenson, Theodore Blegen, and Carl F. Wittke.[14]

In 1951, soon after the end of World War II, Oscar Handlin published *The Uprooted*, a volume that launched a new era in American immigration historiography.[15] Handlin, a scholar of eastern European Jewish heritage, was rooted in the new wave of immigrants that had landed on American shores during the previous half-century. Grounded in the social disorganization model developed by the Chicago School's social scientists, Handlin's almost poetic description of European peasants seeking better lives in the New World was praised for its imagery but criticized for its exaggerations and imprecisions.[16] Clearly, though, Handlin offered a study sympathetic to the dislocation, even tragic isolation, felt by many newcomers who overcame these obstacles only after great struggle. This trajectory had been evident in Handlin's 1941 study of the Irish, *Boston's Immigrants*.[17]

Among Handlin's early critics was Rudolph J. Vecoli in his influential 1964 article "*Contadini* in Chicago: A Critique of *The Uprooted*." Citing the experiences of the Italians who settled in Chicago, Vecoli persuasively refuted Handlin's profile of immigrants, noting in particular that Handlin failed to distinguish among immigrants of different groups who were motivated to migrate by different pushes and pulls and sometimes, as in the case of Italians, preferred seasonal labor migration to permanent emigration until the restrictive legislation of the early 1920s forced them to choose.[18]

Even as Handlin was probing immigration and the immigrant, another eminent scholar was exploring patterns of anti-immigrant sentiment, or nativism, as a perennial element of American culture. John Higham's *Strangers in the Land: Patterns of American Nativism, 1860–1925* (1955) identified three genres of

[14]George M. Stephenson, *History of American Immigration, 1820–1924* (Boston: Ginn, 1926), and *The Religious Aspects of Swedish Immigration: A Study of Immigrant Churches* (Minneapolis: University of Minnesota Press, 1932); Theodore Blegen, *Norwegian Migration to America, 1825–1860* (Northfield, Minn.: Norwegian-American Historical Association, 1931); Carl F. Wittke, *We Who Built America, the Saga of the Immigrant* (New York: Prentice-Hall, 1939).

[15]Oscar Handlin, *The Uprooted: The Epic Story of the Great Migrations That Made the American People* (Boston: Little, Brown, 1951).

[16]The social disorganization model of human behavior posited that in traditional peasant societies the individual was subjected to influences that were consistent and uniform, predictable, and generally the basis of a socially harmonious society. In contrast, modern Western civilization might be characterized as inconsistent, conflict-filled, and disorganized. Immigrants leaving the Old World for the New found themselves battered by the sudden transformation as they moved from the organized to the disorganized social milieu.

[17]Oscar Handlin, *Boston's Immigrants, 1790–1865: A Study in Acculturation* (Cambridge, Mass.: Harvard University Press, 1941).

[18]Rudolph J. Vecoli, "*Contadini* in Chicago: A Critique of *The Uprooted*," *Journal of American History* 51 (1964): 404–17.

nativism: anti-Catholic, racial, and antiradical.[19] Later, Higham concluded that anti-Semitism was a fourth category rather than a subset of either racial or anti-radical nativism.[20] Opposition was hardly from old-stock, white, Anglo-Saxon Protestants alone. Often first- and second-generation newcomers of different groups struggled against each other. Ronald H. Bayor was among the first to treat these intergroup rivalries by exploring the conflicts among New York City's Irish, Germans, Jews, and Italians.[21] Later work by Gary R. Mormino and George E. Pozzetta on Spanish, Cuban, and Italian cigar makers of Tampa suggested that cooperation among different immigrant groups was also possible.[22]

A decade after Handlin, Maldwyn Allen Jones's *American Immigration* (1960) recognized that the foreign-born arrived at different times, but he downplayed the significance of these differences by abandoning the distinction between old immigrants from northern and central Europe and new immigrants from southern and eastern Europe. Jones, a British scholar, emphasized the continuity of the larger social process of immigration.[23] Another British scholar, Philip Taylor, in *The Distant Magnet: European Emigration to the U.S.A.* (1971), also detected more similarities than differences among the experiences of successive immigrant groups.[24] Flawed by a Eurocentrism that largely neglected the significant migration of Asians, Latin Americans, and people from the Caribbean, Taylor's book offers the misleading notion that all those on the move from their respective countries were drawn to the United States. By emphasizing broad social forces that encouraged transoceanic migration, both Jones and Taylor missed the distinctive quality of each group's experiences and the major changes in American society from the 1840s and 1850s, when the Irish and Germans were most numerous among the newcomers, to the end of the nineteenth and early twentieth centuries, when southern and eastern Europeans, Asians, and Latin Americans dominated the flow. Two later overviews, Thomas Archdeacon's *Becoming Americans: An Ethnic History* (1983) and Roger Daniels's *Coming to America: A History of Immigration and Ethnicity in American Life* (1990), corrected such flaws.[25]

[19]John Higham, *Strangers in the Land: Patterns of American Nativism, 1860–1925* (New Brunswick, N.J.: Rutgers University Press, 1955). Earlier anti-Catholicism in the first half of the nineteenth century had been probed by Ray Allen Billington in *The Protestant Crusade, 1800–1860* (New York: Macmillan, 1938).

[20]John Higham, "Another Look at Nativism," in *"Send These to Me," Jews and Other Immigrants in Urban America* (New York: Atheneum, 1975), 102–15.

[21]Ronald H. Bayor, *Neighbors in Conflict: The Irish, Germans, Jews and Italians of New York City, 1929–1941* (Baltimore: Johns Hopkins University Press, 1978).

[22]Gary R. Mormino and George E. Pozzetta, *The Immigrant World of Ybor City: Italians and Their Latin Neighbors in Tampa, 1885–1985* (Urbana: University of Illinois Press, 1987).

[23]Maldwyn Allen Jones, *American Immigration* (Chicago: University of Chicago Press, 1960).

[24]Philip Taylor, *The Distant Magnet: European Emigration to the U.S.A.* (New York: Harper and Row, 1971).

[25]Thomas J. Archdeacon, *Becoming American: An Ethnic History* (New York: Free Press, 1983); Roger Daniels, *Coming to America: A History of Immigration and Ethnicity in American Life* (New York: HarperCollins, 1990).

An increasing number of scholars sought to study immigration as an international phenomenon. In a brilliant 1960 essay, Frank Thistlethwaite turned historians away from a view of immigration as "American fever" and called for a paradigmatic shift that placed migration in a larger international context. He wanted studies of different groups and local conditions that caused people to consider migration as an escape from poverty and persecution, and he urged the study of chain migration patterns to understand where migrants went and why.[26]

From the 1960s through the 1980s an increasing number of scholars had begun to study groups previously neglected in the mainstream narrative of American history—slaves, women, workers, and immigrants. While that mainstream narrative had long been distilled from the words and actions of a white, male, native-born elite, the new paradigm for studying the past, history from the bottom up, required historical studies done from the perspective of previously marginalized groups. There was an explosion of immigration monographs, many of them reflecting Thistlethwaite's sensibilities. A new generation of scholars, many the children or grandchildren of immigrants who arrived in the late nineteenth and early twentieth centuries, was emerging from the nation's finest graduate schools. Monographs by Moses Rischin on the eastern European Jews, Theodore Saloutos on the Greeks, Virginia Yans-McLaughlin on the Italians, and Josef F. Barton on the Italians, Rumanians, and Slovaks are notable examples of such studies.[27] Historians who treated immigrant groups arriving prior to the Civil War included Kerby A. Miller on the Irish, Kathleen Conzen on the Germans, and Jon Gjerde on the Norwegians. Later, Mark Wyman explored the experiences of European immigrants who returned to their homelands.[28] Nor were Asian immigrants

[26] Frank Thistlethwaite, "Migration from Europe Overseas in the Nineteenth and Twentieth Centuries," in Rudolph J. Vecoli and Suzanne M. Sinke, eds., *A Century of European Migrations* (Urbana: University of Illinois Press, 1991), reprinted from Xie Congres International des Sciences Historiques, *Rapports*, Uppsala (1960): 5:32–60.

[27] Moses Rischin, *The Promised City, New York's Jews, 1870–1914* (Cambridge, Mass.: Harvard University Press, 1962); Theodore Saloutos, *The Greeks in the United States* (Cambridge, Mass.: Harvard University Press, 1964); Virginia Yans-McLaughlin, *Family and Community: Italian Immigrants in Buffalo, 1880–1930* (Ithaca, N.Y.: Cornell University Press, 1971); Josef F. Barton, *Peasants and Strangers: Italians, Rumanians, and Slovaks in an American City, 1890–1950* (Cambridge, Mass.: Harvard University Press, 1975). In addition to new work, older monographs were reprinted, especially those written contemporaneously with the turn-of-the-century immigration, such as Robert Foerster, *Italian Emigration of Our Times* (Cambridge, Mass.: Harvard University Press, 1919; reprinted 1968); William I. Thomas and Florian Znaniecki, *The Polish Peasant in Europe and America* (Boston: Graham Press, 1918; reprinted Urbana: University of Illinois Press, 1984); Emily Balch, *Our Slavic Fellow Citizens* (New York: Charities Publication Committee, 1910; reprinted New York: Arno Press, 1969).

[28] Kerby A. Miller, *Emigrants and Exiles: Ireland and the Irish Exodus to North America* (New York: Oxford University Press, 1985); Kathleen Neils Conzen, *Immigrant Milwaukee, 1836–1860: Accommodation and Community in a Frontier City* (Cambridge, Mass.: Harvard University Press, 1976); Jon Gjerde, *From Peasants to Farmers: The Migration from Balestrand, Norway to the Upper Middle West* (Cambridge, Mass.: Cambridge University Press, 1985); Mark Wyman, *Round-Trip to America: The Immigrants Return to Europe, 1880–1930* (Ithaca, N.Y.: Cornell University Press, 1993).

neglected. Betty Lee Sung's work on Chinese immigrants and Harry Kitano's and William Petersen's studies of Japanese arrivals initiated a new era in Asian immigrant studies.[29]

Post–World War II scholarship increasingly emphasized how immigrants were able to make choices that shaped their experience. They could select their destinations, residences, and occupations, for example, but such choices were often circumscribed by larger social forces to which they and their families were subjected. The ebb and flow of commerce, industrial development, and labor limited an individual's options. Social historian Herbert Gutman argued that immigrants—as well as slaves, poor free blacks, and union and nonunion workers—must be understood in terms of how effectively they dealt with large social forces by making deliberate choices among perceived options.[30] Though their options might be limited, immigrants were never reduced to being merely passive victims. Gutman's view informed my own 1982 volume, *The Huddled Masses: The Immigrant in American Society, 1880–1921.* John Bodnar's *The Transplanted: A History of Immigrants in Urban America* (1985) shared that perspective and traced migration decisions in response to capitalism's opportunities to family and community in donor countries.[31]

In the years since these two volumes appeared, immigration and ethnic history has been transformed by reconceptualizations and new approaches. Central to these changes has been the substitution of the term *migration* for *immigration.* The broader perspective of *migration* suggests that the movement of individuals and groups from one place to another may or may not be voluntary and often requires several stages. It is best viewed from a variety of perspectives, not merely that of the host society.

The notion of transnationalism is another key revision to the older immigration paradigm of a one-way flow of migration from donor to host nation. The term *transnationalism* was first used in 1916 by writer and critic Randolph Bourne to describe a cultural pluralism that pushed beyond parochial national boundaries.[32] For Bourne, transnationalism constituted an optimistic vision of a new American cosmopolitanism. However, today's social scientists use the term to describe how migrations often proceed fluidly, swirling in response to broad economic and political forces rather than simply back and forth between two

[29]Betty Lee Sung, *Mountain of Gold: The Story of the Chinese in America* (New York: Macmillan, 1967); Harry Kitano, *Japanese Americans: The Evolution of a Subculture* (New York: Spectrum, 1969); William Petersen, *Japanese Americans: Oppression and Success* (New York: Random House, 1971).

[30]Herbert G. Gutman, "Labor History and the 'Sartre Question,'" *Humanities* I (September/October 1980).

[31]Alan M. Kraut, *The Huddled Masses: The Immigrant in American Society, 1880–1921* (1982; 2nd ed. Wheeling, Ill.: Harlan Davidson, 2001); John Bodnar, *The Transplanted: A History of Immigrants in Urban America* (Bloomington: Indiana University Press, 1985).

[32]Randolph Bourne, "Trans-National America," *Atlantic Monthly* (July 1916): 86–97.

nation-states.[33] Transnational migrants often maintain some combination of the social, political, and cultural networks, activities, and patterns that span borders and nations. They live neither in donor or host societies alone but in both simultaneously.

Today's migration scholars frequently use the term *diaspora* to refer to the dispersal of a population in flight from persecution, starvation, or some other trauma. Students of the Irish migration of the mid-nineteenth century speak of the "Irish diaspora" because Irish migrants pushed by poverty, oppression, and starvation emigrated to a variety of countries, including Canada, Australia, and Latin American countries, not just to the United States.[34]

Finally, the term *incorporation* has increasingly been substituted for the term *assimilation*, although not all scholars agree to do so. In his essential 1964 volume, *Assimilation in American Life: The Role of Race, Religion and National Origins*, sociologist Milton Gordon posited a variety of models by which one American people might be fashioned out of many, including Anglo-conformity, melting pot, and structural pluralism.[35] The notion that all Americans conformed to an English model of society and culture seemed rigidly reductionist. The melting pot model, especially popular after World War II, was derived from J. Hector St. John de Crèvecoeur's eighteenth-century notion of the American as a "new man" possessing a "strange mixture of blood, which you will find in no other country."[36] The model was named after a play about immigrants assimilating, *The Melting Pot* (1908), by a British Jew, Israel Zangwill. Others thought that the most important melting occurred in a "triple melting pot" defined by religion. According to this model, Catholic, Protestant, and Jewish subcultures were three melting pots in which highly diverse groups could find a place. However, the model failed to account for race; African Americans, Asians, and others were often left "unmelted."[37] Gordon's consideration of structural pluralism as the best model was informed by the earlier notion of cultural pluralism developed by

[33]Linda Basch, Nina Glick Schiller, and Cristina Szanton Blanton, *Nations Unbound: Transnational Projects, Postcolonial Predicaments, and Deterritorialized Nation-States* (Amsterdam: Gordon and Breach Publishers, 1994), and Basch, Schiller, and Blanton, eds., *Towards a Transnational Perspective on Migration, Race, Class, Ethnicity and Nationalism Reconsidered* (New York: New York Academy of Science, 1992).

[34]Robin Cohen, *Global Diasporas: An Introduction* (Seattle: University of Washington Press, 1997).

[35]Milton M. Gordon, *Assimilation in American Life: The Role of Race, Religion, and National Origins* (New York: Oxford University Press, 1964).

[36]J. Hector St. John Crèvecoeur, *Letters from an American Farmer* (New York: Albert and Charles Boni, 1925), 54–55.

[37]Will Herberg, *Protestant, Catholic, Jew* (New York: Doubleday and Company, 1955). Ruby Jo Reeves Kennedy, "Single or Triple Melting Pot? Intermarriage Trends in New Haven, 1870–1940," *American Journal of Sociology* 49 (January 1944): 331–39, and "Single or Triple Melting Pot? Intermarriage in New Haven, 1870–1950," *American Journal of Sociology* 58 (July 1952): 56–59.

1920s philosopher Horace Kallen.[38] The separation of Americans by religion, occupation, and class as well as culture accounted for the diversity Gordon said he observed.[39]

A fourth model, the pluralist integration model (or "salad bowl model," as some call it), was advanced by historian John Higham. Seeking to account for both the integrative power of American culture and the distinctiveness of different groups' identities and experiences, plural integrationists suggest that, as a salad, American society and culture constitute a single entity whose component parts can still be clearly identified.[40] Scholars uncomfortable with the problematic notion of one people absorbing another, as implied by the term *assimilation*, have sought other words to describe the process; still, scholars such as Russell A. Kazal continue to find the term *assimilation* a useful characterization of how the American population has been forged.[41]

This fresh perspective on the movement of peoples and their presence in the American population has been complemented by the increasing attention paid to ethnicity and race as factors in shaping the experience of newcomers to the United States. Immigration scholars interested in when newcomers ceased being foreigners argued that there was an intermediate stage before newcomers and their children were fully assimilated. They dubbed this intermediate identity "ethnic American." In a seminal 1990 paper, "The Invention of Ethnicity: A Perspective from the USA," five scholars—Kathleen Neils Conzen, David A. Gerber, Ewa Morawska, George E. Pozzetta, and Rudolph J. Vecoli—explored the process whereby ethnicity is formed in the United States. They concluded that "ethnicity itself is to be understood as a cultural construction accomplished over historical time. Ethnic groups in modern settings are constantly recreating themselves and ethnicity is continuously being reinvented in response to changing realities both within the group and the host society." These scholars perceived a dynamic process whereby "ethnic group boundaries . . . must be repeatedly renegotiated, while expressive symbols of ethnicity (ethnic traditions) must be repeatedly reinterpreted." Immigrant groups were hardly homogeneous upon their arrival, and after arrival the newcomers negotiated their identity not only with the dominant culture but also among various other immigrant groups. It was by such a process, for example, that a Sicilian from a small village became an "Italian American" and was expected by the native-born to be familiar with the customs and cuisine of Romans and Genoese as if they were his own. Ethnic

[38]Horace Kallen, *Culture and Democracy in the United States* (New York: Boni and Liveright, 1924).

[39]Gordon, *Assimilation in American Life*, 159.

[40]Higham, *"Send These to Me,"* 140.

[41]Russell A. Kazal, "Revisiting Assimilation: The Rise, Fall, and Reappraisal of a Concept in American Ethnic History," *American Historical Review* 100 (April 1995): 437–71.

identifications and their renegotiation were recognized by scholars, then, as crucial to the larger assimilation or incorporation process.[42]

As some scholars wrestled with definitions of assimilation and ethnicity, others addressed the experiences of groups swelling the migration stream. Inspired by the civil rights movement of the 1960s, post-1970 migration trends, and a new generation of immigration scholars, many of them Latino or Asian, late-twentieth-century and early twenty-first-century scholarship has paid increasing attention to migration from the Pacific Rim, the Caribbean, and Latin America. Volumes by John Kuo Wei Tchen, Sucheng Chan, Erika Lee, Madeline Y. Hsu, and Eiichiro Azuma are among the best of the new studies of the Asian immigrant experience.[43] Chan's volume on the Chinese in California agriculture also shifted the story of the Asian immigration experience from the East Coast urban-industrial environment to western rural lands.

The size of the legal and undocumented migration from Mexico and the growth in the influence of Latino culture in the United States have encouraged scholarship about all Latino groups, especially about the Mexicans. Some of the best work on Mexicans in the United States includes the work of Albert Camarillo, Mario T. Garcia, and Ricardo Romo.[44] Vicki Ruiz added an important gender component to the corpus with her 1987 work *Cannery Women, Cannery Lives: Mexican Women, Unionization, and the California Food Processing Industry, 1930–1950.* David Montejano's *Anglos and Mexicans in the Making of Texas,*

[42]Kathleen Neils Conzen, David A. Gerber, Ewa Morawska, George E. Pozzetta, and Rudolph Vecoli, "The Invention of Ethnicity: A Perspective from the USA," *Altreitalie* 3 (April 1990): 37–62. For a case study see Timothy J. Meagher, *Inventing Irish America: Generation, Class and Ethnic Identity in a New England City, 1880–1928* (South Bend, Ind.: Notre Dame University Press, 2000).

[43]Paul C. P. Sui, edited by John Kuo Wei Tchen, *The Chinese Laundryman: A Study of Social Isolation* (New York: New York University Press, 1988), and Tchen, *New York before Chinatown: Orientalism and the Shaping of American Culture* (Baltimore: Johns Hopkins University Press, 2001); Sucheng Chan, *This Bittersweet Soil: The Chinese in California Agriculture, 1860–1910* (Berkeley: University of California Press, 1986); Erika Lee, *At America's Gates: Chinese Immigration during the Exclusion Era, 1882–1943* (Chapel Hill: University of North Carolina Press, 2003); Madeline Y. Hsu, *Dreaming of Gold, Dreaming of Home: Transnationalism and Migration between the United States and South China, 1882–1943* (Stanford, Calif.: Stanford University Press, 2000); Eiichiro Azuma, *Between Two Empires: Race, History, and Transnationalism in Japanese America* (New York: Oxford University Press, 2005).

[44]Albert Camarillo, *Chicanos in a Changing Society: From Mexican Pueblos to American Barrios in Santa Barbara and Southern California, 1848–1930* (Cambridge, Mass.: Harvard University Press, 1979; reprinted Dallas: Southern Methodist University Press, 2005); Mario T. Garcia, *Desert Immigrants: The Mexicans of El Paso, 1880–1920* (New Haven, Conn.: Yale University Press, 1981), and *Mexican Americans: Leadership, Ideology, and Identity, 1930–1960* (New Haven, Conn.: Yale University Press, 1989); Ricardo Romo, *History of a Barrio, East Los Angeles* (Austin: University of Texas Press, 1983).

1836–1986 (1987) treats relations between Anglos and Mexicans, while George J. Sánchez's *Becoming Mexican American: Ethnicity, Culture and Identity in Chicano Los Angeles, 1900–1945* (1993) treats the development of a Mexican American ethnicity. Zaragosa Vargas's 1993 volume, *Proletarians of the North*, offers a valuable study of Mexicans not in the fields as migrant laborers but as industrial workers outside the Southwest. Neil Foley's volume on race and ethnicity in Texas, *The White Scourge: Mexicans, Blacks, and Poor Whites in Texas Cotton Culture* (1997), is an especially nuanced and sophisticated discussion of multiracial relations. Racial complexities complicating the migration experience are also the subject of literature on the Caribbean migration, including Irma Watkins-Owens's *Blood Relations: Caribbean Immigrants and the Harlem Community, 1900–1930* (1996) and Mary C. Waters's *Black Identities: West Indian Immigrant Dreams and American Realities* (1999).[45]

Scholars, many of them social scientists or social reformers, had begun to focus on the experience of women immigrants in the early part of the twentieth century.[46] Later in the twentieth century, female immigrants were often included in the scholarship on women and work, such as the studies by Leslie Woodstock Tentler, Alice Kessler-Harris, and Eileen Boris.[47] During the 1970s and 1980s, a new generation of women's historians, feminist scholars, and experts on particular immigrant groups shed fresh light on immigrant women. Donna R. Gabaccia's *From the Other Side: Women, Gender, and Immigrant Life in the U.S., 1820–1990* (1994) is an important overview. Other scholars focused on women in

[45]Vicki L. Ruiz, *Cannery Women, Cannery Lives: Mexican Women, Unionization, and the California Food Processing Industry, 1930–1950* (Albuquerque: University of New Mexico Press, 1987), and *From Out of the Shadows: Mexican Women in Twentieth-Century America* (New York: Oxford University Press, 1998); David Montejano, *Anglos and Mexicans in the Making of Texas, 1836–1986* (Austin: University of Texas Press, 1987); George J. Sánchez, *Becoming Mexican American: Ethnicity, Culture and Identity in Chicano Los Angeles, 1900–1945* (New York: Oxford University Press, 1993); Zaragosa Vargas, *Proletarians of the North: A History of Mexican Industrial Workers in Detroit and the Midwest, 1917–1933* (Berkeley: University of California Press, 1993); Neil Foley, *The White Scourge: Mexicans, Blacks, and Poor Whites in Texas Cotton Culture* (Berkeley: University of California Press, 1997); Irma Watkins-Owens, *Blood Relations: Caribbean Immigrants and the Harlem Community, 1900–1930* (Bloomington: Indiana University Press, 1996); Mary C. Waters, *Black Identities: West Indian Immigrant Dreams and American Realities* (Cambridge, Mass.: Harvard University Press, 1999).

[46]Elizabeth Beadsley Butler, *Woman and Her Trades: Pittsburgh, 1907–1908* (New York: Charities Publication Committee, 1909); Louise Odencrantz, *Italian Women in Industry* (New York: Russell Sage Foundation, 1919); Bessie Pehotsky, *The Slavic Immigrant Woman* (Cincinnati: Powell and White, 1925); Mary Van Kleeck, *Artificial Flower Makers* (New York: Russell Sage Foundation, 1913); Louise C. Odencrantz, *Italian Women in Industry: A Study in Conditions in New York City* (New York: Russell Sage Foundation, 1919).

[47]Leslie Woodstock Tentler, *Wage-Earning Women: Industrial Work and Family Life in the United States, 1900–1930* (New York: Oxford University Press, 1979); Alice Kessler-Harris, *Out of Work: A History of Wage-Earning Women in the United States* (New York: Oxford University Press, 1982); Eileen Boris, *Home to Work: Motherhood and the Politics of Industrial Homework in the United States* (New York: Cambridge University Press, 1994).

particular immigrant groups.[48] Recent scholarship is also treating long neglected topics such as marriage and desertion.[49]

Race more than gender occupied center stage beginning in the 1980s. A new generation of scholars argued that race was the most crucial element of an individual immigrant's ethnic identity in determining how he or she would be received by native-born Caucasian Americans.[50] In the vanguard of this fresh scholarly sensibility were the architects of "whiteness studies." Whiteness scholars contend that the fundamental partition in American life has been racial. The definitive quality of race as a social category was not news. Gunner Myrdal's 1944 classic study, *An American Dilemma,* had opened a new era in the study of ethnicity by examining the centrality of race.[51] However, what the whiteness scholars observed was that being defined as white was synonymous with holding power in American life. European immigrants soon after arrival understood that to make common cause with African Americans, Chinese, or Latinos condemned them to the category of powerlessness and society's bottom rung. Racial categories and hierarchies trumped class solidarity, according to Alexander Saxton and David Roediger. Within a generation after arrival, newcomers rejected alliances of the oppressed and instead choose membership in the dominant "white fraternity."[52] If Latinos, Asians, and Africans could not become white, at least Irish, Italians

---

[48]Donna Gabaccia, *From the Other Side: Women, Gender, and Immigrant Life in the U.S., 1820–1990* (Bloomington: Indiana University Press, 1994); also Gabaccia, ed., *Seeking Common Ground: Multidisciplinary Studies of Immigrant Women in the United States* (Westport, Conn.: Praeger, 1992); Hasia Diner, *Erin's Daughters in America: Irish Immigrant Women in the Nineteenth Century* (Baltimore: Johns Hopkins University Press, 1983); Elizabeth Ewen, *Immigrant Women in the Land of Dollars: Life and Culture on the Lower East Side, 1890–1925* (New York: Monthly Review Press, 1985); Susan A. Glenn, *Daughters of the Shtetl: Life and Labor in the Immigrant Generation* (Ithaca, N.Y.: Cornell University Press, 1990); Miriam Cohen, *Workshop to Office: Two Generations of Italian Women in New York City, 1900–1950* (Ithaca, N.Y.: Cornell University Press, 1992); Ruiz, *Cannery Women, Cannery Lives;* Judy Yung, *Unbound Feet: A Social History of Chinese Women in San Francisco* (Berkeley: University of California Press, 1995).

[49]Anna R. Igra, *Wives without Husbands: Marriage, Desertion and Welfare in New York, 1900–1935* (Chapel Hill: University of North Carolina Press, 2007).

[50]The struggle over racial nationalism is best explicated by Gary Gerstle, *American Crucible: Race and Nation in the Twentieth Century* (Princeton, N.J.: Princeton University Press, 2001).

[51]Gunner Myrdal, *An American Dilemma: The Negro Problem and Modern Democracy* (New York: Harper and Brothers, 1944).

[52]Alexander Saxton, *The Indispensable Enemy: Labor and the Anti-Chinese Movement in California* (Berkeley: University of California Press, 1971), and *The Rise and Fall of the White Republic: Class, Politics and Mass Culture in Nineteenth-Century America* (New York: Verso, 1990). Especially important on the role of race in the forging of the American working class is the work of David Roediger, *The Wages of Whiteness: Race and the Making of the American Working Class* (New York: Verso, 1991), and *Working toward Whiteness: How America's Immigrants Became White: The Strange Journey from Ellis Island to the Suburbs* (New York: Basic Books, 2005).

(even swarthy Sicilians), and eastern European Jews could do so, according to scholars such as Noel Ignatiev, Matthew Frye Jacobson, Thomas A. Gugliemo, Jennifer Gugliemo, and Karen Brodkin. The complexities of Jewish racial categorization are deftly treated by Eric L. Goldstein.[53]

Whiteness studies are hardly without critics.[54] Those who focus on the history of class formation and labor history, especially, are dissatisfied with the whiteness narrative, which they regard as one-directional and monocausal, little different than other narratives created to explain the dominance of a particular group in overly simplistic terms. Constructing such a narrative seems to them a reductionist perspective on the complexities of the American past, especially the struggle for social justice. Labor historian Eric Arnesen, among others, has challenged the vagueness of the term *whiteness* as well as the notion that southern Italians oppressed by the landowners of the north or eastern European Jews seeking refuge from the czar and Cossacks sought refuge in white supremacy after arrival. Nor can Arnesen accept the notion that members of these groups had ever experienced being nonwhite in the same way that African Americans or Chinese had experienced it. Nineteenth-century historian Barbara Fields finds the whiteness construct unnecessarily convoluted and, ultimately, superfluous. For Fields racism is explanation enough for discriminatory social patterns, especially if class, gender, religion, and other such variables are taken into account in the analysis of racist social patterns.[55]

While whiteness remains a controversial explanation of the immigrant experience after arrival, the term *assimilation* remains equally so. Trying to accurately describe the integration or incorporation of newcomers into a society remains a subject of lively debate. For how many generations after arrival do ethnic identifications grounded in identification with other cultures and national experiences persist? In *Postethnic America: Beyond Multiculturalism* (1995), David Hollinger

---

[53]Noel Ignatiev, *How the Irish Became White* (New York: Routledge, 1995); Matthew Frye Jacobson, *Whiteness of a Different Color: European Immigrants and the Alchemy of Race* (Cambridge, Mass.: Harvard University Press, 1998); Thomas A. Gugliemo, *White on Arrival: Italians, Race, Color and Power in Chicago, 1890–1945* (New York: Oxford University Press, 2003); Jennifer Gugliemo and Salvatore Salerno, *Are the Italians White? How Race Is Made in America* (New York: Routledge, 2003); Karen Brodken, *How Jews Became White Folks and What That Says about Race in America* (New Brunswick, N.J.: Rutgers University Press, 1998); Eric L. Goldstein, *The Price of Whiteness: Jews, Race, and American Identity* (Princeton, N.J.: Princeton University Press, 2006).

[54]Some scholars also speak of "blackness studies" to convey their belief that blackness, like whiteness, is culturally constructed. See Deborah Thomas and Kamarie Clarke, eds., *Globalization and Race: Transformations in the Cultural Production of Blackness* (Durham, N.C.: Duke University Press, 2006).

[55]Both Eric Arnesen's and Barbara J. Fields's comments were made at a 2001 symposium on labor and working-class history and were later published. See Arnesen, "Whiteness and the Historians' Imagination," *International Labor and Working-Class History* 60 (Fall 2001): 20; Fields, "Whiteness, Racism, and Identity," ibid., 48–56.

contends that such identities have not and should not be permitted to dominate American culture and that a "cosmopolitan" identity has often emerged in American history to trump ethnic rivalries.[56] Lawrence Fuchs, too, sees in the United States ever-stronger patterns of civic culture that over time have allowed cultural diversity to become a unifying principle and have promoted toleration of racial diversity as well.[57]

Still, many scholars reject such optimism, pointing to the persistence of race as a barrier to assimilating newcomers of color. The term *segmented assimilation* refers to the notion that newly arrived immigrants of color generally can assimilate only into communities of similar hue; arrivals from Africa, regardless of class, are often permitted assimilation only within the African American community.[58] Especially vociferous has been historian Paul Spickard, who renounces the notion of assimilation, which he regards as Eurocentric and disparagingly dubs "the Ellis Island model." Such a model does not adequately describe the experience of nonwhite groups, he contends. Various peoples of color were forced to become part of the American population and then were marginalized by the white Europeans who dominated the North American continent, Spickard charges. Mexicans did not join the population through immigration; their land and people were taken through conquest. Asians in Hawaii as well as native Hawaiians were not voluntary immigrants, but ended up American through annexation. Few would argue with the primacy of race in such instances, but Spickard's polemical tone and exaggerated claims of originality exacerbate his error of seeing race as ethnicity, denying ethnicity as culture, and then forcing all newcomers into one or another of the racial melting pots he hypothesizes.[59]

Sociologists Richard Alba and Victor Nee disagree with Spickard's view that racism has excluded the possibility of assimilation as historians have long characterized it. Without denying the influence of racism, they contend that assimilation in the twenty-first century proceeds much as it had in the past, observing that changes resulting from civil rights legislation and changes in immigration law allow people of color and their children to more readily participate in an

[56]David A. Hollinger, *Postethnic America: Beyond Multiculturalism* (New York: Basic Books, 1995).

[57]Lawrence H. Fuchs, *The American Kaleidoscope: Race, Ethnicity, and the Civic Culture* (Middletown, Conn.: Wesleyan University Press, 1990).

[58]The term was introduced by Alejandro Portes and Min Zhou, "The New Second Generation: Segmented Assimilation and Its Variants," *Annals of the American Academy of Political and Social Science* 530 (November 1993): 73–96. Also see Min Zhou, "Segmented Assimilation: Issues, Controversies, and Recent Research on the Second Generation," *International Migration Review* 4 (Winter 1997): 975–1008.

[59]Paul Spickard, *Almost All Aliens: Immigration, Race, and Colonialism in American History and Identity* (New York: Routledge, 2007). Spickard's overblown argument is effectively deflated by David Gerber's excellent essay, "What's Wrong with Immigration History?" *Reviews in American History* 36 (2008): 543–56.

assimilation process that resembles the way earlier generations of newcomers became integrated into the American population.[60]

Today, scholarship on immigration and ethnicity is robust. Nancy Foner, an anthropologist with a historical bent, examines similarities and differences among different waves of immigrants in *From Ellis Island to JFK* (2000). Social scientists Alejandro Portes and Rubén G. Rumbaut treat second-generation newcomers.[61] Still other scholars tackle previously neglected aspects of the migration experience, offer new approaches to sources, and explore regions of the country previously neglected or undertreated by migration scholars. In *Silent Travelers: Germs, Genes, and the "Immigrant Menace"* (1994), I focused on the intersection of health, disease, and immigration history.[62] My discussion of the role of disease in stigmatizing newcomers in the eyes of their hosts and in shaping public health policies and practices has been expanded upon by Howard Markel and Amy Fairchild for European immigrants, while Nayan Shah, Natalia Molina, and Emily K. Abel have treated the subject for Asians and Latinos coming into West Coast cities.[63] Other scholars are examining the role of consumerism in both integrating newcomers into the society and turning ethnicity into a salable commodity, often benefiting foreign-born entrepreneurs.[64]

The role of immigrants in recasting public health and consumer patterns are just two of the many ways in which American society and culture have been

[60]Richard Alba and Victor Nee, *Remaking the American Mainstream: Assimilation and Contemporary Immigration* (Cambridge, Mass.: Harvard University Press, 2003). For some of the latest scholarship in this area, see Elliott Barkan, Hasia Diner, and Alan M. Kraut, eds., *From Arrival to Incorporation: Migrants to the U.S. in a Global Era* (New York: New York University Press, 2008).

[61]Nancy Foner, *From Ellis Island to JFK: New York's Two Great Waves of Immigration* (New Haven, Conn.: Yale University Press, 2000); Alejandro Portes and Rubén G. Rumbaut, *Legacies: The Story of the Immigrant Second Generation* (Berkeley: University of California Press, 2001), and *Ethnicities: Children of Immigrants in America* (Berkeley: University of California Press, 2001). See also Philip Kasinitz, John H. Mollenkopf, and Mary C. Waters, eds., *Becoming New Yorkers: Ethnographies of the New Second Generation* (New York: Russell Sage Foundation, 2004).

[62]Alan M. Kraut, *Silent Travelers: Germs, Genes, and the "Immigrant Menace"* (New York: Basic Books, 1994).

[63]Howard Markel, *Quarantine! East European Jewish Immigrants and the New York City Epidemics of 1892* (Baltimore: Johns Hopkins University Press, 1997), and *When Germs Travel: Six Major Epidemics That Have Invaded America since 1900 and the Fears They Have Unleashed* (New York: Pantheon, 2004); Amy L. Fairchild, *Science at the Borders: Immigrant Medical Inspection and the Shaping of the Modern Industrial Labor Force* (Baltimore: Johns Hopkins University Press, 2003); Nayan Shah, *Contagious Divides: Epidemics and Race in San Francisco's Chinatown* (Berkeley: University of California Press, 2001); Natalia Molina, *Fit to Be Citizens? Public Health and Race in Los Angeles, 1879–1939* (Berkeley: University of California Press, 2006); Emily K. Abel, *Tuberculosis and the Politics of Exclusion: A History of Public Health and Migration to Los Angeles* (New Brunswick, N.J.: Rutgers University Press, 2007).

[64]Andrew R. Heinze, *Adapting to Abundance: Jewish Immigration, Mass Consumption, and the Search for an American Identity* (New York: Columbia University Press, 1990); Marilyn Halter, *Shopping for Identity: The Marketing of Ethnicity* (New York: Schocken Books, 2000).

altered by the continuing replenishment of the American population through immigration. Lizabeth Cohen's *Making a New Deal: Industrial Workers in Chicago, 1919–1939* (1990) treats the role of immigrants and their culture in American working-class life. Hasia Diner and Donna Gabaccia contend that American cuisine and the American food industry have been profoundly shaped by the foreign-born.[65] And no discussion of American politics and political institutions, especially urban politics, is possible without a discussion of immigrants' influence. Exploration of urban bossism and the political machine often begins with the wit and wisdom of an Irish "pol" from New York's Tammany Hall, George Washington Plunkitt.[66] An impressive work on the political agendas of ethnic groups and how they were shaped by events abroad, especially by nationalist ideologies, is Matthew Frye Jacobson's *Special Sorrows: The Diasporic Imagination of Irish, Polish, and Jewish Immigrants in the United States* (1995). Jacobson has also explored the racial perspectives that underlay American foreign policy, especially expansionism.[67]

With an increasing number of monographs treating the immigrant outside the Northeast, scholars are also offering broader syntheses of regional experiences, such as Elliott Barkan's and Walter Nugent's studies of the peopling of the American West.[68] Traditional immigration sources, especially immigrant letters, are also receiving fresh analysis.[69] In *Authors of Their Lives: The Personal Correspondence*

[65]Lizabeth Cohen, *Making a New Deal: Industrial Workers in Chicago, 1919–1939* (New York: Cambridge University Press, 1990); Hasia Diner, *Hungering for America: Italian, Irish and Jewish Foodways in the Age of Migration* (Cambridge, Mass.: Harvard University Press, 2001); Donna R. Gabaccia, *We Are What We Eat: Ethnic Food and the Making of Americans* (Cambridge, Mass.: Harvard University Press, 1998).

[66]*Plunkitt of Tammany Hall*, recorded by William L. Riordan and edited by Arthur Mann (New York: E. P. Dutton and Co., 1963). The best volume on Progressive politics and the immigrants is James J. Connolly's *The Triumph of Ethnic Progressivism: Urban Political Culture in Boston, 1900–1925* (Cambridge, Mass.: Harvard University Press, 1998). For voting behavior, see Allan J. Lichtman, *Prejudice and the Old Politics: The Presidential Election of 1928* (Chapel Hill: University of North Carolina Press, 1979).

[67]Matthew Frye Jacobson, *Special Sorrows: The Diasporic Imagination of Irish, Polish, and Jewish Immigrants in the United States* (Cambridge, Mass.: Harvard University Press, 1995), and *Barbarian Virtues: The United States Encounters Foreign Peoples at Home and Abroad, 1876–1917* (New York: Hill and Wang, 2000).

[68]Elliott Robert Barkan, *From All Points: America's Immigrant West, 1870–1952* (Bloomington: Indiana University Press, 2007); Walter Nugent, *Into the West: The Story of Its People* (New York: Knopf, 1999).

[69]Immigration scholars have long turned to Charlotte Erickson's 1972 selection of letters by Englishmen and Scots across the Atlantic in the early nineteenth century and, more recently, to other collections as well. Charlotte Erickson, *Invisible Immigrants: The Adaptation of English and Scottish Immigrants in 19th Century America* (Leicester, U.K.: Leicester University Press, 1972); Solveig Zempel, *In Their Own Words: Letters from Norwegian Immigrants* (Minneapolis: University of Minnesota Press, 1991); Walter D. Kamphoefner, Wolfgang Helbich, and Ulrike Sommer, eds., *News from the Land of Freedom: German Immigrants Write Home* (Ithaca, N.Y.: Cornell University Press, 1993); Kerby A. Miller, Arnold Schrier, Bruce Boling, and David N. Doyle, eds., *Irish Immigrants in the Land of Canaan: Letters and Memoirs from*

of British Immigrants to North America in the Nineteenth Century (2006), David A. Gerber examines the letters of British immigrants to the United States and Canada, offering an unprecedented focus on how letters sustained relationships challenged by separation, provided continuity in lives disrupted by travel and distance, and offered emotional and psychic support to those engaged in such correspondence.[70]

The wave of immigration that began in the last decades of the twentieth century, largely from nations in Asia and Latin America, has continued into the first decade of the twenty-first. Contemporary debate, such as that over immigration policy, especially with respect to an increasing number of unauthorized immigrants, is part of the nation's political discourse and has become part of historians' agenda. Aristide Zolberg characterizes U.S. immigration policy as a tool of nation building, while Roger Daniels sees it as inconsistent, even illogical at times. Mae Ngai has observed that at least some immigration legislation, especially the Immigration Act of 1965, had the unintended consequence of making unauthorized immigration a major policy issue and a matter of national debate.[71]

Musing on his choice of subject in the early 1950s, historian Oscar Handlin wrote, "Once I thought to write a history of the immigrants in America. Then I discovered that the immigrants were American history."[72] Handlin's statement was something of an exaggeration. Conquest, annexation, and the forced migration of slaves were also mechanisms for the peopling of the United States. Still, all that happens when individuals come from somewhere else to make their homes in the United States is likely to remain an important field of historical inquiry and one perennially nourished by current events, even as it is today.

Colonial and Revolutionary America, 1675–1815 (New York: Oxford University Press, 2003); Walter D. Kamphoefner, Wolfgang Helbich, and Susan Carter Vogel, eds., *Germans in the Civil War: The Letters They Wrote Home* (Chapel Hill: University of North Carolina Press, 2006).

[70]David A. Gerber, *Authors of Their Lives: The Personal Correspondence of British Immigrants to North America in the Nineteenth Century* (New York: New York University Press, 2006). Gerber explores how the letters of ordinary housewives, farmers, and factory laborers were crafted in styles and in accordance with conventions that can be identified and understood in ways that help to decode immigrants' deepest thoughts and feelings. Also, Gerber, Bruce S. Elliott, and Suzanne M. Sinke, *Letters across Borders: The Epistolary Practices of International Migrants* (New York: Palgrave, 2006).

[71]Aristide R. Zolberg, *A Nation by Design: Immigration Policy in the Fashioning of America* (Cambridge, Mass.: Harvard University Press, 2006); Roger Daniels, *Guarding the Golden Door: American Immigration Policy and Immigrants since 1882* (New York: Hill and Wang, 2004); Mae M. Ngai, *Impossible Subjects: Illegal Aliens and the Making of Modern America* (Princeton, N.J.: Princeton University Press, 2004).

[72]Handlin, *Uprooted*, 3.

David M. Wrobel

Regionalism and Sectionalism in American Historical Writing

In 1884, when the American Historical Association was founded, the memories of the nation's Civil War, far from fading, were resurrected in the presidential campaign between Democratic nominee Grover Cleveland and Republican James G. Blaine. The Republicans "waved the bloody shirt" by associating Democratic Party support with disloyalty to the Union; sectionalism was very much in the air. That same year, a young man who was later to become America's most significant historian of regionalism and sectionalism, Frederick Jackson Turner, graduated from the University of Wisconsin. Four years later, in September 1888, in the midst of another presidential campaign in which the Republicans again unfurled the bloody shirt, Turner began his Ph.D. studies at Johns Hopkins University. In the spring of that academic year, Turner met future president Woodrow Wilson at the university. So began the story of regionalism and sectionalism in American historiography, in the midst of bitter political campaigns and filiopietistic writings about the Civil War. A southerner, Wilson, and a northerner and westerner (or midwesterner, depending on one's definition), Turner, met at the first center of American history doctoral training in the former border state of Maryland.

In 1893, five years after this meeting, Turner delivered his now-famous essay, "The Significance of the Frontier in American History," at the annual meeting of the still fledgling AHA held in Chicago in conjunction with the World's Fair. In that essay, the single most influential piece of writing by any American historian, Turner was responding to the lack of interest at Johns Hopkins about the American western frontier and to the work of one of his mentors, Herbert Baxter Adams. The latter was a leading proponent of the Teutonic "germ theory" that European democratic ideas had been transplanted to the New World rather than having emerged there independently. Turner, by contrast, argued that the demanding experience of settling the western frontier forged a composite American type from the stock that derived from the mixing of a range of northwestern European nations. Moreover, he contended that the

I am grateful to my colleague Joseph A. Fry, Distinguished Professor of History at the University of Nevada Las Vegas, for his careful reading of this essay and for his excellent suggestions concerning the historiography of southern regionalism and sectionalism.

frontier experience nurtured democracy, individualism, nationalism, and a pragmatic American mindset. While noting that the frontier process was not by any
means a universally positive one, Turner's frontier thesis nonetheless presented
the nation with a largely triumphalist master narrative, one that essentially gave
academic legitimacy to a wide range of commonly held assumptions in the late
nineteenth century concerning the uniquely benign nature of the heritage of the
United States. Turner made the story of the nation's newest region, the West, the
story of the entire United States and the shifting western frontier the embodiment of the nation's highest ideals.

   Young Woodrow Wilson responded positively to Turner's frontier thesis, as
did a generation of Turner's students, who defended it vigorously into the 1930s.
Interestingly, though, Wilson might actually have been drawn most favorably to
that aspect of Turner's thesis that most worried its author. Turner had mentioned
three times in the essay that the frontier no longer existed and emphasized that
the first phase of the nation's history had closed with its passing. At the turn of the
new century, Wilson welcomed the end of that first phase in an 1897 essay in the
Atlantic Monthly entitled "The Making of the Nation." He looked forward, in
the absence of the frontier, to a nation without an East and a West, and, as the
wounds of the Civil War slowly healed, to a nation without a North and a South.
"As the country grows," Wilson wrote, "it will inevitably grow more homogenous," and that homogeneity, in his estimation, would be a thoroughly healthy
development.[1] It was Lincoln, a Republican, who at his party's June 1858 state
convention in Springfield, Illinois, echoed the words of Jesus in the New Testament in advancing the celebrated conviction that "a house divided against itself
cannot stand." The Democrat Wilson (himself the son of a Presbyterian preacher)
clearly shared that sentiment and hoped that the nation's future would be free of
regional divisions, particularly if its national center of gravity followed a southern
cultural orientation.

   But as Wilson envisioned a new United States without frontiers and without
sections, Turner came to find in sectionalism, or regionalism, the salvation for a
post-frontier nation. One only wishes Turner had used the latter term, not the
former, since *sectionalism*, even two generations after the end of the Civil War,
elicited painful memories of the nation's peoples and places embroiled in bitter
conflict. Moreover, *regionalism*, by the beginning of the twentieth century, was
suggestive of local color, cultural distinctions rooted in place, and culture that
collectively made the nation stronger. Whatever the case, if the frontier had been
the wellspring of the nation's most benign qualities, what would become of the
United States, Turner wondered and worried, in the wake of the frontier's passing? Would the nation come to mirror its European progenitors as its democratic
underpinnings crumbled? The second half of Turner's career, from around 1910
until his death in 1932, was marked by a deep anxiety deriving from his percep-

----

[1]Woodrow Wilson, "The Making of the Nation," *Atlantic Monthly* LXXX (1897): 1–14.

tion that the frontier had closed.[2] During those years he wrote a series of essays on sectionalism, which he determined to be the best salvation for a frontierless nation. The nation comprised different regions, Turner contended, and each had been formed through the process of particular cultural mixes of people entering particular physical environments at particular moments.

Turner insisted that the presence of regional differences was no cause for concern. The varied regions complemented one another and together composed a varied, but nonetheless functional and united, nation. The regions were, Turner wrote in his 1922 essay "Sections and Nation," the foundational blocks that would enable the United States "to build from our past a nobler structure, in which each section will find its place as a fit room for a worthy house."[3] He began his best-known essay on the topic, "The Significance of the Section in American History" (1925) with the claim that the post-frontier United States was now "more like Europe, and our sections are more and more becoming the American version of the European nation." He closed the essay with the powerful assertion that "we must shape our national action to the fact of a vast and varied union of unlike sections."[4]

But President Wilson's insistence on "one-hundred-percent Americanism" on the home front during World War I rejected both ethnic and sectional fault lines. Wilson had no regrets over the frontier's disappearance and deemed Turner's sections or regions painful reminders of the fractures that had separated North from South and East from West in the second half of the nineteenth century. Interestingly, as the nation emerged from its second major war in Turner and Wilson's lifetime, the historian had offered the president a potential solution to Europe's postwar political problems. Turner's friend and Harvard University colleague Charles Homer Haskins had presented to the American delegation in Paris in December 1918 Turner's memo titled "International Political Parties in a Durable League of Nations." In that memo, Turner suggested that a system of European-wide political parties could effectively mirror the American system of national political parties and, thereby, work across regional lines in a large geographic area to help ensure peace in war-ravaged Europe. Turner's memorandum, in all likelihood, had no discernible impact on the peace negotiations; it is unclear whether Wilson (who by then had known Turner for three decades) even

---

[2]For more on the topic of frontier anxiety in American thought, see David M. Wrobel, *The End of American Exceptionalism: Frontier Anxiety from the Old West to the New Deal* (Lawrence: University Press of Kansas, 1993).

[3]Frederick Jackson Turner, "Sections and Nation," *Yale Review* 12 (October 1922), reprinted in Frederick Jackson Turner, *"The Significance of the Frontier in American History" and Other Essays*, ed. John Mack Faragher (New York: Henry Holt, 1994), 181–200, quotation from 200.

[4]Frederick Jackson Turner, "The Significance of the Section in American History," *Wisconsin Magazine of History* 8 (March 1925), republished in Turner, *"The Significance of the Frontier in American History" and Other Essays*, 201–24, quotations from 202, 224.

read the document. But we can safely conclude that if Wilson had read Turner's memorandum, he would not have agreed with its key arguments.

In the story of Turner and Wilson and of American sections and regions as well as the political reconstruction of postwar Europe, we have a fascinating microcosm of the key contours of historical scholarship on sectionalism and regionalism in the last century. Turner had, unfortunately, adopted the term *sectionalism*, which served as a reminder to many besides Wilson of the Civil War that had torn the nation apart. Had Turner used the word *regionalism*—which conjured up images of healthy differences among places and of benign cultural folkways deeply rooted in place, of what the Harvard philosopher-historian Josiah Royce called a "wise provincialism"—in the essays he wrote in the second half of his career, one wonders whether they might have had an impact on the national heritage as profound as the influence of his earlier frontier thesis.[5]

Still, it is worth considering that Turner's posthumously published collection, *The Significance of Sections in American History* (1932), was awarded the Pulitzer Prize for American History in 1932. Furthermore, it is worth remembering that in the early decades of the twentieth century, regionalism was starting to become a vital component of historical writing in the United States. Regional organizations developed in the first four decades of the twentieth century, and the 1920s and 1930s constituted the golden age of American regionalism. The Pacific Coast Branch of the American Historical Association (PCB-AHA) was formed in 1903 to serve the needs of historians residing in the far western United States and Canada. A few years later, in 1907, the Mississippi Valley Historical Association (MVHA), the first incarnation of the Organization of American Historians, formed from seven historical organizations in the Mississippi Valley. National meetings of the AHA were almost invariably held on the East Coast, which made travel long and costly for historians in the West. The formation of the PCB-AHA and the MVHA can be seen as part of, or at least a precursor of sorts to, what historian Robert Dorman has called *The Revolt of the Provinces* (1993).[6]

Moreover, as a regionalist orientation in literature and the arts became more common and popular in the interwar years, it became increasingly acceptable for historians to write about the history of their own places of residence.[7] A clas-

---

[5]Josiah Royce, *California, from the Conquest in 1846 to the Second Vigilance Committee in San Francisco: A Study of American Character* (Boston: Houghton Mifflin, 1886). For an excellent analysis of Royce's pathbreaking study of community in a new American region, see Robert V. Hine, "Josiah Royce: The West as Community," in Richard Etulain, ed., *Writing Western History: Essays on Major Western Historians* (Reno and Las Vegas: University of Nevada Press, 2002), 19–41.

[6]Robert Dorman, *The Revolt of the Provinces: The Regionalist Movement in America, 1920–1945* (Chapel Hill: University of North Carolina Press, 1993). While Dorman focused on the interwar years, there are numerous examples of significant regionalist expression in the United States in the preceding two decades.

[7]For more on regionalism in history, literature, and art in the interwar period, see Richard W. Etulain, *Re-Imagining the Modern American West: A Century of Fiction, History, and Art* (Tucson: University of Arizona Press, 1996).

sic example of this trend is Walter Prescott Webb's seminal work *The Great Plains* (1931), which appeared the year before Turner died. Webb emphasized the regional distinctiveness of the arid West, treating it as a clearly discernible, mappable "place," rather than as part of a frontier "process." "The Great Plains environment," Webb wrote, "constitutes a geographic unity whose influences have been so powerful as to put a characteristic mark upon everything that survives within its borders."[8] A geographic unity, yes, but not an embodiment of the nation, the claim Turner had made for the western frontier in 1893. Webb's arid West was very much its own place and very unlike the East.

An equally influential expression of regional consciousness emerged from the South around the same time and also assumed a position outside national norms and trends. *I'll Take My Stand: The South and the Agrarian Tradition* (1930), a remarkable set of essays, was the collective effort of a group of twelve southern writers, including John Crowe Ransom, Robert Penn Warren, Allen Tate, Herman Clarence Nixon, and Donald Davidson. The group, whose members labeled themselves the Southern Agrarians, lauded the rural culture of the Old South and contrasted its benefits with the perils of state planning.[9] During the New Deal years, the Southern Agrarians criticized Franklin D. Roosevelt's programs, including the massive Tennessee Valley Authority, on the grounds of overcentralization and lack of sensitivity to regional distinctiveness.

In 1934, a few years after the publication of *I'll Take My Stand* and *The Great Plains*, the Southern Historical Association was formed to promote historical scholarship on that region. Then, in 1937, one of the most polemical and politically motivated regionalist tracts of the New Deal years appeared, Walter Prescott Webb's *Divided We Stand: The Crisis of a Frontierless Democracy*. Echoing the title and the concerns of the Southern Agrarians, Webb railed against the financial power and influence of the industrial Northeast. He called on the South and the West to unite in opposition to the colonial status that the monopolistic North had enforced upon them, especially in the wake of the closing of the frontier.[10] The antimonopolistic and generally anti-big-business rhetoric that Roosevelt increasingly adopted in support of his reformist Second New Deal programs in the late 1930s may actually have owed something to Webb's book. Copies of the book reached Roosevelt and some Democratic congressmen soon after its publication, and the president utilized some of its ideas in a nationally aired radio speech in January 1938.[11]

[8]Walter Prescott Webb, *The Great Plains* (Boston: Ginn, 1931), quotation from vi.

[9]Twelve Southerners, *I'll Take My Stand: The South and the Agrarian Tradition* (New York: Harper and Brothers, 1930), republished with an introduction by Susan V. Donaldson (Baton Rouge: Louisiana State University Press, 2006). Donald Davidson, one of the original twelve southerners, also authored *The Attack on Leviathan: Regionalism and Nationalism in the United States* (Chapel Hill: University of North Carolina Press, 1938). See also Howard W. Odum and Harry Estill Moore, *American Regionalism* (New York: Henry Holt, 1938).

[10]Walter Prescott Webb, *Divided We Stand: The Crisis of a Frontierless Democracy* (New York: Farrar and Rinehart, 1937).

[11]For more on Webb's influence on FDR's policies, see Walter Rundell, Jr., "A Historian's Impact on Federal Policy: W. P. Webb as a Case Study," *Prologue* 15 (Winter 1983): 215–28.

Webb's scholarly engagement with the politics of the present in pursuit of a regional agenda, like Turner's effort a generation earlier to influence the treaty negotiations in Versailles (and Turner's posthumous Pulitzer Prize in 1933), underscores the importance of regionalist thinking among historians in the interwar years. Regionalist thinking, albeit on a larger geographic scale, received a further boost when Turner's former student Herbert Eugene Bolton delivered his 1932 presidential address, "The Epic of Greater America," to the AHA.[12] Drawing on the History of the Americas course he had been teaching at the University of California at Berkeley, Bolton encouraged his colleagues to think transnationally about a region that stretched from Alaska to Patagonia and illuminated the meaning of a wide range of local histories by placing them in comparative context. A decade earlier Bolton's pathbreaking book, *The Spanish Borderlands: A Chronicle of Old Florida and the Southwest* (1921), had given birth to the field of Southwest Borderlands history, which today is one of the most exciting and innovative subfields in the history of the Americas.[13] Notably, in the course of his remarkable career, Bolton had the great honor of two Festschrifts dedicated to him by his students: *New Spain and the Anglo-American West* (1932) and *Greater America* (1945).[14] *The Spanish Borderlands* and *Greater America* (1945) are bookends of sorts to the golden age of regionalism in American historical scholarship in the interwar years.

W. J. Cash's enormously influential study, *The Mind of the South* (1941), was a complicating presence during this renaissance of regional scholarship. The overwhelming tendency of regionalist scholars during the interwar years was to extol the virtues of America's regions. Regions were viewed either as "fit rooms for a worthy house," as Turner insisted, or as victims of an overbearing state, as the Southern Agrarians contended, or of another region that forced them into colonial status, as Webb argued. But Cash's book presented the South as the victim of its own deeply rooted regional dysfunctionalities. Cash's South was marked by a strong historical and cultural continuity from its earliest beginnings right up to the 1930s. Committed to white supremacy, thoroughly unprogressive and immune or even antagonistic to outside criticisms or innovations, the South, in Cash's estimation, was mired in its past and thus unprepared for its future. *The Mind of the South* was the dominant work on southern regional identity for a quarter century after its publication, though it would become the subject of

[12]Herbert Eugene Bolton, "The Epic of Greater America," *American Historical Review* 38 (April 1933): 448–74.

[13]Herbert Eugene Bolton, *The Spanish Borderlands: A Chronicle of Old Florida and the Southwest* (New Haven, Conn.: Yale University Press, 1921).

[14]*New Spain and the Anglo-American West: Historical Contributions Presented to Herbert Eugene Bolton* (Lancaster, Pa.: Lancaster Press, 1932); Adele Ogden et al., eds., *Greater America: Essays in Honor of Herbert Eugene Bolton* (Berkeley and Los Angeles: University of California Press, 1945).

intense criticism from C. Vann Woodward and other southern historians starting in the late 1960s.[15]

Regionalism was considerably less evident as a force in American historiography in the decades after World War II. While the notion of the interwar years as a period of isolationism in the United States has been overemphasized, there is something to the argument that there was an intellectual turning inward after World War I and that such a course naturally promoted regionalist thinking. After World War II, however, with the multipolar power system in shreds and the United States standing on a bipolar global stage as one of just two superpowers, it is hardly surprising that the nation looked out at the world around it. Moreover, in these years developments in American intellectual history, American political history, and American Studies placed an increasing emphasis on the national distinctiveness or exceptionalism of the United States. "Consensus history" is a problematic label for these historiographical developments, since it fails to account for the important criticisms of the nation's past leveled by a good number of scholars in the 1940s and 1950s.[16] However, it is worth noting that many historians in these years followed Daniel J. Boorstin's lead in *The Genius of American Politics* (1953) and David Potter's in *People of Plenty* (1954) and told an inherently national story that de-emphasized division and conflict in general, whether based on race, class, gender, or region, and emphasized a general agreement among Americans over time on the core principles that guided the nation.[17] However, the story of the western frontier did find a place in that national narrative in the early Cold War years. In fact, there was a rebirth of sorts of the notion of American exceptionalism rooted in the nation's frontier heritage. Ray Allen Billington's *Westward Expansion: A History of the American Frontier* (1949) served as a textbook not only for courses on the history of American frontier expansion but also for general U.S. history courses, and it appeared in five subsequent editions.[18] Billington resurrected the frontier thesis and structured his six-hundred-page study around the key contours of Turner's essay, even ending his coverage in 1890, the date Turner (and the U.S. Census Bureau) had provided

[15]For an excellent overview of the impact and criticisms of Cash's *The Mind of the South* (New York: Knopf, 1941), see James C. Cobb's "Does 'Mind' Still Matter? The South, the Nation, and *The Mind of the South*, 1941–1991," in *Redefining Southern Culture: Mind and Identity in the Modern South* (Athens: University of Georgia Press, 1999).

[16]For more on the problems of the "consensus" label, see Gene Wise's classic study *American Historical Explanations: A Strategy for Grounded Inquiry*, 2nd ed. (Minneapolis: University of Minnesota Press, 1980), 343–47.

[17]Daniel J. Boorstin, *The Genius of American Politics* (Chicago: University of Chicago Press, 1953); David Potter, *People of Plenty: Economic Abundance and the American Character* (Chicago: University of Chicago Press, 1954).

[18]Ray Allen Billington with James Blaine Hedges, *Westward Expansion: A History of the American Frontier* (New York: Macmillan, 1949; 2nd ed., 1960; 3rd ed., 1969; 4th ed., 1974); Billington with Martin Ridge, 5th ed. (New York: Macmillan, 1982); Billington and Martin Ridge, 6th ed., Abridged (Albuquerque: University of New Mexico Press, 2001).

for the frontier's closing. In so doing, Billington presented Americans with a tri-umphalist story of the development of a democratic heritage through frontier set-tlement. Martin Ridge, who served as coauthor for the last editions of the book, emphasized that "the heroes and heroines" who stood at the center of Billing-ton's narrative "helped to set the nation on a remarkable course."[19] This lauda-tory angle of vision on the national past contrasted starkly with the critical story American cold warriors began telling in the late 1940s and 1950s about their adversary as they linked the Soviet Union's totalitarian present to its infamously authoritarian past.

For all of his emphasis on the relevance of Turner's frontier thesis to the Cold War present, Billington had little interest in Turner's sectional thesis. He may have feared, like Woodrow Wilson in the midst of another tumultuous moment a generation earlier, that an emphasis on differences among and between U.S. regions would be damaging to the nation. However, it is worth not-ing that the same year that Billington's *Westward Expansion* first appeared, an important symposium on American regionalism took place at the University of Wisconsin, where Turner had taught for much of his career. The resulting col-lection of essays, *Regionalism in America* (1951) edited by University of Wisconsin historian Merrill Jensen, is a remarkable testament to the survival of regionalist thought in the era of consensus history. In the tradition of Turner's 1920s essays, the contributors to *Regionalism in America* generally emphasized the healthy nature of the nation's regional differences. Jensen himself, interestingly, is best known for his writings on the Articles of Confederation and the American Con-stitution, which placed him well outside the mainstream of consensus interpre-tations that critiqued the former and praised the latter document.[20] Moreover, Henry Nash Smith's enormously influential study, *Virgin Land: The American West as Symbol and Myth* (1950), which emphasized the distinctiveness of the nation's mythological foundations, really amounted to a cautionary tale about their solidity. Smith, echoing Cash's analysis of the South, underscored the incongruity between the nation's modern, industrial, post–World War II present and its dominant creation myth rooted in the agrarian frontier past.[21] Such obser-vations as Jensen's and Smith's were hardly the bedrock of consensus history. Smith was warning the nation of the mythological straightjacket it had to escape if it were to enter the modern world on a sure footing; for him the nation's past (or at least its imaginatively reconstructed past) was something it needed to aban-don. For consensus historians such as Boorstin, on the other hand, the nation's positive and largely conflict-free past was a sure foundation for the present and the future—something to be lauded, not abandoned.

[19]Billington and Ridge, *Westward Expansion*, 6th ed. (1999), x.
[20]Merrill Jensen, ed. *Regionalism in America* (Madison: University of Wisconsin Press, 1951).
[21]Henry Nash Smith, *Virgin Land: The American West as Symbol and Myth* (Cambridge, Mass.: Harvard University Press, 1950).

While consensus history had little place for the notion of American regions as "fit rooms for a worthy house" and less time still for any emphasis on divisions within America's house, the next phase of American historical scholarship, beginning in the 1960s, placed considerable emphasis on differences within the nation, though generally not regional ones. The new social history that developed in the 1960s and 1970s placed the categories of race, class, and gender at the center of the American story but found little place for region as a category of analysis. Historians tended to examine groups of laborers according to trade, socioeconomic status, or racial or ethnic background. Moreover, the primary emphasis in the new racial and ethnic studies programs that began to develop at institutions of higher learning across the country was on the distinctive nature of the experience of each particular racial or ethnic group, rather than on the interplay of those cultural groups within particular geographic spaces. To some degree in these decades, the role of place, or space, in historical analysis was pushed to the periphery as the role of identity moved to the center. Nonetheless, it is certainly worth noting that the Western History Association was formed in 1961 and that the New England Historical Association followed in 1966, two important regional history organizations that are, like the Southern History Association and the Pacific Coast Branch of the American Historical Association, still vibrant elements of the professional history landscape in the United States. Yet it was also in this period that the Mississippi Valley Historical Association, originally conceived as a regional organization, and its journal, the *Mississippi Valley Historical Review*, took on names that better reflected the demographic changes that had taken place in membership and subscriptions as historians from all across the country and around the world found in them a professional home. In 1964 they became, respectively, the Organization of American Historians and the *Journal of American History*.

While a period of relative quiet on the regional front, the mid-1960s were not an era of inactivity. Earl Pomeroy's masterpiece, *The Pacific Slope: A History of California, Oregon, Washington, Idaho, Utah, and Nevada*, one of the most significant regional studies ever written by an American historian, appeared in 1965. Pomeroy insisted that the Far West had been more imitative of the East than innovative in the development of its cultural, political, and economic structures.[22] In addition, a number of important works on American regionalism by cultural geographers appeared in the 1970s, including Wilbur Zelinsky's *The Cultural Geography of the United States* (1973) and Raymond D. Gastil's *Cultural Regions of the United States* (1975).[23]

---

[22]Earl Pomeroy, *The Pacific Slope: A History of California, Oregon, Washington, Idaho, Utah, and Nevada* (New York: Knopf, 1965; republished, Reno and Las Vegas: University of Nevada Press, 2003).

[23]Wilbur Zelinsky, *The Cultural Geography of the United States* (Englewood Cliffs, N.J.: Prentice Hall, 1973; rev. ed., New York: Prentice Hall, 1992); Raymond D. Gastil, *Cultural Regions of the United States* (Seattle: University of Washington Press, 1975).

While certainly never completely moribund in the post–World War II decades, by the 1980s regionalism was making a comeback in the American historical profession. Joel Garreau's *The Nine Nations of North America* (1981) added to the work of Zelinsky and Gastil, as well as to that of Turner in the 1920s, emphasizing the distinctiveness of the cultures that have developed in the various geographic regions of the United States and Canada.[24] The first volume of the most important of all of these geographical histories of America was published in 1986: D. W. Meinig's monumental four-volume work, *The Shaping of America: A Geographical Perspective on 500 Years of History*, comprised Vol. 1: *Atlantic America, 1492–1800* (1986); Vol. 2: *Continental America, 1800–1867* (1993); Vol. 3: *Transcontinental America, 1850–1915* (1998); and Vol. 4: *Global America, 1915–2000* (2004) and viewed "the United States as a gigantic geographic growth with a continually changing geographic character, structure, and system." Meinig's 1,600-page study provides the fullest examination to date of the development of different regional societies in North America, or, as Meinig put it in 1986, of "the human creation of places and networks of relationships among them."[25] Also particularly noteworthy in this regard is David Hackett Fischer's influential cultural history, *Albion's Seed: Four British Folkways in America* (1989), which examines how migration streams from East Anglia into Massachusetts, from the south and west of England into Virginia, from the North Midlands into the Delaware Valley, and from the northern British borderlands of England and Scotland and from Ireland into the American backcountry influenced American regional culture from early settlement to the present.[26]

In addition, the 1980s and 1990s saw an explosion of scholarship on the American West. This work portrayed that region, so central a part of the national self-consciousness, as a distinct geographic place, not a part of a larger frontier process. The authors of this "new western history" consciously distinguished themselves from the practitioners of the "old western history" that had emphasized the frontier. A leading example was Donald Worster's *Rivers of Empire: Water, Aridity, and the Growth of the American West* (1985). Like Webb's *The Great Plains* more than a half-century before, Worster emphasized the environmental fragility of the arid West. He then went on to compare the powerful federal and corporate forces behind the water engineering projects that transformed the region in the twentieth century to those behind the creation of China's "hydraulic society," which German sociologist and historian Karl Wittfogel described in his highly controversial and influential study, *Oriental Despotism: A Comparative Study of Total Power* (1957).[27]

[24]Joel Garreau, *The Nine Nations of North America* (Boston: Houghton Mifflin, 1981).

[25]All four volumes published New Haven, Conn.: Yale University Press. Quotations are from Vol. 1, xv.

[26]David Hackett Fischer, *Albion's Seed: Four British Folkways in America* (New York: Oxford University Press, 1989).

[27]Donald Worster, *Rivers of Empire: Water, Aridity, and the Growth of the American West* (New York: Oxford University Press, 1985); Karl Wittfogel, *Oriental Despotism: A Comparative Study of Total Power* (New Haven, Conn.: Yale University Press, 1957).

Patricia Nelson Limerick's *The Legacy of Conquest: The Unbroken Past of the American West* (1987) has probably been the most influential of all the works of the new western history. Limerick insisted on the need to move beyond the story of Turner's frontier process and its much-discussed termination in 1890. By "closing the frontier" as a conceptual framework for western history, she argued, the story of the twentieth-century West could be more fully opened up as a field of investigation for scholars. In a similar vein, Richard White's influential textbook, *"It's Your Misfortune and None of My Own": A New History of the American West* (1991), departed from Turner's and Billington's interpretations of westward expansion to show the consequences of conquest for the West's diverse residents and for the West's varied natural environments. Like Limerick, White told the story of the West as a region (the book made no mention whatsoever of the word *frontier*), one created by the United States government through war and diplomacy in the nineteenth century and one that continued to be shaped by federal bureaucracies throughout the twentieth.[28]

The new western history certainly helped revive the field of western American history. Works such as Worster's, Limerick's, and White's were a far cry from the rendering of the frontier West as the geographic lodestone of a positive national heritage offered by Turner in the late nineteenth and early twentieth centuries and by Billington during the early Cold War era. Furthermore, the new western history certainly departed from Turner's hopeful envisioning in the nineteen-teens and -twenties of the nation's regions as "fit rooms for a worthy house."

In recent years there has also been something of a renaissance of the regionalism theme in southern history. The increased strength of southern representatives in Congress since 1994 and the presence of southerners in the White House—Bill Clinton and George W. Bush (who despite his eastern background and education assumed a down-home Texas ranch culture southern identity)—may be merely coincidental developments. Yet, the elevated presence of the South in the halls of power may account, at least in part, for a renewed scholarly interest in southern identity issues. Whatever the case, David Goldfield's *Still Fighting the Civil War: The American South and Southern History* (2002) explores the ways in which the legacies of the Civil War and Reconstruction still dominate the cultural landscape of the South. James C. Cobb's *Away Down South: A History of Southern Identity* (2005) examines the South's evolving self-perceptions over time and the changing perceptions of the region on the national level. Joseph A. Fry's *Dixie Looks Abroad: The South and U.S. Foreign Relations, 1789–1973* (2002) is the first comprehensive study of an American

[28]Patricia Nelson Limerick, *The Legacy of Conquest: The Unbroken Past of the American West* (New York: W. W. Norton, 1987; 2nd ed., 2006); Richard White, *"It's Your Misfortune and None of My Own": A New History of the American West* (Norman: University of Oklahoma Press, 1991). For a good introduction to the key contours of the new western history, including Limerick's short essay "What on Earth Is the New Western History?" see Patricia Nelson Limerick, Charles Rankin, and Clyde Milner II, eds., *Trails toward a New Western History* (Lawrence: University Press of Kansas, 1991), and *Something in the Soil: Legacies and Reckonings in the New West* (New York: W. W. Norton, 2000).

region's impact on the nation's foreign policy. And anthropologist James Peacock's *Grounded Globalism: How the South Embraces the World* (2007) further shifts the field away from its general emphasis on the South's adversarial relationship with the nation as the defining factor in its history to examine how the region has been increasingly defined by its global relationships.[29]

Globalism, of course, has its discontents for regionalists, particularly those concerned with the maintenance of a stable regional consciousness. Not surprisingly, then, recent historical scholarship and cultural commentary on regionalism have been marked in part by the development of a "death of region" approach. According to this declensionist vision, evident in works such as William R. Leach's *Country of Exiles: The Destruction of Place in American Life* (2000), the West, the South, indeed all of the nation's formerly distinctive cultural regions are, lamentably, being subsumed within an uninspired homogenous national whole characterized by massive corporate franchise operations.[30] With a Starbucks on every corner and the same big-box stores, motels, restaurants, and home builders in every town and suburb, everywhere, these scholars argue, has become like everywhere else, and through the process of globalization everywhere has become like the United States.[31] In this rendering of the bleak future of American regionalism, the national collective becomes a structure without regional rooms, just one large, bland, soulless structure.

However, in the current trend toward global comparative analysis in western American history—evidenced as early as 1981 in Howard Lamar and Leonard Thompson's important collection, *The Frontier in History: North America and South Africa Compared*, in Walter Nugent's important essay, "Comparing Fron-

[29]David Goldfield, *Still Fighting the Civil War: The American South and Southern History* (Baton Rouge: Louisiana State University Press, 2002); James C. Cobb, *Away Down South: A History of Southern Identity* (New York: Oxford University Press, 2005); Joseph A. Fry, *Dixie Looks Abroad: The South and U.S. Foreign Relations, 1879–1973* (Baton Rouge: Louisiana State University Press, 2002); and James L. Peacock, *Grounded Globalism: How the U.S. South Embraces the World* (Athens: University of Georgia Press, 2007). For more on this last topic, see James C. Cobb and William Stueck, eds., *Globalization and the American South* (Athens: University of Georgia Press, 2005). For an excellent discussion of the deep influence of the South in American national culture in the contemporary era, see James C. Cobb's 1999 presidential address to the Southern Historical Association, "An Epitaph for the North: Reflections on the Politics of Regional and National Identity at the Millennium," *The Journal of Southern History* 66 (February 2000): 203–24. For further discussion of the South's relationship with the North, see Edward L. Ayers, *The Promise of the New South: Life after Reconstruction* (New York: Oxford University Press, 1992).

[30]William R. Leach, *Country of Exiles: The Destruction of Place in American Life* (New York: Vintage, 2000).

[31]These concerns are discussed in Michael Steiner and David M. Wrobel, "Many Wests: Notes toward a Dynamic Western Regionalism," in David M. Wrobel and Michael Steiner, *Many Wests: Place, Culture, and Regional Identity* (Lawrence: University Press of Kansas, 1997), 1–30.

tiers and Empires" (1994), in Limerick's Western History Association presidential address in 2000, "Going West and Ending Up Global" (2001), and in Gunther Peck's *Reinventing Free Labor* (2000), a study of Italian, Greek, and Mexican migrant labor in a North American West that stretches from Mexico to Canada—we see a new and promising set of possibilities for regional history.[32]

The degree to which the history of the West, the South, or any other American region is unique, distinctive, or exceptional can be measured only in relation to other American regions (as the important collection by Edward L. Ayers, Patricia Nelson Limerick, Stephen Nissenbaum, and Peter S. Onuf, *All Over the Map: Rethinking American Regions* [1995] makes clear) and to other regions around the world.[33] As scholars of the West and the South and their counterparts working on the Midwest and New England, as well as those writing the history of region-sized states such as Alaska, California, and Texas, continue to think creatively and expansively about regionalism, we are likely to see more pathbreaking studies along the lines of Samuel P. Truett's recent *Fugitive Landscapes: The Forgotten History of the US–Mexican Borderlands* (2006), which re-centers United States history and Mexican history through its transnational field of vision on the Arizona–Sonora borderlands, and Robert Campbell's *In Darkest Alaska: Travel and Empire along the Inside Passage* (2007), which places the touristic discovery and appropriation of the last U.S. frontier within a larger global context of the Western world's interactions with indigenous peoples.[34] In Truett's work and that of other scholars working on the borderlands between the United States and Mexico and those between the United States and Canada, we see Bolton's vision of a "Greater America" playing out.[35] In Campbell's study, the American frontier

[32]Howard Lamar and Leonard Thompson, *The Frontier in History: North America and South Africa Compared* (New Haven, Conn.: Yale University Press, 1981); Walter Nugent, "Comparing Frontiers and Empires," in Clyde Milner II, Carol A. O'Connor, and Martha Sandweiss, eds., *The Oxford History of the American West* (New York: Oxford University Press, 1994), 803–33; Patricia Nelson Limerick, "Going West and Ending Up Global," *Western Historical Quarterly* 32 (Spring 2001): 6–23; Gunther Peck, *Reinventing Free Labor: Padrones and Immigrant Workers in the North American West* (New York: Cambridge University Press, 2000).

[33]Edward L. Ayers, Patricia Nelson Limerick, Stephen Nissenbaum, and Peter S. Onuf, *All Over the Map: Rethinking American Regions* (Baltimore: Johns Hopkins University Press, 1995).

[34]Samuel P. Truett, *Fugitive Landscapes: The Forgotten History of the U.S.–Mexican Borderlands* (New Haven, Conn.: Yale University Press, 2006); Robert Campbell, *In Darkest Alaska: Travel and Empire along the Inside Passage* (Philadelphia: University of Pennsylvania Press, 2007).

[35]See, for example, Benjamin Heber Johnson and Jeffrey Guske, *Border Town: Odyssey of an American Place* (New Haven, Conn.: Yale University Press, 2008); Benjamin Heber Johnson, *Revolution in Texas: How a Forgotten Rebellion and Its Bloody Suppression Turned Mexicans into Americans* (New Haven, Conn.: Yale University Press, 2003); Elizabeth Jameson, "Dancing on the Rim, Tiptoeing through Minefields: Challenges and Promises of Borderlands," *Pacific Historical Review* 75 (February 2006): 1–24.

(and its last geographic embodiment, Alaska), so long a symbol of national exceptionalism, is woven into a larger global fabric of frontiers, colonies, and empires.
In *Completing the Union: Alaska, Hawai'i, and the Battle for Statehood* (2004),
John Whitehead places these noncontiguous American places firmly within
larger national and Pacific World narratives. In doing so he challenges historians
of the United States to think beyond the confines of continental land masses as
the primary units of study, reminding us of other regional worlds in the past, such
as the Maritime West of New England, a triangular region of trade and commerce that stretched from the northwest coast of the United States up to Russian
America and across to Hawaii and had a prominent place in the mental and
actual cartographic maps of the first half of the nineteenth century.[36]

Just as New England-based commercial entities and the sailors who served
them envisioned a region that made sense to them, so political commentators
more than a century later began writing about a Sunbelt region in the United
States stretching from the southeast coast to Southern California and marked by
a tendency toward political and cultural conservatism manifested in strong support for the Republican Party. Political theorist Kevin Phillips used the term
"Sunbelt" in his study *The Emerging Republican Majority* (1969). Historian Raymond Mohl's excellent anthology, *Searching for the Sunbelt* (1990), featured
essays by a number of historians attempting to assess the significance of this new
region of sorts.[37] A part of common parlance in the last two decades at least and
the site of tremendous urban growth, the Sunbelt probably makes more sense as
a descriptive term to people who live outside the region than to residents of the
southeastern, south central, and southwestern United States and Southern California. Those more established regional definitions are far more likely to be used
by residents as regional identifiers than is "Sunbelter." Meanwhile, the national
news media are likely to continue using the term to describe political, cultural,
economic, and demographic trends within the part of the United States that lies
south of the 37th or 38th parallel. The very ubiquity of the term underscores the
continuing presence of regionalism in America.

Returning to larger contexts beyond the geographic parameters of the nation
in the now vibrant fields of Atlantic World history and Pacific World history, we
see further opportunity for a reenvisioning of American regional history in a
global comparative context. The very scale of the conceptual house has expanded well beyond the footprint that Turner considered, and that development

[36]John S. Whitehead, *Completing the Union: Alaska, Hawai'i, and the Battle for State-
hood* (Albuquerque: University of New Mexico Press, 2004). For more on the Maritime West of
New England, see Whitehead, "Non-Contiguous Wests: Alaska and Hawai'i," in Wrobel and
Steiner, *Many Wests*, 315–41, especially 316–22.

[37]Kevin R. Phillips, *The Emerging Republican Majority* (New Rochelle, N.Y.: Arlington
House, 1969); Raymond A. Mohl, ed., *Searching for the Sunbelt: Historical Perspectives on a
Region* (Knoxville: University of Tennessee Press, 1990). See also Raymond A. Mohl, Robert R.
Fairbanks, and Kathleen Underwood, eds., *Essays on Sunbelt Cities and Recent Urban America*
(College Station: Texas A&M University Press, 1990).

speaks not to the death of American regions but to the dynamism of American regionalism and the scholarship that it has engendered over the course of the last century and seems likely to produce well into the twenty-first century. Moreover, since scholarship on regionalism has so often in the past been inspired by important cultural, economic, and political developments, the region as a unit for historical analysis is unlikely to be absent from the scholarly landscapes of the future. Thus, the debates over whether America's varied regions make it "a house divided," or whether those regions constitute "fit rooms for a worthy house," are likely to continue well into the present century despite any morbid pronouncements about the death of American regions.

Timothy J. Gilfoyle

American Urban Histories

Speaker of the U.S. House of Representatives Thomas P. "Tip" O'Neill was famous for the dictum that "all politics is local."[1] Some local historians argue that the same is true of urban history. For more than a century, historians of North American urbanization have focused on local affairs, parochial problems, and community concerns. From provincial, antiquarian accounts in the nineteenth century to more recent case studies adopting subcultural, interdisciplinary, and postmodern methodologies, urban history continues to be organized around questions affecting local communities. Yet synthetic works by writers such as Arthur M. Schlesinger, Sr., Lewis Mumford, and Sam Bass Warner, Jr., retain considerable influence on a subject that defies easy generalization and definition—the American city.[2]

The earliest examinations of North American urbanization were provincial in outlook and methodology. City biographies and regional studies were the most popular genre, and they frequently sought to promote their subject locales. Embracing a celebratory or booster ideology, these early urban histories equated urbanization with demographic increase, industrial progress, and geographic expansion. Some explored the relationship between specific cities and their agrarian hinterlands during the course of the nineteenth century. Like the earliest county histories published in the same century, urbanists chronicled politics, settlement patterns, commercial growth, and the rise of private institutions—businesses, churches, theaters, schools, and hospitals, among others. Authors of multivolume studies such as James Grant Wilson and Paul Gilbert and Charles Lee Bryson referred to their publications as "memorials" and "monuments" to their subject cities.[3] For these and other authors, urbanization represented modernity.

[1] Tip O'Neill, with Gary Hymel, *All Politics Is Local* (Holbrook, Mass.: Bob Adams, 1994).

[2] More detailed discussion of this and some of the themes below appear in Timothy J. Gilfoyle, "White Cities, Linguistic Turns, and Disneylands: Recent Paradigms in Urban History," *Reviews in American History* 26 (1998): 175–204; reprinted in Louis P. Masur, ed., *The Challenge of American History* (Baltimore: Johns Hopkins University Press, 1999), 175–204; Timothy J. Gilfoyle, "Urbanization," in William L. Barney, ed., *A Companion to Nineteenth-Century America* (Oxford, U.K.: Blackwell, 2001), 152–63.

[3] James Grant Wilson, *Memorial History of the City of New-York and the Hudson River Valley*, 4 vols. (New York: New York Historical Co., 1892–1893); Paul Gilbert and Charles Lee Bryson, *Chicago and Its Makers: A Narrative of Events from the Day of the First White Man to*

The most significant of these publications was I. N. Phelps Stokes's six-volume *The Iconography of Manhattan Island, 1498–1909* (1915–1928). More comprehensive than any study of an American city up to that time, *Iconography* was unique in providing more than an adulatory narrative explaining the "greatness" and "progress" of the city. Stokes's volumes offered a chronological, encyclopedic, and historical guide to "Gotham." He deliberately avoided interpretation in order to allow "the facts and myths . . . to speak for themselves." By emphasizing the physical city, Stokes balanced antiquarian acclaim with an objective account of New York's astonishing growth.[4]

Arthur M. Schlesinger, Sr., was the first professional historian to offer a comprehensive and influential interpretation of American cities. His seminal work, *The Rise of the City, 1878–1898* (1933), was important in at least three ways. First, Schlesinger advanced discussions of cities beyond the adulatory narratives of booster historians. Second, he was among the earliest historians to challenge the popular frontier thesis of Frederick Jackson Turner by situating urban history at the center of debates regarding the character of American society. Finally, by emphasizing social structures and physical environments Schlesinger integrated theories associated with University of Chicago sociologists Louis Wirth, Robert E. Park, and Ernest Burgess, the so-called Chicago school of sociology. "There is a city mentality which is clearly differentiated from the rural mind," wrote Wirth. "The city man thinks in mechanistic terms, in rational terms, while the rustic thinks in naturalistic, magical terms."[5]

Schlesinger agreed: Urbanization was the central theme in the emergence of the modern United States. Growing nineteenth-century cities fostered the assimilation of immigrants, the creation of new cultural institutions, and the growth of political parties and social reform movements. The rise of cities may have widened the economic divisions between urban creditors and rural debtors, Schlesinger acknowledged, but it also contributed to a collective belief in social responsibility. By juxtaposing city and rural life, Schlesinger contended that urbanization epitomized modernity and the rejection of agrarian values. The city, not the frontier, defined the American experience.[6]

---

the Inception of the Second World's Fair, 3 vols. (Chicago: Felix Mendelsohn, 1929). Other representative booster or multivolume histories include A. T. Andreas, *History of Chicago: From the Earliest Period to the Present Time*, 3 vols. (Chicago: A. T. Andreas, 1884–1886); Frank Moss, *The American Metropolis: From Knickerbocker Days to the Present Time, New York City Life in All Its Various Phases*, 3 vols. (New York: Collier, 1897); Jacob Piatt Dunn, *Greater Indianapolis: The History, the Industries, the Institutions, and the People of a City of Homes*, 2 vols. (Chicago: Lewis Publishing Co., 1910); William R. Holloway, *Indianapolis: A Historical and Statistical Sketch of the Railroad City, a Chronicle of Its Social, Municipal, Commercial and Manufacturing Progress, with Full Statistical Tables* (Indianapolis: Indianapolis Journal Print, 1870).

[4]I. N. Phelps Stokes, *The Iconography of Manhattan Island, 1498–1909* (New York: R. H. Dodd, 1915–1928), vol. 4, ix.

[5]Robert Park, Ernest W. Burgess, Roderick D. McKenzie, and Louis Wirth, *The City* (Chicago: University of Chicago Press, 1925), 219.

[6]Arthur M. Schlesinger, Sr., *The Rise of the City, 1878–1898* (New York: Macmillan, 1933).

Schlesinger's metropolitan thesis influenced urbanists for more than a generation. One group of urban historians was especially inspired by the Chicago school of sociology: Caroline Ware on city neighborhoods, Vera Shlakman and Constance McLaughlin Green on factory towns, Carl Bridenbaugh on colonial cities, Clyde Vernon Kiser on racial migration and segregation, and Oscar Handlin on immigration addressed the social and cultural impact of urbanization. Together, their works had a threefold impact. Like Schlesinger, they departed from the biographical approach to urban history and introduced themes largely ignored by the earlier booster generation of writers. Second, they emphasized subjects that soon defined much of urban history and contributed to fragmenting the field at the same time. Finally, their case studies represented some of the earliest applications of "thick descriptive" methodologies later commonplace in cultural anthropology and urban sociology.[7]

Writer and architectural critic Lewis Mumford chartered a different course while accepting Schlesinger's logic that cities were the cultural epicenters of civilization. In many publications beginning in the 1930s and culminating in The City in History (1961), Mumford offered a global history of urbanization. The rise of the city was a development so profound, he argued, that it emancipated humankind from the primitive, irrational life of rural society. Urban structures, in Mumford's mind, were the end result of science and technology and reflected the increasing value attached to rational thought. Tracing large shifts in economic organization, alterations in city geography and the built environment, and the transformation of social life, Mumford's meta-narrative thematically linked culture, politics, and technology within a comprehensive account of Western urbanization.[8]

After 1950, historians expanded upon Schlesinger's and Mumford's interpretations of nineteenth-century North America. Richard C. Wade and John C. Reps concluded that cities were the "spearheads" in peopling the nineteenth-

---

[7]Clyde Vernon Kiser, Sea Island to City: A Study of St. Helena Islanders in Harlem and Other Urban Centers (New York: Columbia University Press, 1932); Caroline F. Ware, Greenwich Village, 1920–1930: A Comment on American Civilization in the Post-War Years (Boston: Houghton Mifflin, 1935); Vera Shlakman, Economic History of a Factory Town: A Study of Chicopee, Massachusetts (Northampton, Mass.: Department of History of Smith College, 1935); Carl Bridenbaugh, Cities in the Wilderness: Urban Life in America, 1625–1742 (New York: Ronald Press, 1938), Cities in Revolt: Urban Life in America, 1743–1776 (New York: Knopf, 1955), and Rebels and Gentlemen: Philadelphia in the Age of Franklin (New York: Reynal, 1942); Constance McLaughlin Green, Holyoke, Massachusetts: A Case Study of the Industrial Revolution in America (New Haven, Conn.: Yale University Press, 1939); Oscar Handlin, Boston's Immigrants: A Study in Acculturation (Cambridge, Mass.: Harvard University Press, 1941). Also see Green, "The Value of Local History" and other essays in Caroline F. Ware, ed., The Cultural Approach to History (New York: Columbia University Press, 1940), 275–86. On thick description, see Clifford Geertz, The Interpretation of Cultures (New York: Basic Books, 1973).

[8]Lewis Mumford, The Culture of Cities (New York: Harcourt, Brace, 1938), and The City in History: Its Origins, Its Transformations, Its Prospects (New York: Harcourt, Brace, 1961).

century continent, that cities and towns were the earliest organized structures in the Euro-American settlement process. Nineteenth-century railroad companies, responsible for much of the urban, town, and community planning in North America, were, they contended, part of a four-hundred-year process dating back to Samuel de Champlain in New France, William Penn in British North America, and Spanish missionaries in the Southwest.[9]

Studies preoccupied with urban networks and national settlement patterns, however, were increasingly supplanted by studies emphasizing social history. A "new urban history" emerged after 1960, characterized by interdisciplinary methodologies (particularly between history and sociology), innovative quantification, and the study of ordinary people.[10] Colonial town studies in particular were initially inspirational.[11] The application of computer-based analysis of underused sources such as manuscript censuses, tax rolls, building permits, church documents, city directories, conveyance records, court indictments, and other unpublished papers offered a level of measurement previously unimaginable. Urbanization was treated as a social and ecological process that synthesized the forces of population growth, social organization, physical environment, and technological change. Indeed, the most significant advances in the literature of social history were frequently focused on those processes linked to urbanization: migration, industrialization, and family life.

Stephan Thernstrom proved to be the historian most influential in examining the lives of common people. His examinations of social and economic mobility in the Massachusetts communities of Newburyport and Boston were not only innovative; they inspired a generation of urbanists to ask similar questions in other cities. Investigations covering large cities such as New York, Philadelphia, and Milwaukee, and smaller communities like Omaha, Nebraska; Kingston, New York; Poughkeepsie, New York; and Hamilton, Ontario, challenged notions of rapid economic mobility and ethnic assimilation by city residents. Taken

[9]Richard C. Wade, *The Urban Frontier: Pioneer Life in Early Pittsburgh, Cincinnati, Lexington, Louisville, and St. Louis* (Cambridge, Mass.: Harvard University Press, 1959); John W. Reps, *The Making of Urban America: A History of City Planning in the United States* (Princeton, N.J.: Princeton University Press, 1965).

[10]Stephan Thernstrom and Richard Sennett, eds., *Nineteenth-Century Cities: Essays in the New Urban History* (New Haven, Conn.: Yale University Press, 1969), vii–xiii; Leo F. Schnore, ed., *The New Urban History: Quantitative Explorations by American Historians* (Princeton, N.J.: Princeton University Press, 1975).

[11]Sumner Chilton Powell, *Puritan Village: The Formation of a New England Town* (Middletown, Conn.: Wesleyan University Press, 1963); Darrett B. Rutman, *Winthrop's Boston: A Portrait of a Puritan Town, 1630–1649* (Chapel Hill: University of North Carolina Press, 1965); John Demos, *A Little Commonwealth: Family Life in Plymouth Colony* (New York: Oxford University Press, 1970); Kenneth A. Lockridge, *A New England Town: The First Hundred Years* (New York: W. W. Norton, 1970); Michael Zuckerman, *Peaceable Kingdoms: New England Towns in the Eighteenth Century* (New York: Knopf, 1970); Philip J. Greven, *Four Generations: Population, Land, and Family in Colonial Andover, Massachusetts* (Ithaca, N.Y.: Cornell University Press, 1970).

together, these studies portrayed nineteenth-century Americans as among the most geographically mobile in the world.[12]

Interdisciplinary approaches also generated new examinations of urban space. Sam Bass Warner, Jr., offered several comparative and influential spatial examinations of urbanization. His case study of the late-nineteenth-century streetcar suburbs of Boston proved to be the initiating text in the explosion of suburban studies in the ensuing decades. Then in two chronologically comparative studies, Warner argued that urbanization was structured around an ideology that valorized market development and the procurement of wealth, a phenomenon he labeled "privatism." Urban communities were created, organized, and, in essence, defined as a fusion of thousands of individual money-making, accumulating citizens and autonomous enterprises, not as a popular consensus originating through public participation.[13]

Warner's attention to spatial questions generated new subfields with rich literatures in suburbanization, physical infrastructures, and city neighborhoods. Suburbs represented perhaps the most significant topic in examinations of metropolitan space. Kenneth T. Jackson's *Crabgrass Frontier: The Suburbanization of the United States* (1985)—a title that reflected urbanists' ongoing engagement with Frederick Jackson Turner—and Robert Fishman's *Bourgeois Utopias: The Rise and Fall of Suburbia* (1987) argued that the automobile suburb that emerged after 1920 was historically unique in its low residential density and valorization of home ownership with big lawns, as well as in the tendency of middle and wealthy classes to live on the periphery of cities and endure long journeys to work. This new, distinctive urban form was the cumulative product of the actions of government agencies, private developers, and residential home consumers.

---

[12]Stephan Thernstrom, *Poverty and Progress: Social Mobility in a Nineteenth-Century City* (Cambridge, Mass.: Harvard University Press, 1964), and *The Other Bostonians: Poverty and Progress in the American Metropolis* (Cambridge, Mass.: Harvard University Press, 1973); Peter R. Knights, *The Plain People of Boston, 1830–1860* (New York: Oxford University Press, 1971); Howard P. Chudacoff, *Mobile Americans: Residential and Social Mobility in Omaha, 1880–1920* (New York: Oxford University Press, 1972); Michael B. Katz, *The People of Hamilton, Canada West: Family and Class in a Mid-Nineteenth-Century City* (Cambridge, Mass.: Harvard University Press, 1975); Kathleen Neils Conzen, *Immigrant Milwaukee, 1836–1860: Accommodation and Community in a Frontier City* (Cambridge, Mass.: Harvard University Press, 1976); Stuart M. Blumin, *The Urban Threshold: Growth and Change in a Nineteenth-Century American Community* (Chicago: University of Chicago Press, 1976); Thomas Kessner, *The Golden Door: Italian and Jewish Mobility in New York City, 1880–1915* (New York: Oxford University Press, 1977); Clyde Griffen and Sally Griffen, *Natives and Newcomers: The Order of Opportunity in Mid-Nineteenth-Century Poughkeepsie* (Cambridge, Mass.: Harvard University Press, 1978); Theodore Hershberg, ed., *Philadelphia: Work, Space, Family, and Group Experience in the 19th Century* (New York: Oxford University Press, 1981).

[13]Sam Bass Warner, Jr., *Streetcar Suburbs: The Process of Growth in Boston, 1870–1900* (Cambridge, Mass.: Harvard University Press, 1962), *The Private City: Philadelphia in Three Periods of Its Growth* (Philadelphia: University of Pennsylvania Press, 1968), and *The Urban Wilderness: A History of the American City* (New York: Harper and Row, 1972).

Both historians revealed how suburbanization gave rise to the residential subdivision and a new vernacular architecture—the shopping mall, the motel, the gas station, the drive-in theater, and the mobile home. For Jackson, the United States was the world's first suburban nation. Just as Schlesinger placed the industrial city at the center of nineteenth-century American history, so Jackson did with the twentieth-century suburb.[14]

The ensuing explosion of research on twentieth-century suburbanization stimulated a new vocabulary by those writing on the subject: megalopolis, spread cities, technoburbs, edge cities, disurbs, and post-suburbs, among others.[15] A considerable literature also addressed the impact of automobiles and transportation systems.[16] Most significant among historians, however, was their growing attention to Sunbelt communities, vaguely defined as cities below the thirty-seventh parallel.[17] These regional historians argued that Sunbelt cities evolved differently than the more studied areas of the Northeast and Midwest. David Goldfield's *Cottonfields and Skyscrapers: Southern City and Region, 1607–1980*

[14]Kenneth T. Jackson, *Crabgrass Frontier: The Suburbanization of the United States* (New York: Oxford University Press, 1985); Robert Fishman, *Bourgeois Utopias: The Rise and Fall of Suburbia* (New York: Basic Books, 1987).

[15]On technoburbs, see Fishman, *Bourgeois Utopias*. On disurbs, see Mark Baldassare, *Trouble in Paradise: The Suburban Transformation of America* (New York: Columbia University Press, 1986). On edge cities, see Joel Garreau, *Edge City: Life on the New Frontier* (New York: Doubleday, 1991). On post-suburbs, see Jon Teaford, *Post-Suburbia: Government and Politics in the Edge Cities* (Baltimore: Johns Hopkins University Press, 1996). On "megalopolis," the classic study is Jean Gottmann, *Megalopolis: The Urbanized Northeast Seaboard of the United States* (New York: Twentieth Century Fund, 1961). On spread cities, see *New York Regional Plan Association, Spread City: Projection of Development Trends* (New York: New York Regional Plan Association, 1962), and Alvin Schwartz, *Central City/Spread City: The Metropolitan Regions Where More and More of Us Spend Our Lives* (New York: Macmillan, 1973).

[16]Clay McShane, *Down the Asphalt Path: The Automobile and the American City* (New York: Columbia University Press, 1994); Joel Tarr and Clay McShane, *The Horse in the City: Living Machines in the Nineteenth Century* (Baltimore: Johns Hopkins University Press, 2007); Mark Rose, *Interstate: Express Highway Politics, 1939–1989* (Lawrence: University Press of Kansas, 1979); Paul Barrett, *The Automobile and Urban Transit: The Formation of Public Policy in Chicago, 1900–1930* (Philadelphia: Temple University Press, 1980); David St. Clair, *The Motorization of American Cities* (New York: Praeger, 1986); Bruce Seely, *Building the American Highway System: Engineers as Policy Makers* (Philadelphia: Temple University Press, 1987); Owen Gutfreund, *Twentieth-Century Sprawl: Highways and the Reshaping of the American Landscape* (New York: Oxford University Press, 2004).

[17]The demarcation for the "Sunshine Belt" first appeared in an Army/Air Force report in the 1940s. The designation of Sunbelt cities often includes western cities north of the thirty-seventh parallel such as Seattle and Portland. See David Goldfield, "Searching for the Sunbelt," *OAH Magazine of History* (October 2003): 3. Gerald Nash was among the first to describe the distinctive qualities of western urbanization in reference to economics, politics, and lifestyles. See Nash, *The American West in the Twentieth Century: A Short History of an Urban Oasis* (Englewood Cliffs, N.J.: Prentice Hall, 1973), and *The American West Transformed: The Impact of the Second World War* (Bloomington: Indiana University Press, 1985).

(1982) explained southern city building as "urbanization without cities," arguing for a distinctive southern urbanization that was more ideologically comparable to antebellum plantations than to northern industrial communities.[18] Similarly, Carl Abbott, in a wide range of publications, found Sunbelt cities "modernizing with northernizing." Southern communities like Washington, D.C., integrated and modernized their transportation and communication systems with the regional networks of the Northeast, with little impact on their southern character. In general, Sunbelt historians challenged the dominance of northern and eastern cities in urban history narratives by contending that the American South and West shared a different, distinctive history: business-dominated politics, low taxes, hostility to organized labor, suburban spatial form, federally subsidized growth, and an emphasis on leisure and tourism.[19]

Some historians even advanced a new model to explain North American urban development. A school of historians and social scientists—dubbed the "L.A. school" as a counterpoise to the old Chicago school—claimed that Sunbelt cities like Los Angeles and Las Vegas were national trendsetters for most of the twentieth century.[20] Urban development theories organized around the densely populated industrial city were replaced by a new urban form that emphasized tourism, leisure centers, and technology production exemplified by Disneyland, Sun City, the Stanford Industrial Park, and Las Vegas. These "magic lands," in the words of John Findlay, mixed fantasy, fun, and nostalgia while developing decentered urban designs that superseded earlier models with demarcated downtowns in the Midwest and Northeast.[21] Most notably, Mike Davis emerged as a caustic postmodern Lewis Mumford attacking this new urbanism for its environmental destruction,

---

[18]David Goldfield, *Cottonfields and Skyscrapers: Southern City and Region, 1607–1980* (Baton Rouge: Louisiana State University Press, 1982); Blaine Brownell and David Goldfield, eds., *The City in Southern History: The Growth of Urban Civilization in the South* (Port Washington, N.Y.: Kennikat Press, 1977).

[19]Carl Abbott, *The New Urban America: Growth and Politics of Sunbelt Cities* (Chapel Hill: University of North Carolina Press, 1981), *The Metropolitan Frontier: Cities in the Modern American West* (Tucson: University of Arizona Press, 1993), *Portland: Planning, Politics, and Growth in a Twentieth-Century City* (Lincoln: University of Nebraska Press, 1983), *The Metropolitan Frontier: Cities in the Modern American West* (Tucson: University of Arizona Press, 1993), and *Political Terrain: Washington, D.C., from Tidewater Town to Global Metropolis* (Chapel Hill: University of North Carolina Press, 1999).

[20]Allen J. Scott and Edward W. Soja, eds., *The City: Los Angeles and Urban Theory at the End of the Twentieth Century* (Berkeley: University of California Press, 1996); Michael J. Dear, H. Eric Schockman, and Greg Hise, eds., *Rethinking Los Angeles* (Thousand Oaks, Calif.: Sage, 1996).

[21]John Findlay, *Magic Lands: Western Cityscapes and American Culture after 1940* (Berkeley: University of California Press, 1992); Margaret O'Mara, *Cities of Knowledge: Cold War Science and the Search for the Next Silicon Valley* (Princeton, N.J.: Princeton University Press, 2005); Eugene P. Moehring, *Resort City in the Sunbelt: Las Vegas, 1930–1970* (Reno: University of Nevada Press, 1989); Hal Rothman, *Neon Metropolis: How Las Vegas Started the Twenty-first Century* (New York: Routledge, 2002).

plutocratic politics, and enslavement to the automobile. Davis's California dystopia replaced Mumford's industrial "Coketown" in these renderings of urban America.[22]

Other suburban studies argued that suburbs were less homogeneous and not as bourgeois as Jackson, Fishman, and others indicated.[23] Examinations of Canadian cities by Richard Harris, of Southern California by Becky Nicolaides, and of African Americans by Andrew Weise revised the history of suburbanization and demonstrated that working-class residents, immigrants, and minorities settled on the undeveloped fringe.[24] Robert Bruegmann's *Sprawl: A Compact History* (2005) challenged the distinctiveness of suburbanization itself, contending that low-density neighborhoods were hardly recent, but rather a timeless urban structure originating in ancient Rome and Mesopotamia.[25]

Like suburban studies, the evolution of physical infrastructures in cities attracted considerable attention after 1970. Robert Caro's *The Power Broker: Robert Moses and the Fall of New York* (1974) was a landmark not only because of Caro's indictment of Moses and his coverage of twentieth-century infrastructures—highways, parks, beaches, stadia, high-rise housing, cultural centers, and office towers—but also because it demonstrated the political import of such projects. Caro challenged earlier self-congratulatory accounts of American urban planning, while building upon the urban critiques of Jane Jacobs.[26] Whereas Moses believed

---

[22]Mike Davis, *City of Quartz: Excavating the Future in Los Angeles* (London: Verso, 1990), and *Ecology of Fear: Los Angeles and the Imagination of Disaster* (New York: Metropolitan Books, 1998).

[23]Other important suburban studies before 1995 included Zane Miller, *Suburb: Neighborhood and Community in Forest Park, Ohio, 1935–1976* (Knoxville: University of Tennessee Press, 1981); Daniel Schaffer, *Garden Cities for America: The Radburn Experience* (Philadelphia: Temple University Press, 1982); John R. Stilgoe, *Borderland: Origins of the American Suburb, 1820–1939* (New Haven, Conn.: Yale University Press, 1988); Matthew Edel, Elliot Sclar, and Philip Luria, *Shaky Palaces: Homeownership and Social Mobility in Boston's Suburbanization* (New York: Columbia University Press, 1984); Henry Binford, *The First Suburbs: Residential Communities on the Boston Periphery, 1815–1860* (Chicago: University of Chicago Press, 1984); Michael H. Ebner, *Creating Chicago's North Shore: A Suburban History* (Chicago: University of Chicago Press, 1988); Ann Durkin Keating, *Building Chicago: Suburban Developers and the Creation of a Divided Metropolis* (Columbus: Ohio State University Press, 1988); Stanley Buder, *Visionaries and Planners: The Garden City Movement and the Modern Community* (New York: Oxford University Press, 1990).

[24]Richard Harris, *Unplanned Suburbs: Toronto's American Tragedy, 1900–1950* (Baltimore: Johns Hopkins University Press, 1996); Becky Nicolaides, *My Blue Heaven: Life and Politics in the Working-Class Suburbs of Los Angeles, 1920–1965* (Chicago: University of Chicago Press, 2002); Andrew Wiese, *Places of Their Own: African American Suburbanization in the Twentieth Century* (Chicago: University of Chicago Press, 2004).

[25]Robert Bruegmann, *Sprawl: A Compact History* (Chicago: University of Chicago Press, 2005).

[26]Robert A. Caro, *The Power Broker: Robert Moses and the Fall of New York City* (New York: Knopf, 1974); Jane Jacobs, *The Death and Life of Great American Cities* (New York: Random House, 1961).

that cities were created by and intended to facilitate traffic, Jacobs insisted that the foundation of cities rested upon neighborhoods, diversity, and density. *The Power Broker* appeared at the height of the postwar "urban crisis"—rising municipal debt, declining city services, growing unemployment, city bankruptcies, and deindustrialization—and that further enhanced Caro's interpretive influence.

Caro's "great man" view of urban history quickly generated reactions. One group of scholars blamed the failures of postwar urban planning less on Moses and more on the social engineering ethos of liberalism, the influence of private developers, the ideologies associated with modernism, or some combination thereof. Moses, they argued, was symptomatic of his time; postwar urban renewal and transportation expansion were national phenomena.[27] More recently, another school of historians has resurrected elements of Moses's reputation. He was not omnipotent, these historians believe, but instead was constrained by federal regulations; the balanced transportation system Moses oversaw and the innovative designs of his parkways before 1950 compare favorably to expressways after 1956; programs promoting middle-class housing, university expansion, and cultural institutions helped retain residents and revive downtowns when suburban migration was at its height.[28]

Caro's stress on a single figure may have presented a misguided rendering of urban history, but his emphasis on the construction of the physical city and its related politics proved enduring. Nineteenth-century city services and innovative infrastructures—sewers, roads, parks, water treatment, fire protection, police, and schools—represented, in Jon Teaford's words, an "unheralded triumph."[29] Careful examinations of the physical city and infrastructure problems also revised older urban political narratives; these new interpretations challenged the corrupt political machine versus benevolent reformer frameworks that originated decades earlier with James Bryce and Lincoln Steffens.[30] The demand for capital investment

---

[27]Joel Schwartz, *The New York Approach: Robert Moses, Urban Liberals, and the Redevelopment of the Inner City* (Columbus: Ohio State University Press, 1993); Thomas Kessner, *Fiorello H. LaGuardia and the Making of Modern New York* (New York: McGraw-Hill, 1989); Leonard Wallock, "The Myth of the Master Builder: Robert Moses, New York, and the Dynamics of Metropolitan Development since World War II," *Journal of Urban History* 17 (1991): 339–62; Jon C. Teaford, *The Rough Road to Renaissance: Urban Revitalization in America, 1940–1985* (Baltimore: Johns Hopkins University Press, 1990).

[28]Hilary Ballon and Kenneth T. Jackson, eds., *Robert Moses and the Modern City: The Transformation of New York* (New York: W. W. Norton, 2007); Thomas O'Connor, *Building a New Boston: Politics and Urban Renewal, 1950 to 1970* (Boston: Northeastern University Press, 1993); Kenneth Fox, *Metropolitan America: Urban Life and Urban Policy in the United States, 1940–1980* (New Brunswick, N.J.: Rutgers University Press, 1985).

[29]Jon Teaford, *The Unheralded Triumph: City Government in America, 1870–1900* (Baltimore: Johns Hopkins University Press, 1984).

[30]James Bryce, *The American Commonwealth*, 3 vols. (New York: Macmillan, 1888); Lincoln Steffens, *The Shame of the Cities* (New York: McClure, Phillips, and Co., 1904). Representative examples include Arthur Mann, *Yankee Reformers in the Urban Age: Social Reform in Boston, 1880–1900* (Cambridge, Mass.: Harvard University Press, 1954); Alexander B. Callow, Jr.,

and new infrastructures, these newer histories contended, forced municipalities to adopt policies of "promotional governance," act as "economic adventurers," and rely on residential property owners for support, not on immigrant or working-class masses looking for political patronage or social services. New municipal agencies generated special-interest factions and pluralistic politics that transcended neighborhood and ethnic loyalties. The result dramatically altered the structures of municipal authority. Even elites were never monolithic, but rather internally divided, constantly competing, and shifting in their political alliances. Engineers and infrastructure experts like George Waring thus replaced elective officials and ward bosses like George Washington Plunkitt in urban political history.[31]

Interest in infrastructures generated increased attention to planning history. Earlier celebratory accounts of American urban planning were superseded by critical interpretations emphasizing the dominance of private market forces over public concerns.[32] Others focused on the emergence of planning as a distinct profession, some arguing that it had emerged in the nineteenth century and others depicting it as a product of Progressive Era reform.[33] Central to debates over

---

The Tweed Ring (New York: Oxford University Press, 1965); Zane L. Miller, *Boss Cox's Cincinnati: Urban Politics in the Progressive Era* (Chicago: University of Chicago Press, 1968); Leo Hershkowitz, *Tweed's New York: Another Look* (Garden City, N.Y.: Anchor Books, 1978).

[31]David C. Hammack, *Power and Society: Greater New York at the Turn of the Twentieth Century* (New York: Russell Sage Foundation, 1982); Harold L. Platt, *City Building in the New South: The Growth of Public Services in Houston, 1830–1915* (Philadelphia: Temple University Press, 1983), and *The Electric City: Energy and the Growth of the Chicago Area, 1880–1930* (Chicago: University of Chicago Press, 1991); Terrence McDonald, *The Parameters of Urban Fiscal Policy: Socioeconomic Change and Political Culture in San Francisco, 1860–1906* (Berkeley: University of California Press, 1986); Eric H. Monkkonen, *America Becomes Urban: The Development of U.S. Cities and Towns, 1780–1980* (Berkeley: University of California Press, 1988), and *The Local State: Public Money and American Cities* (Stanford, Calif.: Stanford University Press, 1995); Robin L. Einhorn, *Property Rules: Political Economy in Chicago, 1833–1872* (Chicago: University of Chicago Press, 1991); Alan Lessoff, *The Nation and Its City: Politics, "Corruption," and Progress in Washington, D.C., 1861–1902* (Baltimore: Johns Hopkins University Press, 1994); Joel Tarr, *The Search for the Ultimate Sink: Urban Pollution in Historical Perspective* (Akron, Ohio: University of Akron Press, 1996).

[32]Mel Scott, *American City Planning since 1890* (Berkeley: University of California Press, 1969); M. Christine Boyer, *Dreaming the Rational City: The Myth of American City Planning* (Cambridge, Mass.: MIT Press, 1983); Richard E. Foglesong, *Planning the Capitalist City: The Colonial Era to the 1920s* (Princeton, N.J.: Princeton University Press, 1986).

[33]On the nineteenth-century origins of urban planning, see Reps, *The Making of Urban America*; Stanley K. Schultz, *Constructing Urban Culture: American Cities and City Planning, 1800–1920* (Philadelphia: Temple University Press, 1989); William H. Wilson, *The City Beautiful Movement* (Baltimore: Johns Hopkins University Press, 1989); Jon A. Peterson, *The Birth of City Planning in the United States: 1840–1917* (Baltimore: Johns Hopkins University Press, 2003). For overviews, see Mary Corbin Sies and Christopher Silver, eds., *Planning the Twentieth-Century American City* (Baltimore: Johns Hopkins University Press, 1996); Daniel Schaffer, ed., *Two Centuries of American Planning* (Baltimore: Johns Hopkins University Press, 1988); Donald Krueckeberg, ed., *Introduction to Planning History in the United States* (New Brunswick, N.J.: Center for Urban Policy Research, 1983); Anthony Sutcliffe, ed., *The Rise of Modern Urban Planning, 1880–1914* (New York: St. Martin's Press, 1980).

urban planning and politics was the park movement. Thomas Bender and David Schuyler emphasized the social vision of planners like Frederick Law Olmsted and Calvert Vaux, who believed that parks were essential to facilitating social interaction and republican values among city inhabitants. In the words of Vaux, parks would "translate Democratic ideas into Trees and Dirt."[34] Later historians such as Roy Rosenzweig and Elizabeth Blackmar proved more skeptical. Focusing on efforts to restrict urban suffrage and electoral participation, they concluded that nineteenth-century reformers like Olmsted resisted expanding local elective democracy, which they considered "not an expression of popular will but a fundamentally corrupt exchange."[35]

Studies of physical infrastructures not only generated reinterpretations of urban political economies but also increased historical attention to urban ecologies. William Cronon in *Nature's Metropolis: Chicago and the Great West* (1991) revisited themes addressed by previous generations of urbanists like Schlesinger, Wade, and Mumford in his attention to the rural frontier, but he also charted a different path by emphasizing environmental questions and the interdependency of regional economies and ecosystems. In particular, Cronon rejected dichotomous portrayals of cities and rural hinterlands in opposition to each other by demonstrating how rural agrarian landscapes often defined as "natural" were the product of human forces, like cities themselves.[36] Martin Melosi and Adam Rome offered renewed attention to environmental concerns in the development of urban infrastructures and suburban landscapes.[37]

Urban environmental problems also generated studies that incorporated gender as an analytic category. "Municipal housekeeping"—female volunteerism, child health care, sanitary reform, juvenile courts, immigrant services, and other gender-stereotyped domestic concerns—attracted considerable attention. Kathryn Sklar's biography of Florence Kelley, Maureen Flanagan's comparison of male and female city clubs in Chicago, Sarah Deutsch's study of women activists in Boston, and Suellen Hoy's examinations of Roman Catholic nuns not

[34]Thomas Bender, *Toward an Urban Vision: Ideas and Institutions in Nineteenth-Century America* (Lexington: University Press of Kentucky, 1975), esp. 159–94; David Schuyler, *The New Urban Landscape: The Redefinition of Urban Form in Nineteenth-Century America* (Baltimore: Johns Hopkins University Press, 1986); Witold Rybczynski, *A Clearing in the Distance: Frederick Law Olmsted and America in the 19th Century* (New York: Simon & Schuster, 1999).

[35]Elizabeth Blackmar and Roy Rosenzweig, *The Park and the People: A History of Central Park* (Ithaca, N.Y.: Cornell University Press, 1992), 136, 278; Alexander von Hoffman, *Local Attachments: The Making of an American Urban Neighborhood* (Baltimore: Johns Hopkins University Press, 1995); Daniel Bluestone, *Constructing Chicago* (New Haven, Conn.: Yale University Press, 1991); David Quigley, *Second Founding: New York City, Reconstruction, and the Making of American Democracy* (New York: Hill and Wang, 2004).

[36]William Cronon, *Nature's Metropolis: Chicago and the Great West* (New York: W. W. Norton, 1991).

[37]Martin Melosi, *The Sanitary City: Urban Infrastructure in America from Colonial Times to the Present* (Baltimore: Johns Hopkins University Press, 2000); Adam Rome, *The Bulldozer in the Countryside: Suburban Sprawl and the Rise of American Environmentalism* (New York: Cambridge University Press, 2001).

only challenged orthodox interpretations of urban charity and social welfare work but also demonstrated that male and female reformers adopted different approaches to urban problems.[38] Some located the origins of the urban welfare state in such female-led city organizations.[39]

In addition to studies of suburbs and infrastructures, neighborhoods and their resident social groups constituted a third subject of spatial analysis. Studies of racial segregation were among the most pathbreaking. Arnold Hirsch's *Making the Second Ghetto: Race and Housing in Chicago, 1940–1960* (1983) challenged the long-held distinction between de jure forms of segregation in the Jim Crow South and de facto patterns of residential discrimination characteristic of the urban North. Hirsch concluded that the social and spatial structures of a major northern city were determined less by the benign factors of the market or social customs and more by government complicity. Between 1940 and 1970 a distinctive form of segregation emerged, supported by white Euro-American "ethnics" defending their "homeowner rights" (sometimes violently) and downtown elites striving to preserve commercial real estate. Hirsch identified this state-sanctioned segregation as a new or "second ghetto." So pervasive was this racial exclusion that, according to Hirsch, it "constituted a new form of de jure segregation."[40]

The second ghetto thesis stimulated new research on other North American cities. Some tested the viability of Hirsch's hypothesis in neighborhoods in Atlanta, Miami, and Cincinnati, and even in other Chicago neighborhoods.[41]

[38]Kathryn Kish Sklar, *Florence Kelley and the Nation's Work: The Rise of Women's Political Culture, 1830–1900* (New Haven, Conn.: Yale University Press, 1995); Sarah Deutsch, *Women and the City: Gender, Space and Power in Boston, 1870–1940* (New York: Oxford University Press, 2000); Maureen A. Flanagan, *Seeing with Their Hearts: Chicago Women and the Vision of the Good City, 1871–1933* (Princeton, N.J.: Princeton University Press, 2002); Suellen Hoy, *Chasing Dirt: The American Pursuit of Cleanliness* (New York: Oxford University Press, 1995), and *Good Hearts: Catholic Sisters in Chicago's Past* (Urbana: University of Illinois Press, 2006).

[39]Maureen Fitzgerald, *Habits of Compassion: Irish Catholic Nuns and the Origins of New York's Welfare System, 1830–1920* (Urbana: University of Illinois, 2006).

[40]Arnold Hirsch, *Making the Second Ghetto: Race and Housing in Chicago, 1940–1960* (New York: Cambridge University Press, 1983; 2nd ed. with new foreword, Chicago: University of Chicago Press, 1998).

[41]Works that acknowledge the influence of the second ghetto thesis include Ronald H. Bayor, *Race and the Shaping of Twentieth-Century Atlanta* (Chapel Hill: University of North Carolina Press, 1996); Raymond Mohl, "Making the Second Ghetto in Metropolitan Miami, 1940–1960," *Journal of Urban History* 21 (1995): 395–427, reprinted in Kenneth W. Goings and Raymond Mohl, eds., *The New African American Urban History* (Thousand Oaks, Calif.: Sage, 1996), 266–98; Charles F. Casey-Leininger, "Making the Second Ghetto in Cincinnati: Avondale, 1925–1970," in Henry Louis Taylor, Jr., ed., *Race and the City: Work, Community, and Protest in Cincinnati, 1820–1970* (Urbana: University of Illinois Press, 1993); Carl Husemoller Nightingale, *On the Edge: A History of Poor Black Children and Their American Dreams* (New York: Basic Books, 1994); Amanda I. Seligman, *Block by Block: Neighborhoods and Public Policy on Chicago's West Side* (Chicago: University of Chicago Press, 2005); Thomas J. Sugrue, *The Origins of the Urban Crisis: Race and Inequality in Postwar Detroit* (Princeton, N.J.: Princeton University Press, 1996), and "Crabgrass-Roots Politics: Race, Rights, and the Reaction against Liberalism in the Urban North, 1940–1964," *Journal of American History* 82 (1995): 551–78.

Thomas Sugrue's *The Origins of the Urban Crisis: Race and Inequality in Postwar Detroit* (1996) and Robert Self's *American Babylon: Race and the Struggle for Postwar Oakland* (2003) reinterpreted the political economies of American cities after 1970 by arguing that the forces contributing to political breakdown, deindustrialization, and conservative politics originated in local resistance to racial integration before the antipoverty programs of the Great Society in the 1960s.[42] Finally, Hirsch was among the earliest historians to invoke the concepts of whiteness and the merging of ethnics as analytical tools for understanding American race relations.[43]

Neighborhood studies of migrant groups relied on anthropological theory, emphasized the construction of certain social identities, and deemphasized the textile and Coketown paradigms of earlier urbanists like Lewis Mumford. In her detailed examination of five working-class communities in early twentieth-century Chicago, Lizabeth Cohen found older ethnic identities subverted by mass consumption and class consciousness, a pattern with national implications for American consumer culture, she argued in a later study.[44] Studies on urban Catholicism, in particular, increasingly emphasized its territorial character. The high rates of white ethnic home ownership, a sacralized attachment to residential property and the neighborhood, devotional Catholicism, and the centrality of the ethnic parish in daily life generated a community identity emotionally linked to physical locale.[45]

Social groups identified less by race, religion, or nationality and more by gender and sexuality constituted a vibrant new subfield after 1980. Kathy Peiss's *Cheap Amusements: Working Women and Leisure in Turn-of-the-Century New York* (1986), Christine Stansell's *City of Women: Sex and Class in New York, 1789–1860* (1986), George Chauncey's *Gay New York: Gender, Urban Culture, and the Making of the Gay Male World* (1994), and other works argued that for gay men, single women, lesbian couples, and other socially marginalized urban migrants, city neighborhoods provided unprecedented opportunities to escape the rigid traditions associated with their families and home communities. The spaces associated with commercialized leisure—dance halls, movie theaters, saloons, and amusement parks—enabled urban residents to create multiple and

---

[42]Sugrue, *Origins of the Urban Crisis*; Robert O. Self, *American Babylon: Race and the Struggle for Postwar Oakland* (Princeton, N.J.: Princeton University Press, 2003).

[43]On Hirsch's being among the earliest to use the term *whiteness*, see Hirsch, *Making the Second Ghetto*, 186.

[44]Lizabeth Cohen, *Making a New Deal: Industrial Workers in Chicago, 1919–1939* (New York: Cambridge University Press, 1990), and *A Consumer's Republic: The Politics of Mass Consumption in Postwar America* (New York: Knopf, 2003).

[45]Robert A. Orsi, *The Madonna of 115th Street: Faith and Community in Italian Harlem, 1880–1950* (New Haven, Conn.: Yale University Press, 1985), *Thank You, St. Jude: Women's Devotion to the Patron Saint of Hopeless Causes* (New Haven, Conn.: Yale University Press, 1996), and "The Center out There, in Here, and Everywhere Else: The Nature of Pilgrimage to the Shrine of St. Jude, 1929–1965," *Journal of Social History* 25 (1991): 213–32; John T. McGreevy, *Parish Boundaries: The Catholic Encounter with Race in the Twentieth-Century Urban North* (Chicago: University of Chicago Press, 1996).

distinctive urban subcultures. The crowded venues, spectacular displays, and sophisticated styles epitomized not only a new urban culture but modernity itself. The "democratic" subversion of gender and ethnic and class boundaries enabled groups characterized as geographically segregated and socially marginalized to carve out a degree of independence and autonomy, especially within the context of their spatial impact.[46]

In 1970, Richard Wade lamented the dearth of research on American cities.[47] Few make such claims today. The recent outpouring of city encyclopedias bespeaks the vitality of the field.[48] Two generations of recent urban history writing has changed the way Americans think about their cities and suburbs. Topics and groups invisible to past generations now occupy center stage. Just as Tip O'Neill emphasized the local while simultaneously shaping national policy, micro-historical studies address larger themes regarding the ecology, politics, and culture of cities. Urban historians may have abandoned the Mumfordian meta-narrative,[49] especially its universal interpretations and romantic portrayal of an organic city that never existed, but the influence and range of study in urban history is now far more profound. Fragmentation and diversity—scholarly cacophony to critics; intellectual vigor to proponents—now characterize how historians write about cities. For most, the sum of urban history is greater than the parts.

[46]Kathy Peiss, *Cheap Amusements: Working Women and Leisure in Turn-of-the-Century New York* (Philadelphia: Temple University Press, 1986); Christine Stansell, *City of Women: Sex and Class in New York, 1789–1860* (New York: Knopf, 1986); Elizabeth Lapovsky Kennedy and Madeline D. Davis, *Boots of Leather, Slippers of Gold: The History of a Lesbian Community* (New York: Routledge, 1993); George Chauncey, *Gay New York: Gender, Urban Culture, and the Making of the Gay Male World* (New York: Basic Books, 1994); Joanne Meyerowitz, *Women Adrift: Independent Wage Earners in Chicago, 1880–1930* (Chicago: University of Chicago Press, 1988); Lewis A. Erenberg, *Steppin' Out: New York Nightlife and the Transformation of American Culture, 1890–1930* (Chicago: University of Chicago Press, 1981); Patricia Cline Cohen, *The Murder of Helen Jewett: The Life and Death of a Prostitute in Nineteenth-Century New York* (New York: Knopf, 1998); Timothy J. Gilfoyle, *City of Eros: New York City, Prostitution, and the Commercialization of Sex, 1790–1920* (New York: W. W. Norton, 1992), and *A Pickpocket's Tale: The Underworld of Nineteenth Century New York* (New York: W. W. Norton, 2006).

[47]Richard Wade, "An Agenda for Urban History," in Herbert J. Bass, ed., *The State of American History* (Chicago: Quadrangle Books, 1970), 43–69.

[48]David D. Van Tassel and John J. Grabowski, eds., *The Encyclopedia of Cleveland History* (Bloomington: Indiana University Press, 1987); David J. Bodenhamer and Robert G. Barrows, eds., *The Encyclopedia of Indianapolis* (Bloomington: Indiana University Press, 1994); Kenneth T. Jackson, ed., *The Encyclopedia of New York City* (New Haven, Conn.: Yale University Press, 1995); Leonard Pitt and Dale Pitt, *Los Angeles A to Z: An Encyclopedia of the City and County* (Berkeley: University of California Press, 1997); Neil Larry Shumsky, ed., *American Cities and Suburbs: An Encyclopedia*, 2 vols. (Santa Barbara, Calif.: ABC-Clio Publishers, 1998); James Grossman, Ann Durkin Keating, and Jan Reiff, eds., *Encyclopedia of Chicago History* (Chicago: University of Chicago Press, 2004); David Goldfield, ed., *Encyclopedia of American Urban History*, 2 vols. (Thousand Oaks, Calif.: Sage, 2007).

[49]Recent exceptions include James T. Lemon, *Liberal Dreams and Nature's Limits: Great Cities in North America since 1600* (New York: Oxford University Press, 1996); Sir Peter Geoffrey Hall, *Cities in Civilization* (New York: Pantheon, 1998).

Donald L. Fixico

The Literature of American Indian History

One hundred years ago, the literature of American Indian history existed mainly in non-scholarly works. Ethnographers and observers, not historians, wrote the early books about the history of Indians and their ways of life, describing the cultures of the indigenous people and providing the earliest information about America's native communities. The writings included James Adair's early *Adair's History of the American Indians* (1775), which described the history and Indian ways of life Adair observed in his travels in the Southeast, and Lewis Henry Morgan's classic *League of the Iroquois* (1851). A third work, Henry Rowe Schoolcraft's *The American Indians: Their History, Condition and Prospects from Original Notes, and Manuscripts* (1851), the work of a geographer and ethnologist traveling among Ojibwas in the Great Lakes region and serving as their Indian agent, recorded a first-person account of Indian activities as living history.[1] As a part of the larger national history, the works of Adair, Morgan, and Schoolcraft laid the foundation for combining ethnographic and historical knowledge to understand the American Indian past.

By the late nineteenth century, charitable impulses added additional momentum to the writing of Indian history. In 1881, Helen Hunt Jackson's celebrated exposé, *A Century of Dishonor: The Early Crusade for Indian Reform*, encouraged the emergence of a reform movement to help Indians.[2] Faulting the federal government for impoverishing Indian reservations, her work inspired Clark Wissler, Alfred Kroeber, and other anthropologists to rush to Indian Country to study native peoples before they passed out of history. Fortunately, the Indian population stabilized and increased in the following decades, although anthropologists, writers, and historians wrote about Indians and their histories as if they were frozen in time with no future.

---

[1] *Adair's History of the American Indians* (Tuscaloosa: University of Alabama Press, 2005; originally published London: Edward and Charles Dilly, 1775); Lewis H. Morgan, *League of the Iroquois* (1851; New York: Corinth Books, 1962); Henry Rowe Schoolcraft, *The American Indians: Their History, Condition and Prospects from Original Notes, and Manuscripts* (Buffalo, N.Y.: Derby, 1851).

[2] Helen Hunt Jackson, *A Century of Dishonor: The Early Crusade for Indian Reform* (New York: Harper and Brothers, 1881). For a biography of Jackson, see Valerie Sherer Mathes, *Helen Hunt Jackson and Her Indian Reform Legacy* (Norman: University of Oklahoma Press, 1990).

Of the hundreds of books written since then on American Indian history, most academics have written "about" native peoples—that is, produced history through their own scholarly eyes, history clearly by non-natives. Yet from the beginning, an insider's view was also needed to construct a full history of the Indians. Most of the books approached the subject from the top down—that is, from the perspective of how government and military officials dealt with Indian people. Most of the authors white, they emphasized white roles in Indian history with native peoples serving principally as the victims or the others.

For all its formative influence on historical writing generally, Frederick Jackson Turner's epochal essay, "The Significance of the Frontier in American History," published in 1893 turned out to have a negative influence on Indian history.[3] While Turner inspired an emerging school of western historians who wrote about the West and included American Indians in their works, many of those historians, like Walter Prescott Webb, portrayed Indians as being less important in the shaping of the West than the white intruders.[4] It would take decades for Indians to appear fully as historical agents in their own history.

Among the first post-Turner historians interested in Indians was Grant Foreman, whose *Indians and Pioneers* (1930) provided new knowledge about early settlers moving into the Southwest and dealing constantly with Indians. Foreman next focused his narrative approach on southeastern Indians who during the 1820s and 1830s were removed to Indian Territory, which became Oklahoma in 1907.[5] Foreman's books strongly influenced a young historian-to-be, Angie Debo, who as a child arrived in Oklahoma before statehood. Later at the University of Oklahoma, she completed her doctoral dissertation, published in 1934 as *The Rise and Fall of the Choctaw Republic*. Her book won the American Historical Association's John H. Dunning award for the best book on U.S. history. In 1940, Debo's most important book, *And Still the Waters Run: The Betrayal of the Five Civilized Tribes*, was published. In telling the story of opportunistic exploitation of American Indians who owned land allotments, Debo set the tone for subsequent histories that portrayed Indians as victims.[6]

Debo's work inspired other historians to write tribal histories, and these caught the attention of Savoie Lottinville, a historian who was also director of the University of Oklahoma Press. Starting in 1929, the press was among the earliest

[3]Frederick Jackson Turner, "The Significance of the Frontier in American History," in Ray Allen Billington, ed., *The Frontier Thesis: Valid Interpretation of American History?* (1893; New York: Holt, Rinehart and Winston, 1966).

[4]Walter Prescott Webb, *The Great Plains* (New York: Grosset and Dunlap, 1931), and *The Great Frontier* (Boston: Houghton Mifflin, 1952).

[5]Grant Foreman, *Indians and Pioneers: The Story of the American Southwest before 1830* (New Haven, Conn.: Yale University Press, 1930); and Foreman, *The Five Civilized Tribes* (Norman: University of Oklahoma Press, 1934).

[6]Angie Debo, *The Rise and Fall of the Choctaw Republic* (Norman: University of Oklahoma Press, 1934), and *And Still the Waters Run: The Betrayal of the Five Civilized Tribes* (Princeton, N.J.: Princeton University Press, 1940).

to publish Indian history books, and it has published over 260 titles in its Civilization of American Indian Series since 1932.[7]

Indian ethnohistory emerged in the late 1940s when scholars in ethnography, linguistics, archaeology, and ecology led the way in analyzing the entirety of Indian cultures, thus broadening both the methods and the findings of Indian history. Interested scholars from these disciplines gathered in 1954 to found the American Society for Ethnohistory, and historians joined this new interdisciplinary community. A new era in Indian historiography had been born. Ethnohistorians began producing studies written from the inside of tribal communities.

Unlike Debo's work, the early books of Wilbur Jacobs—*Diplomacy and Indian Gifts: Anglo-French Rivalry along the Ohio and Northwest Frontiers, 1748–1763* (1950) and *Wilderness Politics and Indian Gifts: The Northern Colonial Frontier, 1748–1763* (1966)—established the importance of Indians involved in trade with British and French traders, whose alliances with the native groups served European interests. Jacobs demonstrated that commercial exchanges between Europeans and tribes caused both groups to become dependent on each other, at least for a time.[8]

During the 1960s, numerous books appeared on Indian history and Indians in general. In its strong narrative treatment, William T. Hagan's *American Indians* (1961) brought the long history of Indians to the attention of a larger reading public.[9] That tumultuous decade's protests over civil rights and the Vietnam War also inspired the emergence of the American Indian Movement and found Indians denouncing the United States for dishonoring their treaty rights. Angry Indian youths convinced universities to offer Indian studies programs along with black and Chicano studies programs. The first Native American studies program was founded in 1968 at San Francisco State University.

This renaissance of interest in American Indians led to Stan Steiner's classic, *The New Indians* (1967), one of the earliest books focusing on modern Indian history.[10] Steiner inaugurated an era of post–World War II Indian history in examining the lives of young native activists who had attended Indian boarding schools and moved to cities during the federal relocation program between 1952 and 1973. Federal policies that attempted to change native cultures, Steiner argued, confused many young Indians about their own identities because they came to see themselves as individual "Indians" rather than as members of tribal communities.

One book that presented the native point of view to a wide public was Dee Brown's widely praised 1970 work (notably, by a non-Indian), *Bury My Heart at Wounded Knee: An Indian History of the American West,* which sold over

[7]The University of Oklahoma Press in Norman, Oklahoma, published its first book in 1929.

[8]Wilbur Jacobs, *Diplomacy and Indian Gifts: Anglo-French Rivalry along the Ohio and Northwest Frontiers, 1748–1763* (Stanford, Calif.: Stanford University Press, 1950), and *Wilderness Politics and Indian Gifts: The Northern Colonial Frontier, 1748–1763* (Lincoln: University of Nebraska Press, 1966).

[9]William T. Hagan, *American Indians* (Chicago: University of Chicago Press, 1961).

[10]Stan Steiner, *The New Indians* (New York: Harper and Row, 1967).

4 million copies and has appeared in seventeen languages.[11] Brown used Indian accounts to explain the American experience in the West and thus released Indians from being locked in time. Slowly, Indian voices were being heard as part of the nation's history.

In the wake of Indian activism and the rise of a politicized Indian identity, Hazel Hertzberg wrote her comprehensive examination of Indian politics in *The Search for an American Indian Identity: Modern Pan-Indian Movements* (1971).[12] Hertzberg's introduction of the term *pan-Indianism* influenced other historians to think in terms of a generic Indian identity. As they voiced their protests, Indians themselves were increasingly affected by contemporary events. Their words, conveyed in the edited interviews in Joseph Cash and Herbert Hoover's *To Be an Indian: An Oral History* (1971), encouraged historians to listen to Indian voices and contributed to including Indian perspectives in native history.[13]

Historians also began to view Indians as individuals, even as heroes. Mari Sandoz's *Crazy Horse: Strange Man of the Oglalas* (1942) remains one of the best biographies. Others have followed, including Hugh A. Dempsey, *Crowfoot: Chief of the Blackfeet* (1972), and Dan Thrapp, *Victorio and the Mimbres Apaches* (1974). Among the best are R. David Edmunds's ethnohistorical biographies *Tecumseh and the Quest for Indian Leadership* (1984) and, about Tecumseh's brother, *The Shawnee Prophet* (1983). Tecumseh and his brother continue to get attention, as in John Sugden's *Tecumseh's Last Stand* (1985), his *Tecumseh: A Life* (1998), and his biography of the Shawnee leader *Blue Jacket: Warrior of the Shawnees* (2000). On western Indian leaders, Stan Hoig and Robert M. Utley have written numerous books, including Hoig's *The Peace Chiefs of the Cheyennes* (1980) and Utley's *Custer and the Great Controversy: The Origin and Development of a Legend* (1962) and *The Lance and the Shield: The Life and Times of Sitting Bull* (1993).[14]

[11]Dee Brown, *Bury My Heart at Wounded Knee: An Indian History of the American West* (New York: Holt, Rinehart and Winston, 1970).

[12]Hazel Hertzberg, *The Search for an American Indian Identity: Modern Pan-Indian Movements* (Syracuse, N.Y.: Syracuse University Press, 1971).

[13]Joseph Cash and Herbert Hoover, eds., *To Be an Indian: An Oral History* (New York: Holt, Rinehart and Winston, 1971).

[14]Hugh A. Dempsey, *Crowfoot: Chief of the Blackfeet* (Norman: University of Oklahoma Press, 1972); Mari Sandoz, *Crazy Horse: The Strange Man of the Oglalas* (1942; Lincoln: University of Nebraska Press, 1961); Dan Thrapp, *Victorio and the Mimbres Apaches* (Norman: University of Oklahoma Press, 1974); Kathleen Chamberlain, *Victorio: Apache Warrior and Chief* (Norman: University of Oklahoma Press, 2007), is an updated biography; R. David Edmunds, *Tecumseh and the Quest for Indian Leadership* (Boston: Little, Brown, 1984), and *The Shawnee Prophet* (Lincoln: University of Nebraska Press, 1983); John Sugden, *Tecumseh's Last Stand* (Norman: University of Oklahoma Press, 1985), *Tecumseh: A Life* (New York: Henry Holt, 1998), and *Blue Jacket: Warrior of the Shawnees* (Lincoln: University of Nebraska Press, 2000); Stan Hoig has written more than twenty books, including *The Peace Chiefs of the Cheyennes* (Norman: University of Oklahoma Press, 1980); Robert M. Utley, a military historian, has also written about forty books, including *Custer and the Great Controversy: The Origin and Development of a Legend* (Los Angeles: Westernlore Press, 1962), and *The Lance and the Shield: The Life and Times of Sitting Bull* (New York: Henry Holt, 1993).

Along the same lines, but in a spirit of activism, *Red Power: The American Indians' Fight for Freedom* (1971), a collection of essays edited by Alvin M. Josephy, Jr., connected warriors of the past to Indian activists of the 1960s. Troy R. Johnson similarly brought current concerns into *The Occupation of Alcatraz Island: Indian Self-Determination and the Rise of Indian Activism* (1996).[15] One of the standard works on Indian activism, Johnson's study is organized around themes of urbanization, occupation, and leadership and uses interviews to tell the story of the eighteen-month Indian occupation of Alcatraz that began in 1969.

Historians of the Indians, like all historians, have been drawn to the study of pivotal eras and events in Indian history. The massive removal of Indians living east of the Mississippi inspired Dale Van Every's major study, *Disinherited: The Lost Birthright of the American Indian* (1966).[16] Van Every showed how the Indian Removal Act of 1830 disrupted the lives of so many native peoples and led to great land losses.

The study of federal relations with Indians throughout the nineteenth century also continued to attract the attention of historians who put the government's treatment of Indians at the center of their studies. For instance, Reginald Horsman argued in his influential *Expansion and American Indian Policy, 1783–1812* (1967) that Thomas Jefferson felt tremendous pressure to develop formal relations with Indian groups while president of the young nation. Horsman's work was the first major study to address the tensions between national and state leaders over who would establish and enforce Indian policy as the nation took shape. In *American Indian Policy in the Formative Years: The Indian Trade and Intercourse Acts, 1790–1834* (1970), Francis Paul Prucha argued against then-standard views that the Indian removal policy of Andrew Jackson's administration did not deserve the criticisms it had long received because, by moving the Indians westward, it helped protect the tribes and their cultures from the predations of settlers in the Southeast.[17]

Since much Indian history rests on U.S.–tribal treaty relations, books have appeared regularly on American Indian legal history. Blue Clark's *Lone Wolf v. Hitchcock: Treaty Rights and Indian Law at the End of the Nineteenth Century*

[15]Books on Indian activism include sociologist Joane Nagel, *American Indian Ethnic Renewal: Red Power and the Resurgence of Identity and Culture* (New York: Oxford University Press, 1996); Alvin M. Josephy, Jr., *Red Power: The American Indians' Fight for Freedom* (Lincoln: University of Nebraska Press, 1999); Troy R. Johnson, *The Occupation of Alcatraz Island: Indian Self-Determination and the Rise of Indian Activism* (Urbana: University of Illinois Press, 1996).

[16]See Paul Chad Smith and Robert Warrior, *Like a Hurricane: The Indian Movement from Alcatraz to Wounded Knee* (New York: The New Press, 1996); Dale Van Every, *Disinherited: The Lost Birthright of the American Indian* (New York: Morrow, 1966).

[17]Reginald Horsman, *Expansion and American Indian Policy, 1783–1812* (East Lansing: Michigan State University Press, 1967); Francis Paul Prucha, *American Indian Policy in the Formative Years: The Indian Trade and Intercourse Acts, 1790–1834* (Lincoln: University of Nebraska Press, 1970).

(1994) addressed one of the most controversial court cases in federal Indian law and argued that Congress wrongfully exercised its plenary power to negate the Treaty of Medicine Lodge. Finally, Francis Paul Prucha, in *American Indian Treaties: The History of a Political Anomaly* (1994), another of his influential works, offered the most comprehensive historical analysis of Indian treaties.[18] This major work is the fullest historical analysis of 374 U.S. Indian treaties.

Another important work from the years in which Indian history was attracting more historians and deeper, fresher study is Henry E. Fritz, *The Movement for Indian Assimilation, 1860–1890* (1963), which focuses on Americans' humanitarian effort to solve the "Indian problem" of poor living conditions by making native people a part of the American mainstream.[19] Fritz's pioneering study influenced other historians to rethink the Indian reform era of the late nineteenth century. At the same time, other historians began to focus on the post-reform years. Lawrence Kelly broke new ground with *The Navajo Indians and Federal Indian Policy, 1900–1935* (1968). Kelly's pioneering work influenced historians to write histories of the tribes during the New Deal era of the 1930s.[20] Tom Holm's 2005 work, *The Great Confusion in Indian Affairs: Native Americans and Whites in the Progressive Era*, boldly challenged previous scholarship on Indians in the early twentieth century. Holm argued that, rather than suffering from the pressures of white society and policies, Indians retained their native identity and lived according to what he calls the "peoplehood" of tribal communities.[21]

Indian history in the 1970s experienced further revision in accounts of federal–Indian relations. In *The Reformers and the American Indian* (1971), Robert W. Mardock dealt with the well-intentioned religious humanitarian reformers who reached out to alleviate conditions on dilapidated tribal reservations. Bernard Sheehan, in *Seeds of Extinction: Jeffersonian Philanthropy and the American Indian* (1973), argued convincingly that Thomas Jefferson was the first president to establish a national Indian policy. Sheehan showed how the westward

[18]Blue Clark, *Lone Wolf v. Hitchcock: Treaty Rights and Indian Law at the End of the Nineteenth Century* (Lincoln: University of Nebraska Press, 1994); Francis Paul Prucha, *American Indian Treaties: The History of a Political Anomaly* (Berkeley: University of California Press, 1994).

[19]Henry E. Fritz, *The Movement for Indian Assimilation, 1860–1890* (Philadelphia: University of Pennsylvania Press, 1963).

[20]Lawrence Kelly, *The Navajo Indians and Federal Indian Policy, 1900–1935* (Tucson: University of Arizona Press, 1968). Related books followed, including Donald Parman, *The Navajos and the New Deal* (New Haven, Conn.: Yale University Press, 1976); Kenneth Philp, *John Collier's Crusade for Indian Reform, 1920–1954* (Tucson: University of Arizona Press, 1977); Graham Taylor, *The New Deal and American Indian Tribalism: The Administration of the Indian Act* (Lincoln: University of Nebraska Press, 1980); Laurence Hauptman, *The Iroquois and the New Deal* (Syracuse, N.Y.: Syracuse University Press, 1981); Tom Bilosi, *Organizing the Lakota: The Political Economy of the New Deal on the Pine Ridge and Rosebud Reservations* (Tucson: University of Arizona Press, 1997).

[21]Tom Holm, *The Great Confusion in Indian Affairs: Native Americans and Whites in the Progressive Era* (Austin: University of Texas Press, 2005).

movement caused problems for Jefferson, whose idealistic approach to the natives clashed with the realities of whites' encroaching on Indian homelands.[22]

In the late 1800s, the federal government implemented policies to assimilate Indians into the mainstream and prepare them for U.S. citizenship, the subject of Frederick E. Hoxie in *The Final Promise: The Campaign to Assimilate the Indians, 1880–1920* (1984). No Indian historiography would be complete without attention to the Christian influence on the tribes and reform efforts. An exemplary work in this vein by one of the leading students of the relations between Indians and whites is Francis Paul Prucha's *American Indian Policy in Crisis: Christian Reformers and the Indian, 1865–1900* (1984), which argues that Protestant values undergirded the gradual assimilation of Indians into the American mainstream. Prucha's crowning achievement is his two-volume comprehensive study of federal–Indian policy, *The Great Father: The United States Government and the American Indians* (1984).[23]

The federal–Indian policy of self-determination emerged in the early 1970s and continues today under the government's policy of encouraging tribal self-government with limited funding support. Jack Forbes evaluates the origin of this policy in the administration of Richard M. Nixon in *Native Americans and Nixon* (1972). Literature on tribal sovereignty and Indian self-government includes Harry A. Kersey, *An Assumption of Sovereignty: Social and Political Transformation among the Florida Seminoles, 1953–1979* (1996). But historians have only begun to focus on tribal self-determination as part of the larger history of Indian Country or to write case studies like Kersey's work.[24]

In the 1970s, an increasing body of work concerned the interaction between native peoples and the European civilization that had taken over the North American continent. Alfred W. Crosby's influential *The Columbian Exchange: Biological and Cultural Consequences of 1492* (1972) made the first important contribution to understanding the consequences of Europeans meeting Indians in the New World. Crosby brought to light the deep impact of microbes, foodstuffs, and different cultures on both populations.[25] His comparative analysis

---

[22]Robert W. Mardock, *The Reformers and the American Indian* (Columbia: University of Missouri Press, 1971); Bernard Sheehan, *Seeds of Extinction: Jeffersonian Philanthropy and the American Indian* (Chapel Hill: University of North Carolina Press, 1973).

[23]Francis Paul Prucha, *American Indian Policy in Crisis: Christian Reformers and the Indian, 1865–1900* (Norman: University of Oklahoma Press, 1984), and *The Great Father: The United States Government and the American Indians*, 2 vols. (Lincoln: University of Nebraska Press, 1984).

[24]Jack Forbes, *Native Americans and Nixon* (Los Angeles: American Indian Studies Center, UCLA, 1972); Harry A. Kersey, Jr., *An Assumption of Sovereignty: Social and Political Transformation among the Florida Seminoles, 1953–1979* (Lincoln: University of Nebraska Press, 1996); George Pierre Castille, *To Show Heart: Native American Self-Determination and Federal–Indian Policy, 1960–1975* (Tucson: University of Arizona Press, 1998), and *Taking Charge: Native American Self-Determination and Federal–Indian Policy, 1975–1993* (Tucson: University of Arizona Press, 2006).

[25]Alfred W. Crosby, Jr., *The Columbian Exchange: Biological and Cultural Consequences of 1492* (Westport, Conn.: Greenwood, 1972).

caused many historians to think differently about their entire approach to Indian studies. In 1975 Francis Jennings's *The Invasion of America: Indians, Colonialism, and the Cant of Conquest* was the first major ethnohistory of American Indians that emphasized the European displacement of native cultures and the costs this entailed. From then on, an increasing proportion of the Indian histories would be written from the inside—that is, by understanding how Indian societies worked on the basis of detailed study of Indian life and culture.

This revisionist turn in Indian history led to the reexamination of many subjects and to the questioning of many earlier approaches. For example, Ronald N. Satz, in *American Indian Policy in the Jacksonian Era* (1975), examined the rhetoric behind Indian removal legislation in 1830. Andrew Jackson has long been at the center of debates about Indian removal. For instance, Michael Paul Rogin, in the distinctive *Fathers and Children: Andrew Jackson and the Subjugation of the American Indian* (1975), offered an early psycho-biographical approach toward understanding Jackson and his relationship with Indians.[26]

One unique book caused historians to think about Indians' relationship with the natural environment. In his controversial *Keepers of the Game: Indian–Animal Relationships and the Fur Trade* (1978), Calvin Martin argued that Indians of the Canadian subarctic region blamed the beaver instead of Europeans for causing the diseases that decimated their tribes.[27] Martin's thesis of Indian revenge against the beaver won few followers. Instead, historians like Arthur J. Ray focused on Indians becoming a part of the Canadian fur trade in *Indians in the Fur Trade: Their Role as Trappers, Hunters, and Middlemen in the Lands Southwest of Hudson's Bay, 1660–1870* (1974). Ray argued that Indians played various roles in a commercial European network that altered their cultures.[28]

One pivotal work caused historians to consider how they had viewed native peoples by exploring the images through which they had portrayed them. Robert F. Berkhofer, Jr.'s, pathbreaking study, *The White Man's Indian: Images of the Indian from Columbus to the Present* (1978), pressed historians to analyze earlier perceptions of native peoples and to see how misrepresentations of Indians as being little more than wild savages had affected both Indian history and

[26]Francis Jennings, *The Invasion of America: Indians, Colonialism, and the Cant of Conquest* (Chapel Hill: University of North Carolina Press, 1975); Ronald N. Satz, *American Indian Policy in the Jacksonian Era* (Lincoln: University of Nebraska Press, 1975); Michael Paul Rogin, *Fathers and Children: Andrew Jackson and the Subjugation of the American Indian* (New York: Random House, 1975). See also Thurman Wilkins, *Cherokee Tragedy: The Story of the Ridge Family and the Decimation of a People* (New York: Macmillan, 1970). Case studies of removal are Arthur DeRosier, Jr., *The Removal of the Choctaw Indians* (Knoxville: University of Tennessee Press, 1970); Michael Green, *The Politics of Removal: Creek Government and Society in Crisis* (Lincoln: University of Nebraska Press, 1982); Andrew Frank, *Creeks and Southerners: Biculturalism on the Early American Frontier* (Lincoln: University of Nebraska Press, 2005).

[27]Calvin Martin, *Keepers of the Game: Indian–Animal Relationships and the Fur Trade* (Berkeley: University of California Press, 1978).

[28]Arthur J. Ray, *Indians in the Fur Trade: Their Role as Trappers, Hunters, and Middlemen in the Lands Southwest of Hudson's Bay, 1660–1870* (Buffalo: University of Toronto Press, 1974).

historiography.[29] Such revisionist currents led Laurence M. Hauptman, for example, to write *Tribes and Tribulations: Misconceptions about American Indians and Their Histories* (1995). Not that historians had failed over the years to address those misconceptions. Rather, Hauptman took on the entirety of Indian history to confront the still-existing ignorance of the Indian past and did so by incorporating Indian views into his work. A careful scholar working among tribes and talking to Indians before writing about them, Hauptman put contemporary Indian points of view into the record and made them part of the body of Indian history literature. Consonant with Hauptman's approach is Daniel K. Richter's *Facing East from Indian Country: A Native History of Early America* (2001). Richter's work has prompted early Americanists to consider natives' views of their history when trying to construct the full story of colonial–Indian relations. In this same light, Colin G. Calloway's *One Vast Winter Count: The Native American West before Lewis and Clark* (2003) persuades historians to consider native views of the West before the arrival of white settlers.[30]

As study of the Indian past branched out into new areas during the 1970s, Indian education became an important subject of research. As a part of the reform efforts of the late 1800s, boarding schools were established to educate and assimilate Indian youths into mainstream America. Margaret Connell Szasz's *Education and the American Indian: The Road to Self-Determination since 1928* (1974) set the standard for this rapidly evolving literature, and Francis Paul Prucha followed with a study of Indian boarding schools, *The Churches and Indian Schools, 1888–1912* (1979). Since then, Szasz's and Prucha's works have led to several additional boarding school studies.[31]

In the 1980s, James Axtell extended Francis Jennings's ethnohistorical approach with *The European and the Indian: Essays in the Ethnohistory of Colonial*

[29]Robert F. Berkhofer, Jr., *The White Man's Indian: Images of the Indian from Columbus to the Present* (New York: Knopf, 1978); Richard Drinnon, *Facing West: The Metaphysics of Indian Hating and Empire Building* (New York: New American Library Press, 1980); Brian W. Dippie, *The Vanishing American: White Attitudes and U.S. Indian Policy* (Middletown, Conn.: Wesleyan University Press, 1982).

[30]Laurence M. Hauptman, *Tribes and Tribulations: Misconceptions about American Indians and Their Histories* (Albuquerque: University of New Mexico Press, 1995); Daniel Richter, *Facing East from Indian Country: A Native History of Early America* (Cambridge, Mass.: Harvard University Press, 2001); Colin G. Calloway, *One Vast Winter Count: The Native American West before Lewis and Clark* (Lincoln: University of Nebraska Press, 2003).

[31]Margaret Connell Szasz, *Education and the American Indian: The Road to Self-Determination since 1928* (Albuquerque: University of New Mexico Press, 1974); Francis Paul Prucha, *The Churches and Indian Schools, 1888–1912* (Lincoln: University of Nebraska Press, 1979). Works on the place of Indian boarding schools in Indian history include Robert Trennert, *The Phoenix Indian School: Forced Assimilation in Arizona, 1891–1935* (Norman: University of Oklahoma Press, 1988); K. Tsianina Lomanwaima, *They Called It Prairie Light: Story of Chilocco Indian School* (Lincoln: University of Nebraska Press, 1994); David Wallace Adams, *Education for Extinction* (Lawrence: University Press of Kansas, 1995); Clyde Ellis, *To Change Them Forever: Indian Education at the Rainy Mountain Boarding School, 1893–1920* (Norman: University of Oklahoma Press, 1996).

America (1981) and *The Invasion Within: The Contest of Cultures in Colonial North America* (1985). Like Jennings, Axtell argued that the displacement of Indians by European culture was the principle reason for the downfall of Indian tribes.[32] Taking a different approach, James H. Merrell argued, in *The Indians' New World: Catawbas and Their Neighbors from European Contact through the Era of Removal* (1989), that native communities adopted parts of the invading foreign cultures to enable them to survive. The idea of both Europeans and Indians influencing and changing one another is the emphasis of Colin G. Calloway's *New Worlds for All: Indians, Europeans, and the Remaking of Early America* (1997).[33] Why Europeans invaded Indian lands is the focus of Reginald Horsman's *Race and Manifest Destiny: The Origins of American Racial Anglo-Saxonism* (1981).[34]

Even in the era of ethnohistorical studies, the venerable subject of federal–Indian relations, especially the modern federal policy known as termination, remained of central interest to historians. The post–World War II policy of termination called for dissolving the tribal trust relations with the United States government of 109 tribes, communities, and bands as a means of assimilating Indians into mainstream American society. Two relevant books on this subject are Larry W. Burt, *Tribalism in Crisis: Federal Indian Policy, 1951–1961* (1985), and Donald L. Fixico, *Termination and Relocation: Federal Indian Policy, 1945–1960* (1986). Burt's political history focused on the Eisenhower years of termination. Looking at a larger picture, Fixico explained that the origin of termination policy emerged from the changing attitude of bureaucrats due to World War II.[35]

As more historians examined modern Indian history, others remained focused on the 1700s and 1800s. The 1990s saw the publication of a pivotal book that changed most thinking about early Indian history. In *The Middle Ground: Indians, Empires, and Republics in the Great Lakes, 1650–1815* (1991), a Pulitzer

[32]James Axtell, *The European and the Indian: Essays in the Ethnohistory of Colonial America* (New York: Oxford University Press, 1981), *The Invasion Within: The Contest of Cultures in Colonial North America* (New York: Oxford University Press, 1985), and *After Columbus: Essays in the Ethnohistory of Colonial America* (New York: Oxford University Press, 1988).

[33]James H. Merrell, *The Indians' New World: Catawbas and Their Neighbors from European Contact through the Era of Removal* (Chapel Hill: University of North Carolina Press, 1989); Colin G. Calloway, *New Worlds for All: Indians, Europeans and the Remaking of Early America* (Baltimore: Johns Hopkins University Press, 1997).

[34]Reginald Horsman, *Race and Manifest Destiny: The Origins of American Racial Anglo-Saxonism* (Cambridge, Mass.: Harvard University Press, 1981).

[35]See Nicholas Peroff, *Menominee Drums: Tribal Termination and Restoration, 1954–1974* (Norman: University of Oklahoma Press, 1982); Larry W. Burt, *Tribalism in Crisis: Federal Indian Policy, 1951–1961* (Albuquerque: University of New Mexico Press, 1985); Donald L. Fixico, *Termination and Relocation: Federal Indian Policy, 1945–1960* (Albuquerque: University of New Mexico Press, 1986). See also Kenneth R. Philp, *Termination Revisited: American Indians on the Trail to Self-Determination, 1933–1953* (Lincoln: University of Nebraska Press, 1999); R. Warren Metcalf, *Termination's Legacy: The Discarded Indians of Utah* (Lincoln: University of Nebraska Press, 2002); Edward Valandra, *Not without Our Consent: Lakota Resistance to Termination, 1950–59* (Urbana: University of Illinois Press, 2006).

Prize finalist, Richard White, interpreted European movement toward the west as a shared experience of whites and Indians.[36] White's middle-ground concept of Indians and Europeans shaping history together rejected the previous view of Indians as passive peoples subject to European actions rather than as agents of change in their own right. His approach showed how Indians and settlers of the Great Lakes coexisted and developed a new understanding of each other through the War of 1812. In a recent study about another region of empires and native peoples, *Violence over the Land: Indians and Empires in the Early American West* (2006), Ned Blackhawk convincingly argues that the Great Basin and the Shoshone and its other indigenous people survived tremendous violence inflicted on them by Utes, Navajos, and Comanches as well as by the Spanish and Americans.[37] Tribal dynasties and Indian empires are the focus of an important work by Pekka Hämäläine, *The Comanche Empire* (2008).[38]

While historians of Indians maintained a deep interest in the colonial and early national roots of Indian–European relations, they have also written about native peoples fighting for the United States, as in Colin G. Calloway's *The American Revolution in Indian Country* (1994). Historians have also intensified their research into modern Indian history, with Indian participation in World War II of special interest. Pioneering works on this subject are Allison Bernstein's *American Indians in World War II: Toward a New Era in Indian Affairs* (1991) and Jere Bishop Franco's *Crossing the Pond: The Native American Effort in World War II* (1999).[39] Bernstein's study evaluated the patriotism of some twenty-five thousand young Indian men serving in the armed services and the Bureau of Indian Affairs during the war. In contrast, Franco focused on the way Native Americans fighting in the war served as role models to other Indians and non-Indians and influenced Indian integration into American society.

At the end of the twentieth century, gender history emerged as an important subject of Indian history, especially with Theda Perdue's award-winning *Cherokee Women: Gender and Culture Change, 1700–1835* (1998) and *Mixed-Blood Indians: Racial Construction in the Early South* (2003), the second of which raised the issue of Indian identity and how it has changed. The new century has seen the emergence of a new emphasis on borderlands history, most notably in James Brooks's award-winning *Captives and Cousins: Slavery, Kinship, and Community in the Southwest Borderlands* (2002). The combination of borderlands,

[36]Richard White, *The Middle Ground: Indians, Empires, and Republics in the Great Lakes, 1650–1815* (New York: Cambridge University Press, 1991).

[37]Ned Blackhawk, *Violence over the Land: Indians and Empires in the Early American West* (Cambridge, Mass.: Harvard University Press, 2006).

[38]Pekka Hämäläine, *The Comanche Empire* (New Haven, Conn.: Yale University Press, 2008).

[39]Colin G. Calloway, *The American Revolution in Indian Country* (New York: Cambridge University Press, 1994); Allison Bernstein, *American Indians in World War II: Toward a New Era in Indian Affairs* (Norman: University of Oklahoma Press, 1991); Jere Bishop Franco, *Crossing the Pond: The Native American Effort in World War II* (Denton: University of North Texas Press, 1999).

gender, and women's history has been impressively woven together in Juliana Barr's *Peace Came in the Form of a Woman: Indians and Spaniards in the Texas Borderlands* (2007).[40]

Research into Indians' approaches to natural resources emerged as a fresh subject as issues of environmental use and degradation rose to the forefront of political and social concern. A nationwide study of Indian natural resources is Donald L. Fixico, *The Invasion of Indian Country in the Twentieth Century: American Capitalism and Tribal Natural Resources* (1998), which shows how native leaders and their tribal communities have defended their natural resources against energy companies and federal paternalism.[41]

Another recent subject of historical interest has been American Indians' place in the U.S. economy. Works on this subject include Brian C. Hosmer, *American Indians in the Market Place: Persistence and Innovation among the Menominees and Metlakatlans, 1870–1920* (1999), and Colleen O'Neill, *Working the Navajo Way: Labor and Culture in the Twentieth Century* (2005).[42] Hosmer demonstrates how Indian people shaped Indian history as native communities became part of the modern business world while retaining their tribal identity. O'Neill pursues the subject of Indian labor history in her study of the Navajos as laborers working for a non-Indian company on the Navajo reservation.

With the turn of the twenty-first century, American Indian history expanded into new topics and extended earlier ones. Historians of American Indians, recognizing at last that American Indians are now as much urban dwellers as residents of reservations, began a long-delayed look at Indians in the nation's cities. Edmund J. Danziger, Jr., pioneered urban Indian history with his case study, *Survival and Regeneration: Detroit's American Indian Community* (1991), which argued that native people redefined Indian communities to consist of more than one tribe in urban areas. A comprehensive study is Donald L. Fixico, *The Urban Indian Experience in America* (2000) covering urban Indians throughout the nation, which argues that relocated Indians survived identity crises after resettling in cities. Case studies of urban Indians include James B. LaGrand's *Indian Metropolis: Native Americans in Chicago, 1945–75* (2002). LaGrand argues that

---

[40]Theda Purdue, *Cherokee Women: Gender and Culture Change, 1700–1835* (Lincoln: University of Nebraska Press, 1998), and *Mixed-Blood Indians: Racial Construction in the Early South* (Athens: University of Georgia Press, 2003); James Brooks, *Captives and Cousins: Slavery, Kinship, and Community in the Southwest Borderlands* (Chapel Hill: University of North Carolina Press, 2002); Juliana Barr, *Peace Came in the Form of a Woman: Indians and Spaniards in the Texas Borderlands* (Chapel Hill: University of North Carolina Press, 2007).

[41]Marjane Ambler, *Breaking Iron Bonds: Indian Control of Energy Development* (Lawrence: University Press of Kansas, 1990); Donald L. Fixico, *The Invasion of Indian Country in the Twentieth Century: American Capitalism and Tribal Natural Resources* (Niwot: University Press of Colorado, 1998).

[42]Brian C. Hosmer, *American Indians in the Market Place: Persistence and Innovation among the Menominees and Metlakatlans, 1870–1920* (Lawrence: University Press of Kansas, 1999); Colleen O'Neill, *Working the Navajo Way: Labor and Culture in the Twentieth Century* (Lawrence: University Press of Kansas, 2005).

Indians of various tribes adapted well to living in Chicago and made a permanent community there.[43]

In the first decade of the twenty-first century, the literature of American Indian history is growing larger as more historians enter the field. The works of Gary Anderson, Steven Crum, Peter Iverson, George Moses, Sherry Smith, Elliott West, and John Wunder, among others, are now making important contributions to this historiography.[44] With more than five hundred Indian nations open to historical investigation, historians of the native people of the United States will no doubt continue to add to our general understanding of the larger nation's history, as well as to tribal histories. Even more noteworthy is the fact that historians of other countries—especially of Germany, Great Britain, Canada, Australia, and Japan—have begun to turn to the history of American natives to gain a foothold on the recent histories in their own countries' indigenous communities.[45] One would never have imagined a century ago that American Indian history would break out into the general historiography of the United States, to say nothing of influencing the writing of history elsewhere. Clearly, the history of American Indians has come of age.

---

[43]Edmund Danziger, Jr., *Survival and Regeneration: Detroit's American Indian Community* (Detroit: Wayne State University Press, 1991); Donald L. Fixico, *The Urban Indian Experience in America* (Albuquerque: University of New Mexico Press, 2000). See also the case studies of Indians moving to cities in Jeanne Guillemin, *Urban Renegades: The Cultural Strategy of American Indians* (New York: Columbia University Press, 1975) on the Micmacs in Boston; and James B. LaGrand, *Indian Metropolis: Native Americans in Chicago, 1945–75* (Urbana: University of Illinois Press, 2002).

[44]Gary Anderson, *The Conquest of Texas: Ethnic Cleansing in the Promised Land, 1820–1875* (Norman: University of Oklahoma Press, 2005), and *The Indian Southwest, 1580–1830: Ethnogenesis and Reinvention* (Norman: University of Oklahoma Press, 1999); Steven Crum, *The Road on Which We Came: Po'i Pentun Tammen Kimmappeh* (Salt Lake City: University of Utah Press, 1994); Peter Iverson, *Dine: A History of the Navajos* (Albuquerque: University of New Mexico Press, 2002), and *We Are Still Here: American Indians in the Twentieth Century* (Wheeling, Ill.: Harlan Davidson, 1998); George Moses, *Wild West Shows and the Images of American Indians, 1883–1933* (Albuquerque: University of New Mexico Press, 1996); Sherry Smith, *Reimagining Indians: Native Americans through Anglo Eyes, 1880–1940* (New York: Oxford University Press, 2000); *The View from Officers' Row: Army Perceptions of Western Indians* (Tucson: University of Arizona Press, 1990); Elliott West, *The Contested Plains: Indians, Goldseekers, and the Rush to Colorado* (Lawrence: University Press of Kansas, 1998); John Wunder, *Retained by the People: A History of American Indians and the Bill of Rights* (New York: Oxford University Press, 1994).

[45]See Anna Haebich, *Broken Circles: Fragmenting Indigenous Families, 1800–2000* (Fremantle, Australia: Fremantle Arts Centre Press, 2000); Olive Patricia Dickason, *Canada's First Nations: A History of Founding Peoples from Earliest Times* (Norman: University of Oklahoma Press, 1992).